MW01626412

EYES IN THE SEA

"A fascinating read. By the time you are finished you will understand the reasons for our country to know more, much more about the oceans. As if BP didn't make that point already. Bob Wicklund is not a desk scientist. He is a diver and thus a teacher who all can understand. An exciting, no holds barred story of earth's greatest natural resource. A must for teenagers and senior citizens alike."

—**Lowell P. Weicker,** *former U.S. Senator and Governor of the State of Connecticut and served as Chairman of the Senate Appropriations Subcommittee with jurisdiction over the oceans*

"In *Eyes in the Sea* Bob Wicklund takes you on a voyage into the wonders beneath the waves. His carefully researched and dramatically described expeditions of his underwater adventures is certain to intrigue the readers and make them wish to learn more about the mysteries lurking in the depths, if not incite them to take up diving and see the wonders for themselves."

—**Clive Cussler,** *bestselling author and founder of the National Underwater & Marine Agency (NUMA)*

"Bob Wicklund writes of a time when the depths of the oceans were a vast unknown and a few brave souls were shining a light into that darkness. In honest, compelling prose, he shares personal highlights from the golden age of undersea exploration."

—**Dr. Joe MacInnis,** *physician, deep-sea explorer, motivational speaker and author of* Aliens of the Deep

"Few people have seen, touched, or experienced the wonders of the sea but now you can through—*Eyes in the Sea*—a book that all lovers of the sea need to read."

—**Dr. Robert D. Ballard,** *deep-sea explorer, president of the Institute for Exploration, and Explorer-in-Residence, National Geographic Society*

"In his book, *Eyes in the Sea*, Bob Wicklund brings the reader along on an undersea rollercoaster ride as he recounts his adventures in the early days of diving, ocean exploration, and coral reef research. Along with his vivid tales of undersea living and marine life, he brings us along as he ventures into the high-power politics of Washington, DC, and fends off drug-runners while running a marine research station on a remote island in the Bahamas. It is an entertaining and informative book that in the end showcases how our love and neglect of the sea have changed it forever."

—**Ellen Prager,** *PhD, marine scientist and author of popular earth and ocean science books, previously chief scientist at Aquarius Reef Base and the former Chair of the Federal Ocean Research and Resources Advisory Panel*

"This rough-and-tumble kid with a brave heart embarked on a lifetime of bringing science to the underwater world that fascinated him. And what a lifetime it's been—diving with the likes of Prince Charles and Fidel Castro, living for weeks in submerged habitats, working in the Senate. Wicklund shares with us an amazing string of record-breaking, breathtaking, dangerous, and dazzling adventures under the sea."

—**Linda K. Glover,** *oceanographer and diver, spent decades pursuing ocean science and policy for NOAA and the Navy*

EYES IN THE SEA

EYES IN THE SEA
Adventures of an Undersea Pioneer

Robert I. Wicklund

Foreword by Sylvia A. Earle

MARINER
PUBLISHING

1 3 5 7 9 10 8 6 4 2

Library of Congress Control Number: 2010939146
Eyes in the Sea
Adventures of an Undersea Pioneer
Robert I. Wicklund
Includes Index

p. cm.
1. Undersea Research Exploration 2. Marine Animals 3. Coral Reefs 4. SCUBA 5. Ecology of Oceans 6. Diving Expeditions 7. *Hydro-Lab* Undersea Research Program 8. Submersible Vehicles

I. Wicklund, Robert I., 1938– II. Title.

ISBN 13: 978-0-9849214-0-9 (hardcover: alk. paper)

ISBN 13: 978-0-9841128-7-6 (softcover: alk. paper)

Edited by Judy Rogers and Gerri Wenz

Cover Design by Sarah Brown ◆ Book Design by Charles Ober

Mariner Publishing
A division of
Mariner Media, Inc.
131 West 21st St.
Buena Vista, VA 24416
Tel: 540-264-0021
www.MarinerMedia.com

Printed in the United States of America

This book is printed on acid-free paper meeting the requirements of the American Standard for Permanence of Paper for Printed Library Materials.

DEDICATION

For my Family

My wife, Gerri
My mom, Florence
My children and their spouses:
Bob and Janine
Joan and Bob
Karen and Rich
Mike and Chris
And my grandchildren:
Lauren
Eric
Chris
Tom
Kaitlin
Sarah
Kyle
Caroline

In their hearts—
All Children of the Sea

CONTENTS

FOREWORD

I AM AMONG many who for years have urged, pleaded, cajoled, and begged Robert Wicklund to write this book. Time and again he said, "Aw, who would read it?"

I am not sure who or what finally worked the magic needed to break loose the astonishing sea stories collected here, but here they are—some terrifying, some wise, some break-out-laughing hilarious, others painful sagas of loss, both of treasured friends and of treasured places in the sea. Insights into how policies and laws are made are included too, based on years of working closely with state and federal agencies and legislators, especially the U.S. Senator and later Governor of Connecticut Lowell Weicker.

There are also rare insights into the behavior of sea creatures, especially fish, acquired by Wicklund who, as a scientist during thousands of hours of direct observation, has unraveled numerous puzzles about what goes on under the surface of the sea. Few scientists—actually, few people of any kind—have been immersed in the sea as long, as deep, and in circumstances as varied as the author of this book. In love with the New Jersey shore as a boy, Wicklund has become one of the best friends an ocean ever had, and one of its most articulate voices.

Of the events described, from underwater encounters with Cuban President Fidel Castro to face-to-face meetings with near-frozen fish in icy Arctic waters and standoffs with drug smugglers, all share the single element that makes them at once entrancing and enduring—they are all true.

Today, millions of men, women, and now even children experience the transformative effect of breathing compressed air underwater with scuba, sharing the sensation that Jacques Cousteau described as "flying without wings." Wicklund is not only one of the first to master the use of scuba for scientific research, he is also a pioneer in the use of saturation diving—the sophisticated method developed in the 1960s and 1970s that involves staying submerged and breathing compressed air or a mixture of gases for days and weeks at a time.

Wicklund became the underwater equivalent of a test pilot, subjecting himself to theoretically safe mixtures of gases for breathing longer and deeper than scuba divers descend—verifying the accuracy of the calculations with his own body. I am one of hundreds of scientists who have entrusted their lives to his skill at managing the underwater laboratory *Hydro-Lab* during years of research projects near Freeport, Bahamas. How he, Gerri Wenz, and Dick Clarke successfully operated an underwater laboratory-hotel for years with pathetically slender resources is one of the great unsolved mysteries of the sea.

I witnessed examples of his hands-on technical savvy and diplomatic skills many times during weeks of adventures shared at Lee Stocking Island when he and Gerri managed the research facilities on behalf of the National Oceanic and Atmospheric Administration (NOAA) and the island's owner, businessman and engineering genius John Perry. On an island, all sorts of things go wrong with no handy electrician, plumber, doctor, carpenter, policeman, fireman, lineman, mechanic, psychoanalyst, or other experts to help put things right. Some of the inventive ways such problems were dealt with are recounted here; others may form the basis of future legends or stories passed along as yarns so outrageous that they simply could not be fabricated.

It is true, and I am a witness, that when given a chance to pilot the one-person submersible *Deep Rover* in 1986, Wicklund listened to about an hour of instructions, climbed in, descended to 1,500 feet, and explored the face of a steep underwater slope before calmly returning to the surface—demonstrating the fastest learning curve of anyone who had ever piloted the little sub.

Many books have been written giving technical details of the 20th century breakthroughs that have made unprecedented access to the sea possible, but Wicklund was there for much of the action as a participant and driving force that helped make it happen. In this volume, he shares an insider's view of historic events, spiced with personal glimpses of people and how they behave (and sometimes misbehave) while they are literally working under pressure in close quarters under the sea. Just as intriguing are his accounts of what happens on the surface, when humans act, well, like humans, with all of the good and not-so-good elements included.

When Robert Wicklund first put his face in the ocean more than half a century ago, he discovered a world that no longer exists. Since then, about half of the coral reefs that once circled the globe like a jeweled belt have disappeared or are in a state of sharp decline. Ninety percent of many kinds of fish are gone, beaches are slathered with trash, and seawater, the living liquid that makes life on Earth possible, humankind included, is becoming increasingly acidic and polluted. It is hard for those who see the ocean now for the first time to imagine how much and how swiftly it has changed—more since the middle of the 20th century than during all preceding human history.

At the same time, more has been learned about how the ocean functions, how it governs climate, weather, temperature, the water cycle, the oxygen cycle, the carbon cycle, and much more. Now we know the living ocean makes Earth a hospitable haven in a universe of beautiful but barren planets, comets, and stars. Now we know the ocean is vulnerable—and therefore, so are we. Knowing is the key to caring, and with caring, there is hope that we will do what it takes to reverse the disastrous decline of systems that preceded humankind by hundreds of millions of years.

"Ultimately, we are inseparable from the sea," says Wicklund. "Whatever we do to it, we do to ourselves."

—Sylvia A. Earle, PhD
Explorer-in-Residence at the National Geographic Society, author, documentary film producer, founder of two companies—Deep Ocean Engineering and Deep Ocean Technologies, and former Chief Scientist at NOAA

PREFACE

EACH TIME I venture below the sea's surface, I experience a genuine intimacy. I think that the body, being mostly water anyway, doesn't just sink, it folds into the sea and is welcomed back like a long-lost child.

The undersea world became my passion in the early 60s when scientific diving was still relatively new. For fifty-plus years my involvement with the oceans, pioneering techniques for undersea research, exploring the depths in tiny research submarines, and living in undersea laboratories provided me many opportunities to see and experience what had never before been seen or accomplished.

This book is about my sometimes dangerous, mostly exciting, and always rewarding journeys below the surface to study the oceans—it is a chronicle of encounters with marine animals, interesting and amusing people, and downright good times. Through photographs and true stories, I describe and share some of these experiences. Even the most seasoned diver may say, *I never knew that.* Many of the images and adventures have never been published and are known only to the scientists who dared to bring their eyes into the sea.

In the past, the three-dimensional oceans were studied using two-dimensional science. Ships plied the ocean surface blindly lowering probes to measure the physical world of the shallow seas. Nets were sent down into the dark abyss to capture bits and pieces of the deep-sea realm. Much was learned using these techniques.

We learned that the oceans are not simply homogeneous bodies of water but intricate and diverse arrays of complex current patterns, temperatures, and internal waves, sometimes larger than those on the surface. The bounty of the nets allowed scientists to identify many marine organisms, offering a glimmer of the vastness and richness of the world's oceans.

But the story was incomplete and there was no true understanding of the natural order of the ocean ecosystem. Missing was the ability to observe and touch and think inside the ocean environment. Our knowledge of the sea comes not only from probes, instruments, and nets, but also from placing human eyes, hands, and minds directly into its depths.

Jules Verne took the world on an imaginary journey, *20,000 Leagues Under the Sea*, in 1869. The *real* story goes beyond fiction—beyond anything we could imagine.

ACKNOWLEDGMENTS

THERE ARE MANY people responsible for the contents of this book including divers, scientists, politicians, authors, family, and friends. After years of telling and retelling my stories of our undersea adventures, the people closest to me started to urge a book—the idea being it would be quieter when its cover was closed. But it would take nothing less than amending the Constitution to silence me. All joking aside, it has been rewarding to work with, and I would like to acknowledge, the people who have helped me, in many ways, to pull this book together.

First, I want to thank the late Dr. Lionel Walford who long ago showed a young man the power and poetry of words. My thanks go also to John Muncie for his advice on portions of the early manuscript; to the University of North Carolina Wilmington and Dr. Carol Chase Thomas for proofreading; to Gerri Wenz for her tireless editing and guidance; to Dick Clarke and Denny Breese for ideas and photographs; to Jim English for his review; and to Andy Wolfe, Judy Rogers, and the crew at Mariner Media for their professional rendering of this book.

INTRODUCTION

A FLASH OF bright light penetrating the clear Bahamian sea announced the arrival of a swiftly swimming fish. Bursts of sunlight reflected off the silvery scales of the cero mackerel as it started to swim in circles 40 feet above my position on the ocean bottom.

On this summer morning in 1973, under clear skies and in calm winds, the water temperature was about 80°F and the surface of the ocean was absolutely flat, almost oily in appearance. In the gin-clear water, I could see schools of grunts and snapper among the soft coral outcroppings; a grouper moved from one coral head to another, ignoring me. A large barracuda floated among the grunts, waiting for a breakfast opportunity.

I watched the reef creatures for a short while, then looked up to see the sleek cero swimming just below a large circle on the surface, the so-called "window in the sea," a phenomenon that occurs when light rays change speed—refracting, or bending, as they move through media of different densities—in this case, from air to ocean.

For divers, this refraction means that you can look up through clear water and view a circle at the sea's surface—the "window in the sea"—through which you can see out to the sky above. As a diver moves, the window is always above, moving with him. Beyond the edges of the circle, around the window, the sea surface is opaque.

I could see the cero framed by the "window." It appeared to be swimming, not in the ocean, but in the blue sky and white clouds above. I was transfixed by the fish and its graceful movements. A dark frigate bird suddenly appeared in the window, soaring in the sky above the mackerel, maybe 200 feet from the ocean's surface.

Within the circular window, fish and bird swam and flew as if in a celebratory dance of life. Two species moving effortlessly in the two separate worlds to which evolution had brought them to live. I don't know how long I watched them intertwine—I lost all sense of time, all sense of breathing.

I never saw anything like it again. And yet, I can close my eyes and remember it as clearly as yesterday, perhaps because it seemed so perfectly symbolic of how close—and yet at the same time—how distant the ocean realm is to us and to the terrestrial and atmospheric world in which we are confined.

The sea can be a hostile place for land creatures. We have to bring our own atmosphere along if we want to stay for any length of time. Millions of years have separated us from our ocean-dwelling ancestors; we now stand on the shoreline, looking back at our distant, distant cousins.

I feel privileged to have lived in both worlds, even though time in the sea has been ever so brief. My years of exploration and discovery were not the only wonders of diving—there was also the pure joy of being embraced by the sea and moving about in three dimensions like a weightless bird.

Years of experience make diving mechanically efficient, something like a walk in an underwater park. You move slowly and smoothly, the swimming motion almost forgotten, willing yourself through the water. But any dive can be dangerous; any dive could be your last. Bends, embolism, equipment failure, getting lost, and drowning are all possible. Even moderate currents can be trouble. Water is many times denser than air and swimming against a moderate current can be similar, in terrestrial terms, to taking a stroll against a category-one hurricane.

All my underwater experiences have been memorable, but I especially recall the first time I saw a tropical coral reef. I'd been diving for years in the cold and mostly murky waters off the coast of New Jersey. In 1967, the Smithsonian Institution and famed ocean explorer Ed Link invited me to participate in a diving expedition to the Berry Islands in the Bahamas.

Link, inventor of the Link Trainer, which has trained thousands of military and commercial pilots since World War II, turned his attention from aviation to undersea research and exploration in the 1950s, and then to building submarines that divers could enter and exit underwater.

He didn't have to ask me twice. After a plane ride from New Jersey to Nassau and an eight-hour trip to the northern Berrys aboard Link's ship, *Sea Diver*, I was surrounded by the warm, clear seas I'd explored only in my dreams. Having seen many photos of Caribbean coral reefs, I thought I knew what to expect. I was wrong.

When I broke through the calm surface of the warm Bahamian sea and adjusted my eyes to the colors of the reef below me, I was dazzled. I could see for 100 feet in all directions. I had the sensation of falling through the clear water. It was the absolute antithesis of diving off the coast of New Jersey.

A myriad of brightly colored snapper, grunts, parrotfish, goatfish, and other species drifted slowly among the reds and greens, yellows and browns of the corals, sponges, feather worms, and other reef creatures—all completely new to me. Schools of small silvery fish moved about, packed closely together for safety. I was overwhelmed by the abundance of life.

I saw my first barracuda, which had looked so menacing in photos but here appeared almost docile, hanging motionless over the reef, surrounded by many fish that I imagined were its prey. Nassau grouper moved about as if they owned the reef and examined me closely with curious eyes that flicked back and forth.

More than 500 species of fish can be found on a Caribbean reef and thousands of invertebrates—corals, sponges, crabs, lobsters, crinoids, shrimp, tiny mysids, worms, conch and other snails, octopi and other mollusks—all living together, all dependent on each other, vital parts of an intricate tapestry woven by millions of evolutionary years.

That first dive into tropical waters was the beginning of my intimate relationship with coral reefs. The ocean, now embedded in my soul, has taken me on a long journey—a lifelong adventure that began in a polluted New Jersey bay many years ago.

1
FIRST TOUCH

The two-second image of a tiny, black and yellow fish burned into my brain 57 years ago. It was a tropical juvenile that came from a southern spawning ground in its egg or larval stage, carried north by the swift currents of the Gulf Stream. It had hitched a ride on an eddy and was carried to a shallow salt marsh along the shores of Raritan Bay, New Jersey. That fish is symbolic of my life-long passion—to see, explore, and discover as much as I could about the oceans.

I spent a number of my formative years near the waters of the murky and sometimes polluted Raritan Bay. Storms, particularly Nor'easters, would occasionally threaten my family's home, as happened during the 1950 Thanksgiving storm, which wiped out the entire community of Morgan Beach, New Jersey. Our house, pounded by huge waves that rode inshore on the storm's surge, floated intact about 1,000 feet from its foundation. Little was left to salvage. Fortunately, we were away at my grandparents' house on Long Island, New York. Our German Shepherd, being cared for by neighbors, jumped through a window and swam to safety. Not so fortunate was a puppy that was also inside.

After another storm hit a few years later, the community was bulldozed and has remained an empty beach until this day. This was my first lesson about the power of the ocean and the respect it deserves. Many experiences over the years have only strengthened that respect.

We moved to Cliffwood Beach, still on Raritan Bay, where I continued swimming and free diving for many hours over the summers, always without a mask and always trying to imagine what the blurry movements were that passed in front of my wide-open eyes. Large, dark shadows became monstrous sharks in my mind, which was actually not too far from reality. Only five miles down coast in Keyport and Matawan, a large white shark had killed or maimed several people in 1916, which became one of the most cited shark attacks on record in U.S. history. I'm not sure I knew about this at the time, for the only real fear I had was swimming face first into the tentacles of a large jellyfish, which happened frequently. The experience of tangling in the stinging tentacles, some extending an easy five feet from a body eight inches or more in diameter, was unforgettable, and it took days of pain to recover. They were almost impossible to see underwater.

Toward the end of one summer I read about the adventures of the Navy UDT Frogmen and their daring beach assaults during World War II. I was particularly intrigued by their ability to see clearly underwater by wearing a simple mask that sealed a space between their eyes and the surrounding water. I wanted to see underwater like the Frogmen and a mask would be the answer, so one day I set out to build one based on pictures hanging on my bedroom wall. I cut a basic pattern of a mask from an old tire tube, with the front ready to receive a round piece of glass and the back with straps to be fastened together with a safety pin. The glass was rough-cut and had little resemblance to a circle, as I had originally intended. Many attempts to seal the glass to the rubber tube were fruitless, but I decided to give it its first test anyway.

The next morning and late in the summer season, I entered shallow water near a marsh on the edge of the bay. The water visibility on that day was exceptionally clear for the area, exceeding 10 feet. My first test resulted in the mask filling up with water coming not only from the unsealed glass, but also from the poor seal around my face. I saw nothing but rushing water. After tightening the straps, I tried again and this time I was able to clearly see a blade of seagrass for a second or two before the leaking mask filled. Again and again I dove for only a glimpse of the grass bed or sandy bottom.

I actually observed a fish in the wild as if it were in an aquarium tank. It was poetry. It was to be the rest of my life.

Then, on about the tenth dive, and for only about two seconds, the small juvenile fish was framed by the somewhat circular mask before the water once again rushed in to blur the scene. It was the most exciting and wonderful thing I had ever seen. It was magic. I actually observed a fish in the wild as if it were in an aquarium tank. It was poetry. It was to be the rest of my life.

The fish was a species that to this day I still cannot identify, even with years of experience observing marine organisms. Perhaps I just want to preserve the mystery of that very special day forever. It was definitely a tropical species as were many we found over the coming years. Young tropicals, including angelfish, lookdowns, snowy grouper, filefish, and others normally associated with coral reefs, were found regularly in the summer months throughout the waters of the northeastern and mid-Atlantic states—unlucky riders as eggs and larvae on the powerful Gulf Stream currents.

Many tropical fish and other marine organisms spawn in open water and their fertilized eggs float to the surface where they are at the mercy of currents and wind, sometimes for weeks. The strategy of these animals is to release millions of eggs into the water, with less than one percent fortunate enough to make their nursery grounds and survive to become adults. Their normal habitats are reefs in Florida or the West Indies where they stay for much of their lives. The young fish that are carried north presumably succumb to hypothermia as the waters cool. Their siblings to the south seek out a tropical or subtropical habitat and grow to adulthood. My fish, which I saw only once and for the briefest of moments, did not live much beyond that summer's day, but it survives in my memory.

Buoyed by the perceived success of the diving mask, my brothers Don and Ken and I took a quantum leap forward and built an underwater breathing system out of an old WWII gas mask, rubber hose, and a bicycle tire pump. It, like the diving mask, was simplicity itself. We removed the chemical canister from the mask and waterproofed the hose into its bottom part. The other end of the 50-foot hose was attached to the pump. Being the eldest, I elected myself test diver and off we went to Cheesequake Creek near the mouth of the bay. I weighted myself with rocks in all the pockets of my shorts, donned the very soft mask, and with one of my brothers pumping air into the mask, I walked from the beach into the water.

At six feet I was completely submerged and the mask immediately collapsed onto my face. There was not enough air to compensate for the increased pressure of the depth and the soft mask simply folded. After a brief debate on the rate of pumping needed, my disgruntled brothers agreed to pump harder, and again we set off to conquer inner space.

This time I walked all the way out to about 10 feet deep and was breathing a mixture of air from the pump and seawater from the leaks in the mask. I couldn't see much through the fuzzy plastic eyepieces, but it was amazing. After about six breaths, however, my surface-support crew got tired and slowed the pumping. My face and the whole front of my head were what could only be described as being eaten alive by the mask. With less than a little grace I emerged from the water, sputtering and a bit scared, while ripping the mask off. My brothers, sensing trouble, split from the beach and were not seen for the rest of the day.

Following the last so-called test dive, I was sitting on the edge of the creek considering our great adventure when a giant fish leaped clean out of the water and crashed back into the creek with a huge splash. It looked about 15 feet long and was shark-like in appearance, but did not have a dorsal fin on the middle of its back. There was no way we were going back into the water that day. In later years, I realized how fortunate I was to have seen what I now know was a large sea sturgeon, probably more like six to eight feet in length. The species, famous for its caviar (eggs), has long since disappeared from these waters and, in fact, from much of the East Coast.

The sturgeon that I saw that day in the brackish waters of the creek was likely returning from an early summer spawning run upstream and heading back to sea. Even though the sturgeon's normal range is the entire East and Gulf of Mexico coasts, that day in the early 1950s is the only time I observed one in the wild and is in all probability the last one I will ever see. Its fate is indicative of the plight of many of our fish populations. Overfishing, pollution of coastal nursery areas, and habitat destruction have put many species on paths to extinction.

When I was very young, I remember accompanying my parents in a rowboat to dig clams in a Brooklyn, New York, creek, if you can imagine that. My father, Irv, later owned an old 35-foot fishing boat in Brooklyn, which he named the *Florence* after my mother. On occasion he would take us fishing on the offshore fishing grounds of the New York Bight. It was during World War II and I still remember stopping by a Coast Guard vessel to sign in and to receive instructions on what to do if a German submarine were spotted. Although it was late in the war and the U-boat fleet had been pretty much compromised, there was still an occasional attack on merchant or military vessels along the U.S. coastline. The small, private boats played an important surveillance role in the war.

Captain Irv taking a break onboard the R/V Challenger *during one of its many research trips to study the New York Bight.*

Irv was not a soldier, but he did his part for the war effort as a shipfitter in the Brooklyn Yards, which turned out the important Liberty ships. Incredibly, these ships were built from the keel to a fully operational vessel in a week or so. I was too young to appreciate the enormity of it, but as the consummate storyteller, he kept us in touch with it all. He had a propensity for embellishment, but his stories always had a basis in truth.

Irv grew up roughshod in Brooklyn, but he always had a connection with the sea. A few years after the war, when he had his second boat, *Wanderer*, he started a charter fishing business out of New Jersey. He would occasionally sneak over to the Sheepshead Bay docks in Brooklyn to hustle stragglers who missed the regular boats. The boats that operated from Sheepshead Bay paid a high fee to work out of there, but Captain Irv would have nothing to do with that. He would keep his boat just off the docks and when the last legitimate boat left for offshore fishing he would quickly move in and announce to the late comers that his boat was leaving in a few minutes. Most of these guys were either coming off a hangover or still drunk from the previous night at the local bars and there were usually plenty of them. Irv would get as many onboard as he could in a few minutes and leave, sometimes with security men chasing him and yelling along the dock. My guess is that he enjoyed pulling a fast one and getting away with it. It was all fair game to him.

Later, my brothers and I worked as his weekend mates in charge of making sure there was plenty of bait, netting caught fish, and running beer and other booze to the clients. For a long time I thought that the sport of deep-sea fishing was supposed to include getting drunk and puking over the side of the boat. Cases and cases of beer and whisky accompanied just about every fishing charter aboard the *Wanderer*. After several hours at sea there would probably be at least one almost comatose person with a fishing line in the water, his bait stolen by a fish long ago. Others, who were still upright, would usually be engaged in a serious card game. One charter was booked by an obvious mob boss. He fished and everyone who came with him was falling all over themselves to make him happy. Irv just shrugged his shoulders and said, "These hoods are a pain in the ass, but they pay well, so who gives a shit."

I remember very vividly one charter that, as usual, included a bunch of heavy drinkers, but they were also serious fishermen. We were out for summer flounder, commonly known as fluke, and I had to make a lot of runs to the container that held the live killifish used for bait. On one trip for bait a fisherman was reaching in, grabbing the live fish, and popping them in his mouth, then washing them down with a swig of beer. I asked him to stop, with no effect. Running back to the captain, I told him that this guy was eating all our bait and Irv just said, "Screw 'em, if they'd rather eat the bait than fish, that's ok by me." Luckily, the idiot got sick and some of the bait was saved, which didn't help much because the fish were just not biting that day.

Toward the end of the trip the fishermen began yelling angrily at the captain. Some of the drunker guys started saying they were going to take over the boat and throw the captain and his kid overboard. Both Irv and I were on the flying bridge, which had one ladder to the deck. Irv started the engine and headed the boat toward home. Since we had been drifting for the fluke, there was no anchor to retrieve. Irv instructed me to take the wheel and stay on the appropriate compass course for home. Captain Irv stood by the ladder with a baseball bat daring them to come up and yelling down, "I'll knock your block off!" I was scared but held on to the boat's steering wheel. After some time and basically a standoff, cooler heads among the fishermen prevailed and everything calmed down. When we reached shore they left without incident and, as I already suspected, there was no tip for me that day.

It was not until I was in my late teens that some friends and I pooled our funds to buy a scuba tank and regulator. With no training in the fundamentals of diving, we ignorantly but gleefully plunged into a lake in nearby Matawan, New Jersey. Fortunately, no one got hurt before we started reading about the bends and particularly the deadly embolism that can result from holding your breath while ascending. Even in shallow water, where a demand regulator compensates for the increased pressure associated with depth, holding your breath while ascending causes the air in your lungs to expand in the presence of an ever-decreasing ambient pressure. This could result in air bubbles passing from your lungs into your bloodstream with possibly devastating results, including paralysis and death, depending where the bubble goes. It is based on a simple rule of physics called Boyle's Law—the volume of a gas at constant temperature varies inversely with the pressure exerted on it—and it puts an untrained or inexperienced scuba diver at serious risk. Any trained diver, even if they cannot quote this law word for word, damn well knows what it means. After about 54 years of diving, I still marvel at the downright good luck we all had in surviving our stupidity, or was it some force of nature that made provisions for future events and allowances for dummies?

After about 54 years of diving, I still marvel at the downright good luck we all had in surviving our stupidity, or was it some force of nature that made provisions for future events and allowances for dummies?

From that point forward, I was destined to spend a good part of my life underwater. So, stupid acts aside, I found a door that led into and under the sea and miraculously, when it opened, its waters did not come rushing out to wash my dreams away.

2

THE EARLY YEARS OF DIVING FOR SCIENCE

IN 1961 THE opportunity of a lifetime came my way. Job prospects for me were grim at best. With no college education and a family on the way, my best bet was to try and establish a career with the Teamsters Union, but those jobs were hard to find. I had just been laid off for the winter months from a Teamster's job with the Allied Moving Company and moved to an apartment in Jersey City, New Jersey, so I could shape-up at the loading docks in Brooklyn.

Every night at midnight, I and about 100 other men faithfully gathered with hopes of being picked to work a shift loading trucks. Each night, some seedy-looking character stood in front of the group and, with an air of arrogance, nodded at a handful of men as the signal that they were the lucky ones to be picked to work that night. Being a fresh face, it would be some time before I was selected to work. It wasn't long until I hated the whole process.

One day I was sitting in my city apartment looking out a window facing an alley with a brick wall on the other side about 10 feet away. A small, white, feathery object floated slowly down. I ran down the four flights and outside to discover a howling blizzard underway. From the apartment window I couldn't even tell that there was a snowstorm outside—how depressing. I craved snowstorms, nature, and the sea and none of it was there. That snowflake might as well have been a brick bouncing off my head.

A week later I read about a new Department of Interior marine laboratory being established on Sandy Hook just outside my hometown of Highlands, New Jersey. I walked into the lab's office and applied for a job. John Clark, assistant director of the Sandy Hook Marine Laboratory, interviewed me. I told him I would do anything, including sweeping floors. I just wanted to be near the ocean and learn about the things that go on at a marine lab. Even though my skills and education were limited, when he learned that I could dive and was pretty good at math, he hired me for one month to work on a recreational fishing creel survey. In pre-computer days that meant pencil-and-paper arithmetic to get averages of fish catches by states, species, regions, etc. Later, a slide rule was added to my pathetic arsenal of tools and, to top it off, a hand-operated adding machine.

At the end of that month, my employment was extended and I had the good fortune of meeting Dr. Lionel Walford, the lab's director. His office was on the second floor of the lab, an old, abandoned World War I Army hospital located at Fort Hancock on the far end of Sandy Hook. The dark wood panels of his office fit his demeanor. He was soft-spoken, thoughtful, brilliant, and, although originally from California, he spoke with an accent befitting an Oxford professor. He wore earth tone clothes and, always, a bow tie. He was tall, slim, and very non-athletic in his appearance. With his thinning hair brushed to the side, Lionel Walford was not exactly an imposing figure, but I sensed great strength of character and intelligence. I found out later that he was a much respected fisheries scientist and author. We hit it off immediately—he, a seasoned and accomplished scientist, and I, a high school-educated knockabout with a very transparent love of, and interest in, the sea.

For the next seven years or so, I was Lionel's student and associate. His own interests in the sea were vast and he had keen instincts for developing scientific protocols. He became particularly interested in my diving experience, as limited as it was at that time. After years of oceanographic studies, he was not satisfied measuring the oceans with nets and probes sent into the depths from the decks of research ships. He knew that much could be accomplished using traditional scientific techniques, but he didn't know how to implement them in the ocean. He felt somewhat blind. As it turns out, he was far ahead of his time.

In a paper he wrote a few years before, Lionel mused over how samples of mid-water organisms caught in a net and dumped on the deck of his research vessel did not tell him how things were ordered before the net did its work. Sure, species diversity, taxonomy, and other things could be determined, but not order. We would talk for hours about how fish school and how they use certain habitats for protection. We can tell a lot about a predator's feeding behavior by studying its stomach contents, but how do they capture their prey and what triggers feeding? How is an ecosystem ordered? Lionel was a man who wanted answers, and he was not satisfied until he got what he wanted. He wanted to know how it felt to dive underwater. Could I see fish and other marine life? Could I tell what fish were doing? Even before Lionel expressed his frustration with working blindly in the sea, French author Gilbert Doukan asked similar questions in his book, *The World Beneath the Waves,* published in 1954.

My underwater experience at this time was limited to the murky waters of New Jersey, but I told Lionel about the tautog, or blackfish, that we hunted with spear guns around the end of rock jetties. I was able to tell him about the fish's behavior of hiding in holes and crevices when threatened and of large striped bass searching along the surf line for prey early in the morning. This was rather basic stuff, but at that time little was known about this or anything else like it below the ocean's surface.

Author taking a lunch break between research dives off the coast of New Jersey.

It was Dr. Walford's scientific curiosity and foresight that gave me the opportunity to advance in marine science. With me as its first dive officer and scientific diver, the Sandy Hook Marine Lab launched one of the original federal diving-for-science programs. It was the dawn of a career that allowed me to spend many thousands of hours in the sea observing and documenting that unknown environment.

The first item to be addressed in starting a diving program at Sandy Hook was getting me certified as its dive officer. Unfortunately, there was no precedent for this at the Department of Interior, so we had to make it up as we proceeded. The lab

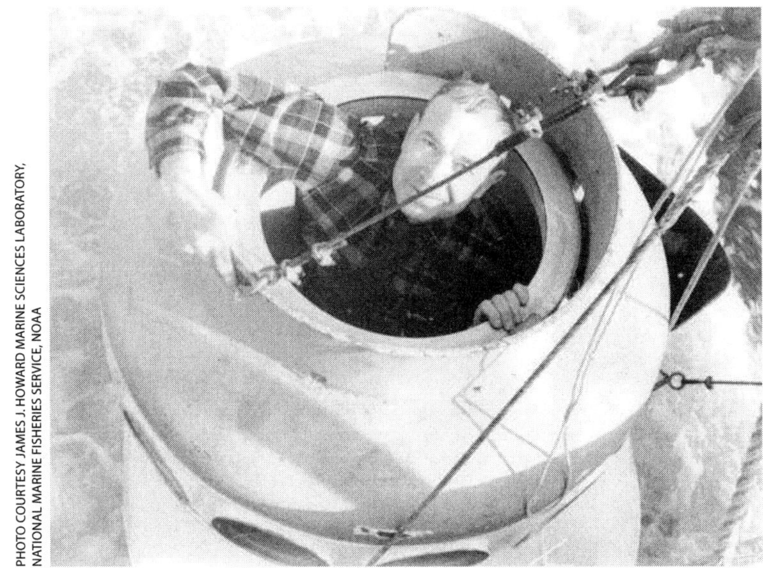

PHOTO COURTESY JAMES J. HOWARD MARINE SCIENCES LABORATORY, NATIONAL MARINE FISHERIES SERVICE, NOAA

Lionel A. Walford preparing to dive in the Shmoo *submersible off the coast of New Jersey*

hired Roy Keiser, a New York YMCA swim and dive instructor, to give me the open-water test. As I was self-taught, he waived the normal requirements and scheduled an open-ocean dive test for me on an artificial reef of discarded rock 70 feet deep off the coast of Fire Island, New York. I had little dive equipment for the test—no tank, regulator, wet suit, or weight belt. I rented a tank and regulator and bought a wet suit for $15 from a friend. There was a little problem with the suit however; its previous owner was six feet three inches tall. I am five feet eight. The only other diving suit I had used previously was a front-entry, thin rubber thing that looked like a condom. It also offered no warmth unless you had clothes on underneath and only then if you could seal the front entry properly—which was just about never. Sometimes these suits would leak so much that the diver could not get out of the water because about 80 pounds of water was trapped around his or her legs. A hole would have to be cut in the foot part of the suit to let the water out.

The swim fins I had for my dive test were ones my grandmother had given me some years before which had diaper pins holding the now broken straps together. To round off my dive equipment ensemble, I had fashioned a weight belt out of some lead weights hung on a piece of rope. I arrived at the boat with all my equipment in a bag and out of sight. If Roy had seen this sorry mess before we left, he most likely would have canceled the trip.

So, on a dreary Saturday morning, our boat left from a Long Island marina and we steamed to the artificial reef for about an hour. After anchoring on the reef area, we prepared to dive. When I appeared on the aft deck Roy looked at me and laughed out loud. I was nervous enough as it was, but I knew that my checkout dive was already in the pits. I stood in front of Roy with a suit draped and baggy on my short body. The diaper pins on my fins were clearly visible. At least I had a slip knot on the weight rope, which I hoped would impress Roy somewhat.

"Bob, do you really want to continue with this?" Roy asked through his now uncontrolled laughter.

"Yes, sir, I really do," I answered with noticeable reservation.

We dove to the 70-foot reef and I did what Roy instructed. Later, in his report to the lab, Roy commented that, under the circumstances of "grossly inadequate dive equipment," I did very well and he recommended I be certified, but only if the lab bought some new gear. So it was, I became the lab's first diver, certified to 70-foot depth —unconventional by today's standards, indeed, but a beginning.

One year later, after some significant experience, I was designated the dive examiner for the entire Northeast region of the Bureau of Sport Fisheries and Wildlife. Anyone who was to dive for the Bureau had to be tested and approved by me. Interestingly enough, I was certifying divers to 120 feet while I was still only technically certified to 70 feet. The bureaucrats were in a dither over this and it took some time to get it all worked out. These were the early years and we had to feel our way along as the scientific diving program was developing.

Just before I received new dive equipment I was tapped to assist a *Life* magazine photographer who wanted still photos of drifters that we used to track currents along the bottom of the New York Bight. They were a very colorful yellow and red and would be published with an article in the magazine on oceanography.

The photographer, his female assistant, John Clark, and I traveled to Shark River Inlet where we could set up the shoot in about 10 feet of water. Scuba gear was not required, but it was early spring and the water was still very cold, so wet suits were in order. Of course I still had the baggy suit that was way too big for me, and to top it off I forgot my swimsuit, so I just put on the rubber suit with nothing underneath.

John saved me from flashing the whole neighborhood when I later walked back to the car, now wearing a towel around my waist.

About an hour later when the shoot was complete, we swam to the jetty and I started to climb up the rocks when John rushed down and pushed me back in the water. What the hell, I thought. What's his problem? It seems that my oversized wet suit had torn along the crotch on some sharp underwater rocks and I was fully exposed. I was so cold I couldn't feel a thing. John saved me from flashing the whole neighborhood when I later walked back to the car, now wearing a towel around my waist. Hypothermia isn't the only danger of diving in frigid waters.

The Sandy Hook Marine Lab was a place of magic for me. I spent hours in the library sucking up knowledge about anything pertaining to the sea, and I spent hours discussing what I was learning with Lionel Walford. I read his book *Living*

Resources of the Sea and heard about his philosophy on fishing and how methods could be improved to help feed the starving people of the world. I learned he was a humanitarian, as well as a scientist. I should have known this right away; his taking me under his wing, so to speak, was a humanitarian act in itself.

When his book was published in 1958, the wisdom of the time was that many standing fish stocks were underutilized. Walford believed this himself, but he was concerned that management of the worldwide fisheries was not based on sound scientific knowledge. Later events proved him right.

The sixties and seventies were the heyday of commercial fishing around the world. Huge fleets from the Soviet Union, Poland, Canada, Cuba, and other countries with trawlers over 200 feet long accompanied by much larger factory ships worked all of the planet's major fisheries. These fleets would often ply the seas off the U.S. East Coast, dragging large nets along the floor of the continental shelf. They would just about scrape the bottom clean of all living things. Some of the nets used by these foreign operations were so large that several 747 jumbo jets could fit inside the "throat" or opening. The fish and just about everything else in the sea did not have a chance.

Management of the fisheries practiced by the fleets back then was called "pulse fishing," meaning that they would fish an area, clean everything out, leave it alone for a little while, and then come back and do it all over again. It doesn't take rocket science to figure out the consequences of these practices. It was common in the sixties to see small mom-and-pop-operated boats from our East Coast fishery bobbing about the huge foreign ships on the edge of the continental shelf during the winter months. The American fleet consisted mostly of 50- to 80-foot wooden-hulled or rusty steel-hulled boats, braving the harsh conditions of winter gales and heavy seas to get their share of the then rich harvests.

> It took almost 50 years of disastrous marine management practices for the bulb to light over our collective undersized brains.

For the next 20 years the oceans were literally raped, putting all of the major worldwide fisheries in jeopardy. Stocks of codfish, the staple of many countries, were almost wiped out. Even the rich Grand Banks fishery off the east coast of Canada, made famous by the book and movie *Captains Courageous*, had to be virtually closed down in later years.

In the early seventies, the U.S. Congress passed the "Magnuson Act," declaring a 200-mile exclusive economic zone and imposing limits on foreign fishing off our coasts. This, in effect, gave back most of the fishing grounds to the U.S. fleet. It did not solve the problem, however, because our own fishery quickly became modernized and eventually over-capitalized, resulting in the continuation of overfishing practices. Quotas were imposed later, but these were so politicized at times by often self-serving interests that they did not work very well and, in fact, not at all in some cases.

In 2004 the U.S. President's Commission on Ocean Policy submitted its report recommending that future marine management practices be based on an "Ecosystem-Wide Protocol," which became buzzwords throughout the oceans' community. In his 1958 book, Walford wrote a whole chapter on the uses of ecological principles. In a nutshell, he said, "Research and thinking...should be directed toward finding principles of ecology...the development of true ecological principles depends on long-continued systematic studies of environments." It took almost 50 years of disastrous marine management practices for the bulb to light over our collective undersized brains.

We cannot afford 50 more years of the same. In fact, we cannot afford five more years, or even one year, of the same. I remember a favorite joke that Lionel often told and which I have repeated over the years. It's funny of itself, but it took me a while to understand how it fits our actions when it comes to the oceans and the environment in general.

It goes like this:

One man confronts another and shouts,

"I say, old man, you have bananas stuck in your ears."

"What did you say?" answers the other man.

"I said, you have bananas stuck in your ears," the first man states once again.

"WHAT?"

"I SAID YOU HAVE BANANAS STICKING OUT OF YOUR EARS!"

"I'm sorry," says the second man, "I can't hear you; I have these damn bananas in my ears."

The man can't hear about his problem because of the problem itself. This can be applied to us and to our policymakers. We can't see our problems of environmental degradation in the oceans or elsewhere, or that the fish are disappearing, because we are the problem itself. We can't see the "forest for the trees." Perhaps another way to put it is, we have our heads stuck up our butts.

3

LEARNING ABOUT THE OCEAN

THE YEARS PASSED at Sandy Hook and I was becoming confident in my ability to contribute something worthwhile to the field of marine science. Diving aside, there was much to know about the oceans. Some of this knowledge came from books, lectures, and the like, but primarily it came from people with vision and creativity I met along the way, and with whom I established a working relationship. Lionel Walford was one, and others that I befriended and trusted during the early years were critical to my success.

One afternoon in my second year at Sandy Hook, Lionel called us together to meet the newest member of our scientific staff. Gathering in the conference room, I noticed a man standing with Lionel, towering over the director's slight six-foot-one frame. In his dry humorous way, Lionel made the introduction, "May I introduce Mr. Bori Olla, the man with a name that reminds me of a northern constellation." Bori was one of the biggest men I had ever seen (although 30 years later, it's common to see kids his size playing on high school football or basketball teams), and little did I imagine at that moment he would become a good friend, mentor, and advisor for much of my career. Brilliant, funny, and complicated, Bori quickly established himself as one of the best scientists in his field of fish behavior and marine science in general. His influence on my ability to think like a scientist and to understand the many things I was seeing underwater was profound.

At first I found his presence intimidating, not because of the difference in our size, but because I felt we were on different intellectual planes. Regardless, we soon became friends, due in part perhaps to similarities in our humble New Jersey upbringings and zest for life that was somewhat on the rough side. As the years passed, however, it became more of a kinship through our love of the sea and mutual respect as our abilities to dig into its many secrets emerged.

Much knowledge came from the lab's library, but the visceral understanding of the sea came from just being there. Watching fish school and feed around the docks, pulling plankton nets at three in the morning to examine their contents, or diving offshore in the winter—these were the things of knowledge that stick to your ribs.

I saw, for instance, juvenile bluefish, referred to locally as snapper, seemingly herding a small school of juvenile menhaden that pulled into a tight circle and swam around and around in the shallow waters of Sandy Hook Bay. Only those that strayed from the group were attacked by the few bluefish that also swam around the outside of the school. Were the bluefish actually herding the menhaden or were the menhaden circling to baffle their attackers? Observations on predator attacks on schools of fish answered that question in later years.

I quickly learned that the physical and biological world below the surface of the oceans was probably more complex than that above. The murky waters within the New York Bight, for example, are influenced by the Hudson River flow that disgorges millions of gallons of fresh and brackish water into the ocean along with pollutants, including organics from farms and sewer systems, chemicals from industries and agriculture, and urban street runoff. The less dense freshwater effluent from the river flows over the top of the higher-salinity ocean water.

During the winter months the water temperature is pretty much uniform from the surface to the bottom, but in the summer a strong thermocline sets up, separating warm surface water from almost winter temperatures below. Once the thermocline is set there is little warming below. During the summer months off the coast of New Jersey, it can be 75°F on the surface, 68°F 25 feet down just on top of the thermocline, and 40°F on the bottom in a depth of only 50 feet. When diving through the thermocline in the summer without a protective hood, it felt like my head was being squeezed in a vise until I acclimated to the cold.

A mass of this cold winter water is trapped every summer in the New York Bight region, extending from just south of Cape Cod, Massachusetts, to south of Cape May, New Jersey, and almost to the edge of the continental shelf. The thermocline acts as a temperature and density barrier to heat reaching the water below. Additionally, oxygen is depleted by bio-activity below and the density difference at the thermocline prevents mixing with rich surface water. This often leads to serious oxygen depletion in bottom water, killing many benthic organisms including fish.

We first discovered this in early September, around 1965, after a hot summer with frequent southerly winds that blew surface water offshore, which was replaced by bottom water that stayed near shore most of the summer. On a number of dives around wrecks and reefs, we saw many lobster, cunner, tautog, hake, several species of crabs, and other animals either dead or dying on the bottom.

In 1969 during an oceanographic cruise, we measured dissolved oxygen levels on the bottom in September that were below 2.0 ppm, not enough to sustain these animals. Organic material coming out of the Hudson River, flowing along the surface and then sinking into the zone below the thermocline, had much to do with the depletion of oxygen on the bottom. In later years this same problem appeared in other coastal regions of the East and the Gulf of Mexico. Each year now, during the summer months, a huge area of the Gulf is declared a "Dead Zone," influenced by organic-laden runoff from the Mississippi River. That the New York Bight region was one of the first "Dead Zones" is not a distinction to crow about.

There were few divers at the Sandy Hook lab, so I had to rely on summer students and a few volunteers to fill in. By the mid-sixties diving had become popularized by Captain Jacques Cousteau, who laid claim to inventing the Self-Contained Underwater Breathing Apparatus (SCUBA) and who was bringing underwater images to the world stage. It was, in part, because of Cousteau that it was getting easier to find people with diving experience. My friend Lee Ward, one of the original guys who chipped in to buy the scuba rig we trained on, would often finish his shift on the DuPont assembly line early in the morning and come right to the boat to fill in as a buddy diver.

Lionel Walford told me one day that he had good news. He had a new volunteer who was a certified diver and had some pretty good underwater photography equipment. He would also be available for the whole summer. Great, I thought, an underwater photographer would be a nice addition to our team. We didn't have any of our own photo equipment at that time and missed recording some interesting fish behavior.

The next day Lionel brought the volunteer down to our office. He was a young boy, only 14 years old. He was a skinny kid with curly black hair and he looked like he was about to fall asleep. After introductions, I looked at Lionel and silently pleaded with him not to do this to me. He's just too young and couldn't be much of a diver, I thought. Lionel was adamant and we were stuck. "Maybe," I told one of our other divers, "we can leave him on deck, but use his cameras." It's a dirty trick, I thought, but, hey, look at him. He'll probably freak out when he bumps into his first fish in the murky water.

On the first dive with our new buddy, David Doubilet, we decided to back off and give him a chance to show us he was capable of the diving tasks. He donned his gear with no trouble and jumped off the *Challenger* with the rest of us, toting a brand new German Rollei camera and underwater housing. Although we watched him very closely, it was obvious that he was a confident diver, which eased our minds considerably. On this and subsequent dives, he did well, took many pictures, and displayed incredible ease in the water.

One time we were lying quietly on the bottom at 60 feet watching some flounder and I motioned to him to take a picture. There was no reaction. I looked closer into his mask and saw that he was asleep—not the last time this would happen. He was a nice and capable kid and we grew fond of him, regardless of his propensity to sleep just about anywhere, even underwater. As it turned out, David became one of the world's most renowned underwater photographers. He now travels the globe photographing for *National Geographic* and many other publications, as well as appearing in documentary television programs and writing or illustrating books on the undersea world. I had the chance to dive with him once again about 20 years later in the Bahamas and he was still a nice kid to me.

Over the next few years, with help from David and other volunteers, we scoured the ocean bottom off the coasts of New Jersey and New York. Although the water visibility was poor most of the time, we were learning a lot about the unknown habits of marine life just a few miles off the most human-populated area in the country. Many times we had to virtually press our face masks against the bottom sediment or rocks to see anything.

On one trip to the Shrewsbury Rocks, which jut out of the sandy bottom just one mile off Monmouth Beach, New Jersey, we were lucky to have over six feet of visibility. The Rocks became a popular sportfishing ground for a number of species and we were interested in surveying their population dynamics. This day we were looking for juvenile habitats among the rocks. While turning over loose stones, we exposed a small blenny-like fish, about two to three inches long. It was darting from place to place.

Soon everywhere we looked there were these strange fish, which we had never seen before. Although well hidden, we determined that this species was the most abundant on the Shrewsbury Rocks. On the next dive in the area we collected a few specimens to key and identify. To our amazement we found that it was the radiated shanny, common in New England waters but never before seen south of Rhode Island. Here was a common species that we found only one mile off the highly populated coast of New Jersey and at a depth of only 35 feet, which was never before known there. Putting our eyes beneath the surface had paid off once again.

A species of fish that we often encountered during our dives was the goosefish, one of the ugliest animals in the sea. It is a cold- and temperate-water species and member of the angler family with a flap of skin on its head that attracts prey into its gigantic mouth. The goosefish can measure over three feet long and up to 50 pounds in weight with much of its length taken up by its head and mouth. When its mouth is open, it presents a gaping tunnel lined with wicked-looking teeth that angle back toward its throat. It got its name from a New Englander who claimed to see a goosefish come to the surface and swallow a whole goose. I believed this because I once found a dead goosefish on the shores of Raritan Bay with two full-sized diving ducks in its stomach.

One of our scientists spent a week aboard a winter bottom trawler in the late sixties and estimated that about 80 percent of the biomass in the catch was goosefish. At that time the fishermen considered these animals of no value and tossed them back into the sea. Now they are considered a delicacy and have been

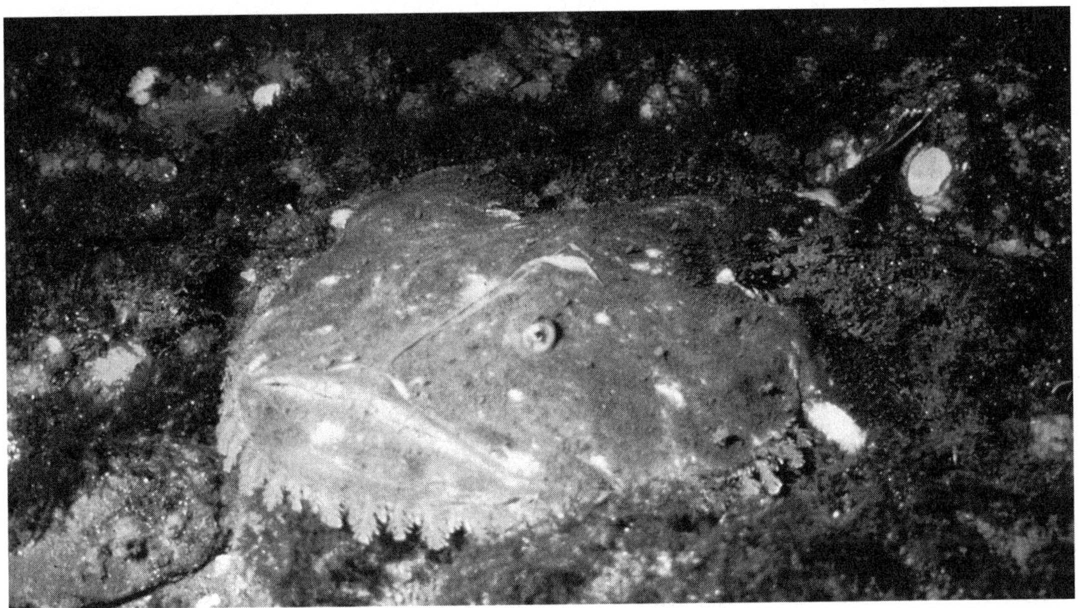

Large goosefish off the coast of New Jersey.

renamed monkfish with the tail section bringing a high market price. Of course, its popularity has resulted in its numbers being significantly reduced.

On more than one occasion while swimming along a sandy area off New Jersey, I had my face pressed fairly close to the bottom as usual because of poor visibility when I noticed an eye looking at me several inches off to one side, then a second eye about the same distance to the other side. Between the eyes I could just make out a mouth with exposed teeth right under my face. It was a goosefish flattened out on the bottom and partially covered with sand. It was lying in ambush of an unsuspecting prey. Each time was a startling experience. My face was within striking distance of a formidable predator with a reputation for being cranky.

On one occasion I pulled upward just as the goosefish snapped at me and quickly swam off. Obviously it was only defending itself against something it perceived as a large predator and not as prey. On another dive off the coast of Massachusetts, I frightened a lobster out of a muddy hole. It was very low visibility and I followed the lobster's muddy trail that led right to a waiting goosefish. The fish opened its huge mouth and swallowed the lobster whole. All I could see were the lobster's crossed claws sticking out of the goosefish's mouth. It is quite a character—ill-tempered, ugly, and, unfortunately for it, good eating. Many people compare the taste of the goosefish's flesh to lobster. Maybe its own taste for lobster gives its meat the same flavor.

4

DRIFTING IN THE NIGHT SEA

During the third year of the diving science program at the Sandy Hook Marine Laboratory, we made a few night dives along the New Jersey coast with homemade lights constructed of headlights from automobiles wired to a 12-volt DC wet cell battery. Our diving depth and horizontal movement were limited by the length of the cable between the light and the battery. This and the murky water allowed us only quick views of bottom organisms moving through the limited lighted area, but it gave us the start for a new project.

I was intrigued by the nighttime behavior of marine organisms in the open mid-water ocean, so I developed a plan to drift around the night sea 30–40 miles off the coast. No one had done this before and we anticipated some exciting sights. The first step was to hang off a line attached to the research vessel *Challenger* and just drift along at about 30 feet deep, observing what we could. With a double set of tanks we could spend a lot of time underwater and a light with a power cable to the surface could shine all night.

By this time we were aware of the presence of large numbers of the great white shark and other potentially dangerous shark species off the New York-New Jersey coast, and we were also aware that most species were active nighttime feeders. So after one test dive, during which we probably spent most of our time looking around for the man-eater that would surely come charging out of the gloom just outside the lighted area and swallow us whole, we changed our plans. We needed a protective cage to make us feel secure enough to concentrate on watching and photographing the activities of the animals in our lights.

We found just what we needed at, of all places, the nearby Earle Naval Ammunition Depot, where ships loaded and unloaded all sorts of military weapons and explosives. As we were a federal agency, the Navy made surplus ammunition crates available to us. The crates were made of heavy steel rods, each one half the size we needed to build a usable underwater cage.

We welded two of the cages together making it four-feet-wide by four-feet-high by eight-feet-long with doors fashioned on both sides. We built underwater lights with two fragile movie spotlights screwed into a 25-cent, rubber outdoor receptacle, waterproofed with a three-inch-wide piece of rubber cut from a bicycle tire tube. We attached this to a 110-volt cable that would bring power from the surface to the lights fastened to the top of the cage. This completed the building phase of our project. The whole thing weighed about 300 pounds and was not easy to move.

The first dive with the cage was on a summer night in 1965. The weather was good, but a steady wind whipped up a three- to four-foot surface chop. The *Challenger* had a cargo mast and boom on the forward deck with which we would lower the cage into the sea and to depth. At about 10 p.m., after a three-hour steam to a site 30 miles offshore, we picked up the cage with *Challenger*'s boom and lowered it to 35 feet. The overall depth was 110 feet. Following the ritual of dressing in wet suits and donning tanks, cameras, and hand lights, Stu Wilk, another scientist at the Sandy Hook lab, and I jumped into the black sea and swam down to the cage with its bright lights illuminating a wide area in two directions. The visibility was good, about 25 feet, being far enough away to avoid the Hudson River runoff. A strong thermocline was detected at 30 feet with a 10°F difference in temperature, from about 68°F at 25 feet deep to about 58°F at 35 feet. We knew there was trouble as soon as we entered the cage.

The *Challenger*, being a round-bottom boat, was rolling in the waves, jerking the cage wildly up and down. It was hard to concentrate on the view outside the cage as we were being hauled up and down through the thermocline, experiencing rapid temperature changes. Not only that, we had to hold on to the cage to ride with it. Otherwise, because we were fairly neutrally buoyant, it would hit us on the way up and again on the way back down. We gutted it out for over an hour and a half and finally gave up when seasickness was added to the mix. The possibility of embolism was also on our minds. Little was seen that night, but we learned a lot about what not to do.

The secret to eliminating the yo-yo effect on the cage by wave action came to us quickly. For the next excursion we simply added a couple of barrels that were positively buoyant. A length of line between the cage and barrels was preset to allow the divers to drift along at 30 feet deep. The differential between the weight of the cage and the buoyancy of the barrels was small, keeping them partially sunk. The waves would flow over the barrels dampening the up and down effect on the cage. The subsequent excursions went well; even in rough seas the cage remained fairly stable.

The only other "bug" in the system was the homemade lighting system on top of the cage. During one of our earlier dives, Stu and I were in our second hour of drifting at about 35 feet when we saw electrical sparking along the top of the cage. There was an obvious leak in our system and it was shorting out. Not understanding

PHOTO COURTESY ROBERT WICKLUND

Preparing the drifting cage for night dives off the New Jersey coast.

the physics of electricity underwater but knowing that 110 volts of electricity mixed with water could be deadly, we decided to bail out before getting fried. Stu opened the cage door and left first.

Within two seconds Stu was back inside the cage, slamming the door shut. He then made the sign that a huge shark came after him out of the darkness. Seeing that the sparking was continuing, I said to myself, screw the shark, and left. Once on the surface I told the crew of the *Challenger* to haul the cage up with Stu inside. I never did see the shark, but Stu was convinced that the shark was after him. The problem of sparking was easily solved with some waterproofing, and it never happened again.

On a good number of nights over the next two years, the *Challenger* headed far offshore where we drifted for hours in the dark sea. We saw some amazing things. The lights on top of the cage attracted many species of planktonic invertebrates and small fish. Of course the lights and the cage itself set up an artificial environment, but many of the natural history aspects of different species were apparent.

On one such night the small fish attracted a small school or pack of young fish, all about four to five inches long. The pack consisted of three species—common mackerel, bluefish, and herring—all appearing to work in unison to attack smaller fish and snap at the larger plankton. The 10 or so individuals stayed pretty much together, only breaking from the school to attack something of interest.

The most remarkable thing about this event was that the three species working together are mortal enemies when they get older and larger. The herring is prey to the mackerel, and both are eaten by the bluefish. Also, adult bluefish and mackerel will prey on all three of the younger fish, which of course is cannibalistic. The system that dictates the interactions of predator and prey in the oceans is basically simple and efficient, but it includes some very complicated and interesting behavioral techniques for capturing prey and avoiding predation.

What we observed that night gave us a wealth of information. It not only showed feeding behaviors; it also illustrated the importance that size plays in the survival of species in the oceans.

In the case of the herring, which is a plankton feeder, it's not clear what advantage there is to joining a pack of predators while feeding. It may be simply that the herring we saw that night became separated from their cohorts and found it safer to join a group of other species than to be by itself.

It's obvious that many predators maintain an advantage when hunting in packs by creating confusion among a school of prey. Our lights disoriented the prey species within the vicinity of the cage, which changed their normal schooling behavior. Their reference point became the lights rather than the school itself and they could be seen scattered about in every position, even upside down. This disorientation of the small fish made a field day for the predators.

What we observed that night gave us a wealth of information. It not only showed feeding behaviors; it also illustrated the importance that size plays in the survival of species in the oceans. Among predators big eat small, including their own kind.

Some marine species are highly specialized to the size of their prey at different times of their lives. An example is a young spiny lobster that I kept in an aquarium in the Bahamas along with a number of juvenile queen conch. The lobster, about four inches long, would attack a small conch about one and a half inches in diameter, turn it over, and then work its legs into the conch shell to pull the animal out. I saw this event several times during a month, and each of the conch prey were about the same size.

When the lobster molted, losing its outer shell, it expanded in size by 20–25 percent. The lobster again attempted to attack the small conch, but it failed. Its legs were now apparently too big to get inside the conch shell, and it would have to move on to larger prey. The juvenile conch, which is slow growing, is spared a whole host of larger lobster predators.

During one long evening we were surrounded by silversides and a number of other juvenile fish species when a pod of 10 squid arrived. They were about 10–12 inches long, including tentacles, but unidentified as to species. The squid moved slowly around the cage in a wide circle, keeping in an amazingly tight group. They swam head first using fins along the sides of their bodies for propulsion. Squid are capable of swimming forward and backward with these fins. They also have a jetting capability by squeezing water through two tubes, which can rapidly propel them forward to escape danger.

The squid continued to swim around the cage for several minutes before one of the 10 moved quickly backwards and away from the pod to capture a small fish with its tentacles. It pulled the hapless prey toward its beak inside the tentacles where they meet the body, then moved quickly back into pod formation while continuing to feed. During a two-hour dive we observed at least a dozen similar attacks by the squid and the same behavior by other groups on subsequent nights.

These observations gave us insight into the squid's social behavior as well as their feeding behavior. Their techniques for hunting and at the same time keeping safe depend on their cooperation. Observations of other species of squid confirmed that they are very complex animals.

Perhaps my fingers looked like another squid, but whatever it was doing was a captivating, almost spiritual experience, and it gave me reservations about my next calamari meal.

On several occasions some years later in the Bahamas, I floated quietly on the surface during daylight watching groups of squid, which became curious about my presence. Most stayed some distance away swimming around my motionless body, but a few bold individuals would cautiously approach, tentacles first. One actually approached my outreached hand and gently caressed my fingers with its tentacles. This was most likely out of curiosity, and not an attempt by the squid to find out if my fingers were good to eat. It didn't grab; it used its tentacles to feel and explore. Perhaps my fingers looked like another squid, but whatever it was doing was a captivating almost spiritual experience, and it gave me reservations about my next calamari meal.

This same species displayed a remarkable escape mechanism when startled. Several times when approached by a squid, I conducted a simple experiment by slapping the surface of the water near the animal. It responded by blanching to white from an almost black color, shooting ink, which took on the shape of a squid of the same size, and jetting rapidly away. All of this appeared to be done instantaneously and at once. The ink held the squid shape for 20 seconds or so. It was obvious that the squid's strategy was to leave a decoy behind as it escaped. If a predator attacked this species of squid, it would most likely go for the ink shape that replaced the departing, now almost invisible prey.

The most exciting evening we spent drifting about off the New Jersey coast was in the summer of 1965. It was a perfect night with little wind and almost dead calm seas. As we approached the 20-mile mark straight off Monmouth Beach, we could see the surface of the ocean roiling in all directions. The sea surface was dimly illuminated by our vessel's lights, and the disturbance, which we identified as a school of fish, seemed to go on for miles as we traveled eastward.

Excited, we decided to stop there and drift though the school. Two of us entered the cage at about 11 p.m. with hand lights and a camera. Within a few minutes, and with many thousands of fish in our view, we identified the fish as round herring, a small, cigar-shaped northern species. They were everywhere and typically oriented to the lights on top of the cage. Within the lighted area the fish moved in all directions. Squid appeared to feed on smaller fish also attracted to the lights; the round herring were apparently too big to eat.

After drifting through this huge school of fish for about a half hour with little action recorded, all of the fish in our view suddenly turned and pointed in one direction. At first and for about 30 seconds, the herring did not advance very far. Then the group around us started to move slowly in unison and in one direction.

It was the sound that startled me. It started as a dull roar and ended with a crescendo that sounded like being on the edge of a large waterfall as the fish moved through the cage at full speed. It became absolutely chaotic; we were totally disoriented.

Moments later the group around the cage was out of sight, but they were followed by thousands more moving at a slightly faster pace. In another couple minutes we were clearly watching the massive school passing by. We could not see much beyond the cage because every inch of ocean in our view was filled with rapidly swimming fish. The parade of herring continued for some time, swimming faster and faster. Within five minutes or so the school was in a panic and moving so fast that thousands came right through the cage, pelting us like hailstones. I tried to take photographs, but the fish were too dense inside the cage, and I only captured blurry images on film.

It was the sound that startled me. It started as a dull roar and ended with a crescendo that sounded like being on the edge of a large waterfall as the fish moved through the cage at full speed. It became absolutely chaotic; we were totally disoriented.

What had prompted this panic in the round herring school? The roaring sound was coming not only from the fish that were hitting the cage, but also from the school itself. The millions of fish swimming at great speeds were making their own sound. Eventually the school thinned out, but became more chaotic with the fish swimming from side to side. It was the back end of the school, and it was then that we saw what had thrown the fish into panic.

Large bluefish, the wolves of the sea, appeared and were attacking the herring. They came out of the darkness and into the lights like waterborne rockets, snapping the herring in two or swallowing them whole. Within seconds our view was filled with hundreds of herring with the bottom halves of their bodies bitten off, still alive and spinning helplessly in circles. The bluefish, each about two feet in length, continued their carnage as the last of the school of herring passed by.

Knowing there were a lot of bioluminescent organisms in the water, we switched off the lights and observed an even more amazing sight. Small, blue-green streaks of bioluminescence were everywhere, looking like a disorganized meteorite shower. The movements of the fleeing prey were stimulating millions of tiny organisms, causing them to flash.

There were longer, heavier streaks of light as the larger bluefish continued to attack. It didn't seem to matter to the predators whether the lights over our cage were on or off. We were awestruck. Watching the lightshow I became so engrossed I forgot where I was. Suddenly the light streaks were gone. When we turned on the lights again the sea appeared empty. It was one of the most dramatic natural history events of my life.

Piecing it all together, we concluded that we were somewhere in the middle of the enormous school of round herring, and when we first saw the fish turn in unison, the bluefish had already started their attack on the edge of the school some distance away. The signal that they were under attack rippled through the school.

As the fish all pointed and started to move in one direction, it appeared they knew where the attack was originating. The school moved faster as the attack intensified and as the bluefish moved closer. The fact that we were inside a massive school of fish afforded us a rare and perhaps once-in-a-lifetime look at their behavior under siege. Millions of fish taking so much time to pass by, even though they were swimming very fast, meant that when the attack began the bluefish were perhaps as far as a mile away, yet the herring in our view knew there was danger and responded.

This experience illustrated to me that the survival of schooling prey species depends not only on numbers but also on their ability to communicate danger to each other.

5

THE JERSEY SEA SERPENT

In addition to the night project, we made many exploratory dives during the day. On one such dive in the summer of 1963, we were interested in observing bluefish behavior and selected a sportfishing ground about 10 miles east of the northern New Jersey shore. Once the bluefish arrived in the summer months, the area became inundated with fishing boats of all sizes, from small, outboard-driven open boats to "head" boats over 100 feet long and carrying up to 100 day sportfishers. Most of the boats drifted and ladled out chum slicks of ground menhaden to attract the hungry bluefish. We had this crazy idea that this would be a good place to dive and observe the bluefish.

We arrived onsite at mid-morning. The skies were cloudy, but otherwise it was a nice day with little wind and calm seas. There were perhaps 200 boats already fishing and chumming up their quarry. We could see bluefish coming onboard boats everywhere and the pungent smell of the oily menhaden chum was pervasive.

The captain positioned the *Challenger* so we could work nearby the fleet, but not so close that we risked getting entangled with the fishing boats. This could be dangerous, especially with divers in the water, not to mention being bad for PR. We decided to stay near the surface and came up frequently to check the position of our boat, so we wouldn't get too far away. We carried a line and float in the form of a plastic, one-gallon bottle to mark our position.

Once in the water we descended to about 25 feet for 10 minutes and didn't see a thing. The visibility was only about 15 feet. It was much deeper, but we figured that the bluefish would be attracted to the surface by the chum slick. The first time we came to the surface the *Challenger* was only 50 feet away. We repeated the dive and on the second ascent we found ourselves near a school of fish jumping out of the water being chased by a large shark with a triangular dorsal fin, which we later identified as a great white. This gave us some hesitation about continuing the dives, but we did two more anyway.

When we finished, my dive partner swam to the boat, but before I started back, something caught my eye just under the surface.

I dove to about 10 feet and saw a long, almost ribbon-like organism, its length disappearing into the murky water 15 feet away. Its body was nine to twelve inches deep and less than three inches wide and it appeared translucent. It was the strangest thing I had ever seen underwater.

I came to the surface and shouted, "You have to come over here and see this!"

By this time my partner was aboard our boat and the captain moved it closer to my position. By luck, Lionel Walford was onboard and he saw the thing right away. I swam alongside the organism for over 30 feet, but was ordered back as the *Challenger* was drifting into the fishing fleet. I never saw either end of it.

It was an interesting, mysterious encounter, but it was definitely not a menacing creature. In all his experience, Lionel had not seen anything like it.

When we returned to the lab, I pored over the literature to find some reference to it. Surely a creature that size must be known to science, I surmised. The closest we could come to finding a description of the animal was an oarfish. The oarfish, a long ribbon-shaped bony fish said to reach lengths of 56 feet but more like 26 feet, is rarely seen in U.S. waters. In Europe it's also known as the "King of Herrings" from a legend that the fish announced the arrival of herring. Since we didn't see the head or tail of the creature, we will never really know if it was an oarfish, but my guess is that it was indeed this species.

That would have been the end of a fun encounter, except that three weeks later John Devlin, science editor for the *New York Times*, interviewed Lionel about the lab's work. Seeing an opening for publicity for the relatively new institution, Walford told the editor the story of the mysterious sea animal, but not in any sensational way.

The next day a fairly prominent article appeared in the paper with the headline "Sandy Hook Ship Sees 'Sea Serpent,'" announcing that "frogmen" would conduct a search the following night. Well, it was true that we were going on one of our now routine night drift dives in a region known locally as the "Mud Hole," but it wasn't to look for the so-called sea serpent.

The Mud Hole is not a hole at all, but a section of a gorge dug by the Hudson River system thousands of years ago when sea level was lower by hundreds of feet and the sea bottom of the continental shelf there was high and dry. It actually extends all the way to the edge of the shelf where the river also dug the Hudson Canyon.

We chose the site because of its fame as a place where pelagic game fish gather. Bluefish, king mackerel, tuna, bonito, and albacore, to name a few, are all caught by sportfishermen there during the summer months.

Early that evening, while we were preparing for our offshore night dive, one of the local charter fishing boats arrived at the Coast Guard station where the *Challenger* was docked. "Unusual to see you here, Jess," yelled the *Challenger* captain. "What are you up to?"

Jesse Ewing, owner and captain of the *Lynn* answered, "I was hired by a bunch of reporters to follow you so they can photograph and record your capture of the sea serpent."

"What?" I yelled. "There's no sea serpent. We're only going out to do our usual thing studying the behavior of night animals. Are they crazy?"

We had already agreed to let a few reporters onboard our boat, but we didn't realize at that time what was happening. Once the article was published in the *New York Times*, it was "Katy, bar the door!" The reporters either didn't believe us or didn't care what we were really doing offshore. As far as they were concerned, the sea monster was our goal.

This was my first experience with a media feeding-frenzy, and there was a lesson to be learned about staying out of the limelight if you want to keep your reputation intact.

This was my first experience with a media feeding-frenzy, and there was a lesson to be learned about staying out of the limelight if you want to keep your reputation intact. I was actually quoted in one paper saying that we were going out to catch the "thing" and hoped to bring it back alive, which was a total fabrication.

Reporters and photographers from the *London Times, Life* magazine, the now defunct *Journal American* in New York, the *Newark Star Ledger*, and more were jamming onto the *Lynn* to follow us to the Mud Hole. By 6:30 p.m. the Coast Guard dock was in utter chaos. It was a story in the making with no basis in reality. The sea serpent was becoming real right in front of our eyes, and there was no stopping it. We could only try to accomplish our mission for the night and, at the same time, accommodate our guests. After all, the fledgling Sandy Hook Marine Laboratory was about to get some much needed publicity. I know that one person onboard the *Challenger* was having a ball and that was Captain Irv, my father, who loved every minute of the show.

The night went fairly smoothly, save almost losing one of the reporters overboard while he was attempting to transfer from the *Lynn* to the *Challenger*. The two vessels were stern to stern. This guy grabbed the railing of the *Challenger* just as a wave passed by moving the boats apart. His partners held on to his legs and he was stretched to the limit. He finally let go of the railing and his body swung down and slammed against the transom of the *Lynn*. He was quickly hauled aboard feet first. Aside from some bruises and feeling like a complete idiot, the reporter was okay.

We went about our business and dove through the night while flashbulbs popped like strobe lights in a disco hall. Monster or no monster, the press was not to be denied their story. So the madness continued for several hours until seasickness drove the crew on the *Lynn* home and rendered the remaining reporters stationed on the *Challenger* a miserable lot for the rest of the night and into the next morning. The Jersey sea serpent did not fade away gracefully; for months afterward we had to deal with letters and calls offering theories that ranged from alien invasions to thoughtful identifications of the creature. Eventually, and thankfully, the whole thing was just about forgotten and I didn't have to face my future career with a sea serpent around my neck.

6

TALE OF THE *SHMOO*

IN THE MID-SIXTIES Nixon Griffis, a New York City character with a lot of time on his hands and even more money, adopted the Sandy Hook lab as his place to become personally involved with marine science. As typical with someone like Nixon, he was the target of all kinds of people wanting him to support mostly wacky ideas, which would not be funded by any responsible organization. I remember one flaky entrepreneur who wanted him to fund a project farming menhaden in the open waters of the Gulf Stream. Fertilizer and iron were to be dumped into the Stream, theoretically producing phytoplankton to feed the fish. The idea was so off-the-wall that even Nixon with his limited experience saw through it pretty fast and backed off.

Nixon came to us one day and said that he had just bought into a pair of subs invented and built by an Australian engineer, and he would be shipping them to the U.S. in the coming summer. He asked if we would be interested in using them for our research at his expense. The offer hit me like a lightning bolt. The opportunity to have our own sub to explore the local waters was beyond belief, and I advised (would have begged) Dr. Walford to say yes, which he did. Lionel was not a diver or even much of a swimmer, but he had an explorer's blood.

The so-called subs turned out to be one-atmosphere, towed vehicles without their own power source. One was a small one-person vehicle that could dive up to 150 feet deep. The other was much larger and could accommodate two persons with a maximum depth of 600 feet. It was the bigger one we were interested in using. It was somewhat round, larger on the bottom, and smaller on top with a series of windows all around. An entrance hatch was placed on top. It allowed for a pilot to sit in front with a set of wheels on each side of the cabin for moving the dive planes up or down to dive or surface—the only control that he had. A passenger sat in tandem just behind the pilot. Three additional windows were set in the rounded bottom.

Although its official name was the *Bathyscanner*, it immediately reminded us of the *Li'l Abner* cartoon character called the Shmoo, which looked like a fat bowling

PHOTO COURTESY ROBERT WICKLUND

Towed research submersible Shmoo *being prepared for a dive off the coast of New Jersey.*

pin or a pear. The name stuck, and forever after the strange-looking sub was called the *Shmoo.*

Its operation was simple. We fashioned about 900 pounds of lead weights that fit in the bottom and with two people it was made to be positively buoyant. By adding or subtracting lead ballast, depending on the weight of the passengers, we could keep the *Shmoo* at about 50–75 pounds buoyant. Once the boat started to tow the sub, the pilot turned the wheels forward which would orient the dive planes downward, forcing the vehicle underwater. It would come up just as easily when the planes were turned up. If the forward motion stopped, the *Shmoo* would simply float to the surface.

Within several weeks of the *Shmoo*'s delivery to Sandy Hook, the *Challenger* was fitted with an A-frame and a salvaged winch previously used for pulling Navy blimps down into their berthing docks. The *Shmoo* weighed something over a ton and this combination of A-frame and winch allowed us to lift the sub a few feet out of the water and fasten it against the transom of the boat. It was secured against a tire mat hanging off the back of the boat with a hand-operated come-along. There the passengers could enter and emerge from the top hatch of the strange little sub.

Our first test would be manned by the inventor of the sub from Australia, whose name I have forgotten, and me. We planned on a two-hour dive just off the tip of Sandy Hook, primarily to test for stability, handling, and general usefulness as a scientific and exploratory tool. Our efficiency at launch and retrieval was also being tested. Maximum depth would only be about 60 feet or so.

The first and only dive that day went as anticipated for the first hour. The *Shmoo* handled well. We were able to dive to the bottom and bring it back to the surface with relative ease. The simple CO_2 scrubber and oxygen system inside the cabin seemed to be working okay. Communications to the surface vessel was a cheap two-way walkie-talkie attached to a wire strung along the 5/8-inch rope towline.

Sometime into the second hour we both started to feel funny, a little light-headed, and our breathing became heavy. We alerted the boat crew, but told them it was okay for now and we'd continue the dive. Ten minutes later we were feeling worse and breathing became harder. It was obvious that the carbon dioxide levels were rising and we would have to abort the mission. The scrubber fan was still working and the canister was filled with lithium hydroxide that scrubs the CO_2, but we still had problems.

"Topside, this is *Shmoo*—we will have to abort. Our CO_2 levels are rising and we both feel bad."

Unfortunately, the seas had picked up and it took some time to secure us. By the time we got out into fresh air on the deck of the *Challenger*, both the Australian and I were puking our guts out, and we had major headaches for hours afterward. Okay, so the first test had some problems. We'll fix the scrubber and not much else could go wrong, we thought. Captain Irv was not very happy with the situation. He was used to putting things underwater, but not with people inside, and especially not his son. It took some time and a lot of whining to get it straight with him.

After a thorough testing of the life-support system in the *Shmoo* and assuring ourselves that all of the bugs were worked out, we planned our second dive on the Shrewsbury Rocks, a favorite bottom fishing area. The site was an extensive rocky reef in 60–80 feet of water, rising some 5–10 feet above the sandy bottom. We hoped to see how fish, lobster, and other organisms used the reef for shelter and food.

I was the pilot on this dive, accompanied by Joe Deaver, a general technician at the lab. Once we were onsite and all of our safety and operational checks were completed, we entered the *Shmoo*, closed the overhead hatch, and were launched off the stern of the *Challenger*. While we were under a slow tow and the boat crew was letting out the 5/8-inch nylon line, we made the final checks of the oxygen flow of 1.5 liters per minute per person, new CO_2 scrubbing system, dive planes, and communication system.

Once the towline was let out to about three times the planned dive depth, it was secured to a cleat on the *Challenger* and the speed was set for about two knots.

With Joe sitting behind me, I started the dive to the bottom where we hoped to see much of the Shrewsbury Rocks. I turned the diving planes down sharply and we started a smooth descent into the very murky water. We hoped the visibility would improve once we dove below the thermocline.

The *Shmoo* was heavily built and we were confident that everything was okay. Unknown to us at that moment, however, the stainless steel ring that held a lower window in place had been ripped off in the initial crash.

The descent was slower than I expected, and I had to push the dive planes to dig into the water even more. It was soon apparent that the long, heavy towline was acting as a plane itself, tending to pull us upward. Even so, we continued to descend.

Unfortunately, the visibility did not improve below the thermocline, and, in fact, it became a little worse. I had my face pressed against the small round window watching for the bottom, but before I could see it, the *Shmoo* hit the rocky reef with a loud bang, bouncing up off the rocks and then down again, all in an instant.

The *Shmoo* was heavily built and we were confident that everything was okay. Unknown to us at that moment, however, the stainless steel ring that held a lower window in place had been ripped off in the initial crash. The lower windows were difficult to access from our seats, and we couldn't see that one had lost its outer ring. The second crash cracked that window in two. The ten-inch-round windows were five inches thick and made of beveled acrylic to fit into a cone-shaped hole in the sub. The damaged window had a clearly visible crack right down the middle and water was shooting into the *Shmoo*'s cabin.

Fortunately, the differential between the outside ambient pressure of roughly 50 psi and the cabin pressure of 14.7 psi kept the window in place; otherwise, the two pieces of window would have just fallen out and the *Shmoo* would have flooded in moments. As it was, we were rapidly filling with water.

We immediately called the surface crew, told them of our plight, and instructed them to shut down the *Challenger* and pull us up. We realized that by this time we had already lost our buoyancy due to the flooding and added weight of the water. We knew our situation was grave. Some quick decisions had to be made if we had any chance of surviving. We had two scuba tanks and regulators wedged under the seats, but we didn't have enough time to free them. I considered bailing out with the tanks, but Joe was not a diver and it would have been dangerous at best for him. I also considered a free ascent without tanks, but again, Joe would probably not have made it.

The boat crew started slowly winching us to the surface with the towline, and we waited with some trepidation as the water level in the *Shmoo* reached above the seat and up to our waists. At that point we had to shut down the scrubber and fan, which were operated by a 12v motor, and also the oxygen system. Oxygen was not a problem because the flooding increased the cabin pressure, thereby increasing the partial pressure of oxygen. We didn't anticipate being in the sub long enough for increasing CO_2 levels to be a problem. Our main concern was that we were in 80 feet or so of water and flooding rapidly. We kept the communication system out of the rising water so we could keep the surface crew apprised of our situation.

I was thankful that Joe stayed cool even though he was not a diver nor had any experience with subs. When we finally saw the light increasing as we approached the surface, the water was up to the middle of our chests. The *Challenger* crew attached the cable to the *Shmoo* and lifted it high enough above the ocean surface to barely expose the hatch, then quickly pulled the sub against the transom. On cue we opened the hatch and scrambled out of the *Shmoo* and safely onto the vessel's deck. Just before we left the sub after opening the hatch, I saw the broken window fall out as the inside and outside pressures equalized and the *Shmoo* flooded almost to hatch level. When the crew attempted to lift the sub, the increased weight broke the lifting cable and the *Shmoo* went to the bottom. The towline was still attached, so we tied a marker buoy to it and left, intending to come back the next day for a recovery operation.

Captain Irv said good riddance to "that dangerous piece of crap" and wanted it left on the bottom. He then said to me, "If that thing is recovered, why don't we just save time and bury you in it. Two dives and two close calls—not good, damn it!"

He was pissed and scared. I felt bad for him, but the more I experienced being underwater, good or bad, the more I became hooked. My father, an adventurous soul in his own right, recognized this and continued to be supportive, in spite of his well-founded concerns. This was my first experience with in-your-face undersea danger and another life lesson in safety and recognition of our fragility in an alien environment. It would not be the last of these lessons for me, as time has told.

The next day we returned to the site where the *Shmoo* lay on the bottom of the ocean. We dove to attach a heavy lifting cable and within one hour had it snug against the *Challenger*'s transom. On shore we removed all three lower windows and had solid steel plugs manufactured to take their place. We also replaced the towrope with a ¼-inch stainless steel cable that, with much less surface area, would reduce the lifting effect on the sub. With these changes and limiting our study areas offshore to low bottom relief, we were able to operate the *Shmoo* effectively and safely for two summer seasons.

We made several dozen dives in the *Shmoo* and gave a number of people the experience of seeing the ocean world firsthand. Lionel Walford was one, and he was delighted to finally see underwater himself.

On one dive, coming from offshore into the inner New York Bight, we were being towed at four knots right above the thermocline at a 35-foot depth when we came upon a mass of coelenterate jellyfish. We saw the group for at least a mile and, to our amazement, most had from one to several juvenile fish using their two-foot tentacles for protection. We estimated that there were tens of thousands of the jellyfish and at least as many juvenile fish. Among them we could only identify a few jacks, but more importantly, this was our first and last observation of a major group of juveniles using jellyfish for protection in the open ocean. We speculated that this one observation was indicative of a common survival behavior used by a number of species. Nursery grounds are not limited to estuary systems; they can even be living habitats in open ocean water.

All in all, the *Shmoo* performed well after the initial snafus, and we saw a lot of the New York Bight. One major hitch in the design was that, even with the small surface area of the ¼-inch tow cable, we could not dive much deeper than 150 feet. At about that depth the cable's lifting effect took over, which prevented us from going any further.

Captain Irv continued to be skeptical of our operation throughout the two seasons. To add insult, on one dive into cold water I didn't have any warm clothes, so I borrowed my father's hooded sweatshirt. When the dive was completed and we were on the surface waiting to be picked up, a stiff wind started to churn the seas, delaying the time it took to retrieve the sub. The *Shmoo* moved in all directions and, of course, I started to feel queasy. I knew I wouldn't make it until we were hauled out of the water, but if I let go in the sub it would take me days to clean it out. I had no choice but to unzip the sweatshirt and use it as a receptacle. When I climbed out of the *Shmoo*, I handed the folded shirt to the captain. He looked at it, yelled "Son of a bitch!" and threw the sweatshirt overboard. It took some time to smooth that one over.

The *Shmoo* had an inglorious ending. It went from Sandy Hook to a Connecticut engineer's backyard, then on to my farm in Virginia for a few years, and finally into storage at the Fort Fisher Aquarium in North Carolina before winding up as scrap.

7

FLIGHT OF THE ALBATROSS

During my tenure at Sandy Hook I was involved in a project mapping monthly sea-surface temperatures off the New Jersey and New York coasts, up to 100 miles offshore, using a new airborne infrared radiation thermometer. Started by John Clark, it was a joint project between the Sandy Hook lab and the U.S. Coast Guard. Flying in a twin-engine Grumman UF Albatross amphibian plane, normally used by the Coast Guard for search and rescue operations, we took continuous surface temperature measurements as the plane flew at 500 feet above the ocean along 100-mile transects extending just beyond the continental shelf.

We flew and measured two days each month, covering the ocean from Montauk Point, Long Island, to Cape Henlopen, Delaware. At the end of each two-day trip, we drew up an isotherm map to be used to find the best places to fish and to gather general information about the region's physical oceanography. Every month we also threw out five surface drift bottles and five bottom drifters at predetermined stations along the way, each labeled with a reward offer for their return with information such as date, time, and location found. These were designed to determine gross surface and bottom current patterns along the mid-Atlantic shelf.

The flights originated at Floyd Bennett Field in Brooklyn, famous for some of the early pilots, among them Amelia Earhart, Wiley Post, and "Wrong Way" Corrigan, who started out to fly cross-country and wound up in Dublin, Ireland. As the junior member of the two-man team, I drew the unenviable duty of flying all the winter months. The period from about mid-December through the end of March was brutal. On cold days the relatively warm water caused rising air currents. Flying at 500 feet over the sea surface meant our plane was continuously thrown up and down. It was a five-hour roller coaster ride. Winter winds added to the misery. I was airsick on most of my flights, and it didn't help that I had to concentrate on the instrument that was graphing the seawater temperature.

As we approached a drifter station, I had to open a large hatch to throw the drifters out. The latch was often left open, which kept the inside of the cabin frigid, and a safety harness kept me from falling out. I was sick and I was freezing, but I wouldn't have missed it. We often saw whales on the edge of the shelf and small, poor American fishing boats, which would heave in the heavy winter seas while the large Soviet, Polish, and other foreign fleets rolled with ease. On particularly cold days steam rose in spirals from the ocean, looking like smoke from a thousand campfires. I fantasized that the steaming spirals, which we called "smokers," were the spirits of sailors lost at sea over the centuries. In these waters the bones of ships and men are common.

> "Tower, now our port engine is giving us trouble. It's missing on several cylinders. We may not make it to our home base. Please advise." Now we were nervous. Both John and I immediately cinched our seat belts a notch or two tighter.

The first year went well. We produced 12 monthly maps of sea-surface temperatures and developed a sizable mailing list of fishermen, scientists, government agencies, and anyone else who wanted the information. We were particularly interested in the distribution of migratory fish in relation to seawater temperature regimes.

During the second winter, John Clark and I worked the flights together in January. For the second flight that month, we arrived at Floyd Bennett Field at about 6:00 a.m. to set up the temperature recording equipment in preparation for our scheduled 7:00 a.m. takeoff. It was a very cold, windy morning with air temperatures well below freezing. We learned that the chief pilot for this flight would be an older reserve captain needing some flight hours to stay qualified. A regular career Coast Guardsman served as copilot. The infrared camera was mounted on the outside bracket, the recorder calibrated, and the Albatross's engines warmed; we were ready to go.

After takeoff we headed south along the New Jersey shore. We had completed the first half of the monthly course the day before and would pick up the first transect around Barnegat Bay, working south. When we reached the starting point of the transect line right at the shoreline, the pilot turned the plane due east. We were at 500 feet and immediately the plane started bouncing. I knew we were in for a rough five hours. The ocean below was whipped into frothy whitecaps by the wind, and my stomach was already telling me that I shouldn't have eaten that egg sandwich.

A few minutes into the flight heading offshore, one of the engines started to sputter and vibrate violently. John and I, and the three crew members in the back cabin, put on our headsets to listen to the captain's communications. "I just shut down our starboard engine before it tore loose. This craft flies well on one engine, so we'll abort our trip, climb to 1,000 feet, and head back to Brooklyn."

Everything seemed okay and we weren't too concerned. The plane reached 1,000 feet seconds later as we headed west back to the shoreline and then turned north toward home. While listening to the captain's report of our situation to the Floyd Bennett command tower, an irregular sound started coming from the port engine. We could hear it over the captain's voice.

"Tower, now our port engine is giving us trouble. It's missing on several cylinders. We may not make it to our home base. Please advise."

Now we were nervous. Both John and I immediately cinched our seat belts a notch or two tighter. For the next several minutes the captain and copilot discussed possible alternatives. They discussed an ocean landing, but the seas had increased to 8- to 10-foot breaking waves, and even this staunch seaplane would not make it under such conditions.

Barnegat Bay was within sight, but it was entirely covered with rough ice. The port engine was losing power but was still running for the moment. A decision had to be made quickly. Finally, the captain, who was visibly and audibly shaken, decided to belly-land the plane on the ocean beach.

I thought about all the debris on the New Jersey beaches, including logs, barrels, and many other large objects commonly found there that could tear the plane apart. The copilot, a young lieutenant, must have also thought of the consequences of a beach landing and took control of the plane, to the captain's relief we surmised. He decided to head inland for 10 miles to the Lakehurst Naval Air Station. Lakehurst was huge and had been a base for rigid dirigibles in their glory days, including the German Hindenburg that tragically exploded and burned while landing there in 1937.

The Albatross was now headed due west toward Lakehurst. The engine was running at partial power, and we were dropping at about 100 feet per minute. I wondered if we were going to make it. The lieutenant called the Lakehurst station and informed them that he was making an emergency landing at a runway he knew was directly ahead.

The Lakehurst control tower came back and said, "Negative, that runway has been closed for years. Turn north or south and use one of the open runways."

"Can't do it," replied the pilot; "If I turn, the plane will fall out of the sky."

"Be advised, you do not have permission to use that runway!" was the answer from the Lakehurst tower.

The pilot had no time to argue; he severed communications, told us to hold on, and continued to head for the closed runway. By this time we were back down to 500 feet high and dropping fast. We could see the runway ahead.

The plane continued to lose altitude as we skimmed over a stand of pine trees. The landing gear was lowered and moments later we came down hard and fast onto the rough runway. The brakes screamed as we slowed.

When the engine was shut down, we all just sat quietly for a moment. I became aware that I was having trouble breathing and realized that for the last few minutes of our flight I kept tightening my seat belt to the point it was restricting my diaphragm. The young lieutenant had saved our lives. Once the Albatross was secured, he turned around and said to us, "Well, there were a few minutes there when you couldn't have pounded a tenpenny nail up my ass with a sledgehammer."

He was a very cool guy, indeed. Wiley Post, or any of those old pilots that called Floyd Bennett Field home, had nothing on this Coast Guard officer. I wish I could remember his name.

When the drifters were deployed, we had to wait for people to find them. They ended up mainly on the beaches, but sometimes fishermen would find them in the open ocean. The finders were supposed to fill in the information on the card inside the surface drifter or cut off the plastic tag on the bottom drifters and send them to us for the reward.

We received a good many returns except from the remote beaches of Sandy Hook, which created a gap along the coast. Since the entire peninsula was owned by the military, very few people had access to its beaches. The beaches were particularly empty in the winter; the cold winds and frigid temperatures made them very hostile to casual strollers or fishermen.

On very cold nights with the air temperature well below freezing and the wind blowing out of the north, a few hardy souls might build fires on the beaches and "frost fish." This consists of walking the beaches at the surf line where a species of hake often feeds at night and is occasionally exposed to the air in pursuit of its prey. The fish are immediately stunned by the cold and thrown up onto the beach by the waves; the fishermen then collect them by hand. The harshness of the winter beach is even too much for the fish.

During the winter we had to search the several miles of the Sandy Hook coast ourselves for drifters carried by the ocean currents to its beaches. Bori agreed to help, so he, Dave Hanson, a lab technician, and I spent many hours driving along the water's edge in a four-wheel-drive truck owned by the lab looking for the drifters with pretty good success.

On one extremely cold morning when the lab's truck was not available, Dave offered to use his tiny convertible sports car. He argued that it was cold enough for the wet beach to have frozen when the tide went out and his small car wouldn't have a problem negotiating the beach.

Not wanting to miss a day of collection, at 8:00 a.m. the three of us piled into the open car and headed for the beach. The strand near the water's edge was indeed frozen solid, and Dave whipped his prized car along at somewhere around 60 miles an hour. There were straight clean runs of over a mile. Dave hated stopping to pick up drifters. He was there for the thrill of driving in a place few people would ever experience.

At about 10:30 a.m. the tide was starting its flooding stage, and we knew that we had about a half hour of searching time left. Or so we thought. We concerned ourselves with the incoming tide, but didn't calculate the effects of the rising sun on the frozen sand. Around 10:45 a.m. we were moving along nicely when we spotted a drift bottle partially buried in the sand. We stopped and Bori and I walked over to the bottle. He picked it up, turned back toward the car, and yelled. The sun had done its thing and Dave's car had sunk into the now softened sand. Worse yet, his beloved car was below the tidemark, and within an hour or so seawater would completely cover the vehicle making it a candidate for an artificial reef.

Almost instantly Dave's demeanor went from exhilaration to sheer panic. He desperately tried to move the car, but it only dug in deeper. Bori and I ran up the beach to collect driftwood or anything else we could find to place under the wheels. Nothing worked and we could see the ocean moving slowly higher. There was nothing in the world that could be done to stop the impending drowning of Dave's car.

In a final desperate attempt, Bori and I ran to the lab's maintenance garage through snow and sand, reaching it some 20 minutes later. Fortunately there were two workers there; we pleaded with them to bring the four-wheel-drive truck to pull the car off the beach. They weren't happy, but they came anyway. We got it out just in time. The water had surrounded the car, but it wasn't deep enough to do any damage—another heart-stopping moment in the name of science.

8

WINTER DIVING

THE WINTER COASTAL waters off New Jersey are quite cold. Following a fall cooling of surface water, the thermocline becomes unstable and there is a turnover of the water column. The onset of winter cools the ocean uniformly from surface to bottom, and it stays that way until the formation of a new thermocline in late spring to early summer.

The fact that few people had ever attempted to observe the winter behavior of marine organisms off the northeast coast prompted us to spend some time diving in January and February to observe what happens on the ocean bottom during the coldest time of year. The best protection we had was a ¼-inch neoprene wet suit that kept us warm for 20 minutes or so in the more or less 30°F water temperature. Most of our dives lasted 45 minutes or more, and it took a full hour to warm up for the next one.

The *Challenger* was our dive platform for all offshore dives. In the early years, the accommodations were very austere with a heated galley and a few bunks below. The cooking facilities consisted of a sterno stove and a can opener, and the food was canned Dinty Moore stew. Following a long dive, we gathered in the galley and took turns heating the stew right in the cans. We were cold and shivering, but the hot stew warmed us and we were as happy as pigs in a mudhole. Before long we couldn't wait to get back in the ocean.

Many of our dives were in typically murky water. Often we would swim along with our faces only about a foot or so from the bottom, but it was enough to see that few organisms were active. We saw pipefish and seahorses, normally found in the estuaries, lying dormant under seaweed several miles offshore. A number of species of snails were active, especially the moon snail, a large gastropod we observed attacking hibernating blue claw crabs buried six to eight inches in the sand and mud. The snails were somehow able to detect the buried crabs, digging down to envelop and consume them. Most of the time we only saw the tops of the snails, or simply a depression in the sediment. We dug in and pulled the snail out, still attached to the crab. This was the first and, I believe, the only observation of the moon snail as a major winter predator of the commercially important blue claw crab. How the snails find the crabs under the sediment is still a mystery.

In a lab experiment between dives, we measured the heart rate of a summer flounder in a tank at ambient winter temperature ranging from 32°F to 40°F. Over several months the dormant fish was attacked by scores of tiny periwinkle snails that found their way into the water system and were actually eating the flounder alive. Flounder normally migrate to winter grounds near the edge of the continental shelf where the bottom water temperatures are warmer. If for some reason the fish were to fail the migration and stay inshore, their fate would probably be similar to the one in the tank.

On one particularly cold winter morning, we decided to do a little exploring offshore aboard the *Challenger*. The air temperatures hovered around 10°F and Sandy Hook Bay had a thin layer of surface ice ranging from the Coast Guard dock to the tip of the Hook.

We got underway about 7:00 a.m., steering the old wooden-hulled boat through the ice. The thin ice cover easily gave way to the slow movement of the vessel. It was not until we were about 500 yards from the dock that we looked behind us and saw what looked like a bloody trail in our wake.

We realized soon enough that the trail was red bottom paint from the *Challenger*. The captain leaned over the rail, heard a ripping sound, and saw that the sheer ice was cutting into the hull at the waterline like a knife. The boat was literally being cut in half by the ice.

Of course we turned around and followed the broken ice trail back to the dock. Even though the *Challenger* had a thick-planked hull, it was scary to see how easily the ice sliced into the wood. There was an extremely clean cut in the hull extending from the prow to the transom on both sides and almost a half inch deep in some places. If the ice had been thicker, it might have scraped some paint off the hull, but it would not have been able to cut. The sea had taught us another valuable lesson. Luckily, we learned quickly enough to avoid significant damage or, at worst, disaster.

Winter diving off New Jersey was both painful and exhilarating. Even though there was not much to see close to the coast, it was still useful and confirmed what all fishermen already knew—that most fish migrated out to deeper, warmer waters. A few species, such as the small pipefishes and seahorses, lay dormant around shells or seagrass a mile or so offshore.

We later learned, diving under the ice in Newfoundland, that cunner, a common local fish, actually hibernated close to shore in winter. Just a little more information about what goes on in the ocean, even in winter.

9

SHARK COUNTRY

THE SHARK POPULATION in New York and New Jersey waters was quite healthy in the 1960s. Large fishing tournaments targeting sharks took place every summer, resulting in hundreds being brought in by sportfishing boats and hung on the docks for photo ops alongside an often drunk, hairy-chested "sportsman." In retrospect it was obscene that these animals were caught, photographed, and then mostly discarded overboard. Every shark species that inhabited the region was caught in one tournament or another with the mako and great white winning the big prizes.

The knowledge that large catches of sharks were common in the New York Bight did not deter us from diving in its dark, murky waters. We knew they were there, but we simply did not think much about the possibility that we might have been swimming alongside these magnificent, but often scary animals. It might have been better if we had been able see the sharks, but in water that seldom exceeded six-foot visibility, this was unlikely unless they were right on top of us. So we just didn't think about it.

Years later, an old friend and commercial diver, "Big John" McLaughlin, told me a story about a contract he had to repair a Navy buoy in the Tongue of the Ocean in the Bahamas, 180 feet below the surface in gin-clear water.

Descending to the buoy, he saw what appeared to be a large school of fish, which started to swim up to him. As they approached, he saw that they were actually hundreds of sharks swimming all around, sometimes bumping into him. John, who was about the coolest diver alive at that time, couldn't function with the unnerving activity of the sharks. He stopped his descent and quickly swam back up to the surface boat. On deck, the project supervisor was unsympathetic and reminded him that he was under contract to complete the job. So John went back into the water, closed his eyes, and felt his way along the cable leading all the way down to the buoy at 180 feet with the sharks following. He completed his task and then ascended, again with his eyes closed. I guess we did the same kind of thing diving in the murky waters, but we didn't have to shut our eyes, only our brains.

Jack Casey was our resident shark expert at Sandy Hook. An affable fellow and a good friend, Jack spent days at the shark tournaments collecting data on population dynamics, spawning, feeding behavior, and the like. He often set out buoyed lines with baited hooks from the *Challenger* in selected areas specifically to catch sharks for tagging purposes.

Called longline fishing, the rigs were sometimes over a mile long with many surface buoys and hundreds of hooks. After "soaking" for a few hours, the longlines were retrieved and any sharks caught were measured, weight estimated, tagged, and released. On one occasion he set out a longline on the Shrewsbury Rocks, just one mile off the New Jersey beaches. When he pulled in the line several hours later, he had caught about 20 sharks, a number of which were great whites. The whites were young and relatively small, if a 400-pound shark can be called small (a great white can grow to 20 feet long and exceed 4,000 pounds).

This catch on the Shrewsbury Rocks, one of our dive study areas, was a little disconcerting to say the least. We dove with some trepidation for a while, but soon we were able to once again shut down the part of our brain that worried about the danger of shark encounters. Aside from feeling a presence in the murky water or a passing shadow now and again, we had no shark encounters in all our years of diving the waters of the New York Bight.

Captain Irv told me a funny story about one of their shark study adventures. Casey's crew was catching and tagging sharks one summer day only about a mile off the beaches of Coney Island, New York. Many thousands of people used this beach and there could be thousands in the water at one time. One of the sharks brought alongside the *Challenger,* tagged, and released that day was a rather large great white. Unlike other species that could not wait to get away after being released, the white shark stayed on the surface, turned, and attacked the boat, biting the hull.

It did this several times and then turned and swam off along the surface toward shore, straight for the Coney Island beach with all those people in the water. Alarmed, the crew headed the boat inshore and managed to get between the shark and the beach. At this point the great white again attacked the boat. The crew was able to get a gaff into the shark and lift it onboard.

With a sigh of relief they quickly dispatched the shark. From then on their policy was that, due to their unpredictable nature, great whites would not be tagged. We could only imagine the fallout if a pissed-off shark, with an official U.S. government tag on its back, were to eat a Brooklyn bather.

10

THE *BEN FRANKLIN*

IN 1969 A 30-DAY joint expedition was undertaken by the Grumman Aircraft Engineering Corporation and U.S. Navy using the Grumman/PX-15 submersible, or mesoscaphe, also known as the *Ben Franklin*, to drift 1,500 miles in the Gulf Stream from Florida to Maine.

The *Ben Franklin*, designed by famed explorer Jacques Piccard, was relatively large for a research submersible at almost 50 feet in length and 10 feet in diameter. The purpose of the drift project was to observe the Gulf Stream at the sub's depth limit of 2,000 feet, using only the currents for propulsion. This expedition turned out to be rather uneventful and prompted some of the crew to rename the Blake Plateau, a broad, relatively flat part of the Southeast Continental Margin at around 1,500 feet, the Bleak Plateau, since there was little evidence of life in that area.

Following the drift expedition, Grumman and the Navy made the sub available to scientists for short dives on its way back to Florida. As we were becoming more convinced than ever that studying the oceans from an underwater vantage point was extremely valuable, I jumped at the opportunity.

I met the support vessel, *Privateer,* at a dock in Atlantic City. The *Ben Franklin* was tied to the side of the boat. After loading supplies and planning where the dive was going to be made, we left the dock and steamed to the edge of the continental shelf where we could dive to between 1,200 and 2,000 feet. With the *Ben Franklin* under tow, the trip was slow and took all night.

Once onsite the sub crew boarded a rubber dinghy and headed for the *Ben Franklin*, still attached to a towline some 200 feet behind the *Privateer*. The towline was removed and the crew had the sub operational. I transferred over to it in the dinghy, which slid up on the sub's hull and bounced around in the waves. I readied myself at the bow and jumped onto the sub's deck as quickly as possible. After a short climb up a ladder to the top of the conning tower, through the hatch, and down another ladder, I was inside the sub.

Compared to small research subs, the interior of the *Ben Franklin* was enormous. There was plenty of overhead to walk around, a small galley, and a head. Once the dive began and we moved below the thermocline into cold water, the inside of the sub cooled off quickly. I found a blanket and spent the next eight hours with my face against a small porthole where I could see the few feet in front of it that was illuminated. Cruising just off the bottom at about 1,500 feet, the scene was fascinating.

The deepwater grenadier, or rattail, was common near the bottom with their long extended tail fins trailing behind as they swam by slowly. An unidentified, large red deepwater crab species was in our lights most of the dive.

Although relatively small in size, the hagfish was the only "monster" of the deep I observed on that trip. Eel-like in appearance, blind, and ranging in size from one to two feet long and several inches in diameter, the hagfish attaches its jawless mouth to the side of a fish and, with its tongue studded with rasp-like teeth, bores into its hapless victim sucking everything out and leaving behind only skin and bones. On several occasions a hagfish, apparently attracted in some way to the lights coming from the sub, attacked and attached itself to a port. I could see the business end of this rather loathsome-looking animal as it attempted to eviscerate the sub by rasping on the Plexiglas window, without success thankfully. I had read that hagfish attack just about any fish in the ocean, even large sharks, so I guess the *Ben Franklin* was just another fish to this nasty little creature.

The surface-support crew kept the sub pilot apprised of a hurricane that was south of us but not expected to have any effect on our dive. We were to be inshore long before it passed by at sea. By the end of the day however, the storm took a turn and increased its forward motion to over 35 miles an hour. The sea conditions deteriorated rapidly. The captain of the *Privateer* conferred with the sub pilot and they decided the safest course of action was to keep the sub underwater. We moved upslope to a depth of 400 feet and took on ballast water to set the sub on the bottom. There we sat until the next morning.

Reports came back from the surface crew that they were getting beat up pretty badly by the high seas. We, on the other hand, were protected from the storm's effects and sat snugly on the bottom. The hurricane passed offshore of our position, but still produced high winds and seas that left the boat crew thoroughly exhausted.

When we got the all clear to surface, the waves were still over 10 feet high and the narrow-beamed *Privateer* was rolling relentlessly. The large rubber dinghy transported a few of us at a time back to the support ship. As I waited in the conning tower, the violent action, typical of most subs on the surface in heavy seas, got to me again—an undignified ending to an exciting voyage under the sea.

11

DEEP DIVER EXPEDITIONS

SOMETIME IN 1968, the Sandy Hook Marine Lab was visited by Gene Wallen of the Smithsonian Institution. Gene was charged with finding scientists with diving experience to participate in a series of experimental diving expeditions in the West Indies. The Smithsonian had received a grant from inventor and explorer Ed Link and from J. Seward Johnson, co-founder of the Johnson and Johnson Pharmaceutical Company, to fund participation in a new lockout submersible testing expedition in the Bahamas. The submersible *Deep Diver*, designed by Ed Link and built by Perry Oceanographics, Inc., was the world's first lockout sub. It carried a pilot and passenger in a forward compartment and two divers in the aft chamber. The sub was capable of stopping on the ocean bottom, pressurizing the aft dive chamber to the ambient depth, and allowing one or two divers out into open water. The design depth for the sub was 1,200 feet and for a lockout dive it was 1,000 feet.

I was selected to participate in the project along with a few other people, including Rick Waller of the U.S. Bureau of Commercial Fisheries and Dr. Walter Stark from the Rosenstiel School of Marine and Atmospheric Sciences at the University of Miami. It would be my first diving experience in tropical waters. At this point, all of my experience was in the cold, murky waters of the northeastern U.S. coast. I was not sure how it would be to see more than five to six feet underwater.

I had followed Ed Link's adventures for several years before my involvement with the *Deep Diver* project. Ed was the inventor of the Link Trainer, the most famous early flight-training simulator. Later, Ed built the *Sea Diver* research vessel. It was 100 feet long and equipped to launch and retrieve a moderate-size submersible and support extensive diving operations. The *Sea Diver* was a comfortable and seaworthy vessel that even sported a fireplace in the main lounge.

Ed's interest in exploring fabled Port Royal, Jamaica, which had slipped into the sea after an earthquake in 1692, prompted him to build the ship. Most of the city and 2,000 of its inhabitants disappeared beneath the Caribbean Sea. In the mid-fifties, Ed and his wife, Marion, spent several years exploring and retrieving historical artifacts from the city's submerged ruins. They found cannons, remnants of buildings, and thousands of small artifacts, but most importantly from a scientist's viewpoint, Ed was developing the diving skills and tools that would later serve scientific undersea exploration and studies.

The first expedition was to Great Stirrup Cay in the Berry Islands, Bahamas. I met the *Sea Diver* at Riviera Beach, Florida, where we embarked to the Berrys. Onboard were Ed and his wife Marion, Denny Breese, who was the ship's diving expert, sub pilots Roger Cook and George Bezak, and scientist Walter Stark. I was about to experience the alluring tropical ocean of the West Indies.

I was excited beyond reason during the trip across the Gulf Stream, past New Providence Island, and into the Berry Islands. Dolphins played in the bow wake of the boat and flying fish showed off their gliding skills everywhere. The sea was so blue I couldn't look away. I had seen dolphins and porpoise before in northern waters, but not the flying fish. They intrigued me. Their ability to escape a predator by jumping out of the water and gliding on their modified pectoral fins that served as wings was fascinating. The fish also displayed an elongated lower caudal, or tail fin, which they used to give an extra push by sculling the surface of the water when gliding low. In a sense, this was really flying under power rather than gliding.

One evening we anchored just offshore of the Great Stirrup Cay. It was a quiet, windless night and the sea was flat calm, almost like an ice skating rink. I was standing on the deck looking down at small fish attracted to the ship's lights. Off in the distance, beyond the lights where it was pitch black, I suddenly heard a sound like the hissing of a snake. Every few moments the sound was interrupted by a staccato of swishing water. Moments later a flying fish appeared in the lighted area, just above the surface of the water and heading straight for the *Sea Diver*. It was the tip of its lower tail fin, dragging in the water with intermittent sculling that was making the sound and leaving a thin wake in its trail. The fish then hit the side of the boat and flopped into the water.

In the moment before it hit, I saw another, much larger, fish moving with, and just below, the flying fish. The large fish, which I later identified as a dolphin (not the mammal), or mahi-mahi, was attacking the flying fish and amazingly was able to track its prey while it was in the air. Without the advantage of wind, the flying fish was using its tail fin to keep it in the air, but the predator had adapted to its prey's behavior and I'm sure the flying fish was no longer with us after it fell back into the ocean. I was afforded a first look at life and death of these two species—the strategy of escape by the flying fish and the predation skills of the dolphin in full view. Some of the *Sea Diver*'s crew looked at me sideways when I excitedly tried to tell them what I had just seen, probably spitting the words that made little sense to them.

Following the next day's anchoring drill, we quickly donned our diving gear and dove into the clearest water I had ever seen. It was about 35 feet to the bottom, but we soon came to the edge of the shelf that dropped off precipitously into the deep ocean. When I first swam into the deep water and over the ledge where I could see down for almost two hundred feet, I gasped and quickly swam back. The experience of swimming over the ledge took my breath away, and I felt as if I were going to fall into the abyss. This soon passed and I was happily taking in the beauty of the coral reefs and the vast biodiversity associated with them.

During this get-acquainted-with-the-tropical-seas period, Ed Link and his crew were working out some of the bugs in the lockout capabilities of the *Deep Diver*. They installed two sets of diving hoses and helmets, and pressurized the aft chamber several times to check for leaks and flow rates of air. The sub was also equipped with a supply of breathing-grade helium for deep dives in the future. At this point in my diving career, I had little experience with serious nitrogen narcosis which can have a debilitating effect on a person deep diving using pressurized air. The nitrogen in the air becomes almost narcotic under pressure, and the diver can and usually does lose good judgment. The deeper one goes the more serious the effects and, as with alcohol, they are different from person to person.

The experience of swimming over the ledge took my breath away, and I felt as if I were going to fall into the abyss.

Some people start to feel the effects at 70 feet or so, others at 100 feet, and some are unaffected until they reach 150 feet. By replacing all or some of the nitrogen in a diver's breathing supply with helium, the narcotic effect is eliminated. The sub's breathing system was capable of providing mixed gases to accommodate the diving profile. Another consideration was the toxic effect of oxygen on the human body beyond 300 feet deep, or just over 35 atmospheres absolute. If a dive was scheduled for these depths, the partial pressure of oxygen would be reduced accordingly.

Following a long lecture and demonstration of the sub's lockout capabilities and safety checks, we prepared for my first lockout dive from the *Deep Diver*. It was scheduled to be a short and shallow dive just to complete some training and equipment tests. Roger Cook, an ex-Navy Seal and very capable diver, would be my buddy. We entered the aft hatch, which led to the dive chamber and dogged it closed behind us. Several minutes later the *Sea Diver's* crane gently lifted the eight-ton sub off the deck and lowered us into the ocean. A diver quickly unhooked us from the lifting cable and we were on our way. The chamber was cramped with equipment hoses, dive helmets and, of course, the two of us.

As the sub powered away from its mother ship, the pilot started to take on water, causing a blast of air from the ballast tanks, and we began a controlled descent to the bottom. For a first timer, it was pretty exciting. The pilot skillfully maneuvered the *Deep Diver* onto the ocean bottom and weighted the sub down with additional ballast water. Once stabilized, we started pressurizing the chamber to equal that of the ocean depth. After rechecking the diving equipment, we undogged the bottom hatch. We were 60 feet deep and the outside pressure on the hatch was equivalent to almost 30,000 pounds pushing against it, so opening the hatch dogs would not affect the integrity of the sub at all. Not until we reached the ambient pressure would the hatch fall open.

The trick to getting the most time from our dive was to pressurize the chamber as quickly as we could equalize the pressure in our ears. Roger opened the valve to the pressure tanks, which blasted air into the sub's chamber with a deafening roar. The two of us held our noses and continuously blew against our closed nostrils to clear the pressure against our eardrums. As the pressure rose, the heat inside the chamber increased dramatically. Later, when decompressing the chamber after the dive was completed, the opposite effect of cooling air was experienced, providing a simple lesson in physics.

It was a whole new world; we may as well have been preparing to step out onto the moon's surface.

It was a whole new world; we may as well have been preparing to step out onto the moon's surface. Moments later, the pressure inside the chamber was the same as the outside ocean and the hatch fell open on its two hinges. The hatch opening was only about three feet from the ocean bottom and a soft aqua blue glow from light reflected off the sandy bottom contrasted with the relatively dark chamber. It was a beautiful abstract painting beyond the hatch. Since this was a test dive in shallow water, we used scuba rather than the relatively cumbersome helmets and air hoses.

Stepping through the hatch into the ocean, I left the surface environment provided by the sub's chamber and moved instantly and effortlessly into 60 feet of ocean depth. Although the ocean temperature was about 80°F, it felt cool compared to the 100-plus temperature inside the chamber. The rich experience of mind and body, as I passed from the pressurized chamber into the open ocean environment, was hard to take in all at once, and this was only the first of many to come.

The first expedition with the *Deep Diver* was to acquaint us with the tropical seas and the new technology being developed by Ed Link to serve undersea science and exploration. The second expedition, some months later, provided the opportunity to put this technology to the test as a tool for marine science.

The first scientific dive from the lockout sub was at night. Rick Waller and I were in the lockout chamber and Roger Cook was the pilot. We set up three lights on the bottom, powered from the surface—one with a red filter, one with a blue filter, and the third with no filter at all. The simple test would be to see how fish behaved in the presence of each light. Rick and I spent several hours diving from the sub to observe the fish at night.

During daylight, divers set the 110v lights on the sandy bottom at 60 feet. Cables from each led to the surface to be powered by the ship's generator. That evening about 10:00 p.m., Rick and I entered the *Deep Diver's* aft chamber, and following the launch of the sub, we were soon on the bottom not far from the lights. We were now proficient in controlling the sub's diving system and quickly pressurized the chamber to match the sea's ambient level. Again we used scuba gear for our excursions from the sub. We were some distance from the lights which had to be repositioned before they were turned on. Within a half hour the lights were repositioned and lit. Immediately, the plume of lighted ocean from the three lights attracted tens of thousands of small fish, some larger predators, larval forms of invertebrates, and the leptocephalus stages of eels. Most were around the brightest light without a filter.

About an hour later thousands of small squid, each about eight inches long, moved into the lighted area. They were everywhere. At first we thought they were there to feed on the myriads of small fish attracted to the lights, but soon we could see that they were coming together into mating pairs. Normally shy to divers, especially those making quick moves, these squid paid little attention to us, going about their business to spawn; millions of new squid were going to be made this night. The squid swam all around us, sometimes flashing an array of colors. The males were slightly larger and would somehow entice a female to approach and swim onto the top of and against her obvious suitor. Then the male would gently embrace his mate with a number of his tentacles and insert his specialized tentacle containing semen into the female's mantle. Often a second male would vie for the same female, but it was always the intruder that broke away and left the first two alone without a battle.

The normally quiet tropical ocean was now a mass of frenetic activity as the thousands of squid, squeezed into the lighted area, continued through their mating ritual. What was it about the lights that enticed them to spawn here? A large barracuda moved so slowly into the area it appeared to be drifting, and with a flash of silver reflected from the lights off its side, the fish charged through the mass of squid and took one that met its fancy. With one gulp the squid was gone and the barracuda stopped and hovered, looking for another victim. This was like many other attacks I had observed, where a predator bypassed thousands of prey and picked out just one. There was something different about that particular squid that attracted the barracuda to it that night.

Once the mating was complete for a squid couple, the female immediately swam down and placed a sac of gelatinous material filled with the fertilized squid eggs on the bottom. The sac, about two inches long and one-quarter inch in diameter, was pushed into the sand bottom by the female squid. Amazingly, after thousands of squid eggs were placed on the bottom, a pattern emerged with mop-like formations of sacs deposited exactly where the lights were shining. Where two beams crossed, producing the most light, the volume of egg sacs was the heaviest. Had we created a squid farm?

While studying and photographing the mass spawning, we became distracted by four large stingrays that also came into the lighted area and started to dig into the bottom looking for food. The rays were not concerned about our presence at all and would bump into us, swim over the top of us, and stir up the bottom sediment with their wings, cutting visibility down to almost nothing. At first it was fun, but it soon reached an annoying level. Nothing we did dissuaded the pesky animals, including grabbing their wings or kicking at them, and soon we had to give up and retreat back to the *Deep Diver*. The rays obviously liked the lights and were unwilling to leave.

The following morning we dove on the spawning site and saw a vast field of squid egg sacs protruding from the sandy bottom. The now unlit lights marked where the squid had spawned. *National Geographic* photographer Bates Littlehales caught most of the action on film which subsequently appeared in an issue of the Society's magazine. Rick and I published the observations in a scientific journal.

These were limited test dives to evaluate the capabilities of the lockout sub for science. Although we were in shallow water, we were able to study the squid spawning over a long period and we considered the project a success.

12

FIRST SATURATION DIVE FROM A SUBMARINE

Ed Link was now ready to put his invention to the test. The *Deep Diver* performed well as a diver lockout system in shallow water and for short periods, but he was eager to test its capabilities as a research tool in more demanding environments. Following a series of one-atmosphere dives to 1,000 feet, Rick and I prepared to conduct the world's first saturation dive from a submarine. To understand a saturation dive we need to first consider the physics and physiology of pressure and breathing gases on the human body.

Simply put, the deeper a person dives the more nitrogen goes into solution within their blood stream. Also, the longer a person stays under pressure the more nitrogen goes into solution within their blood stream. The combination of the two determines if decompression is necessary and, if so, for how long. After a period of time at a given depth, the body absorbs all of the nitrogen it can, which is called being "saturated." From that point on any decompression debt accumulated at the given depth does not increase, no matter how much longer the diver stays underwater.

A dive, for example, to 50 feet for about 12 hours (about the time it takes to saturate a person's body with dissolved nitrogen) requires a long decompression to return to the surface, which would not change no matter how much longer the dive. So, the advantage of a saturation dive for research or other undersea projects is that a person can stay at a depth for as long as they want or can, with only one long decompression at the end.

Our dive profile was developed by Joe MacInnis, a well-known hyperbaric physician and undersea explorer from Toronto, Canada. It would require us to spend a total of 42 hours at a depth of 120 feet, including an 18-hour decompression period. The dive would be conducted in the *Deep Diver* chamber with freedom to make as many tethered excursions as possible on a helium/oxygen mix of breathing gas. The lightweight helmet provided communications back to the sub. Aside from this being the first saturation dive from a submarine, we were going to test a system that would allow us to breathe straight air for a part of the mission to see if we could save some very expensive helium. Manning the forward compartment was

Roger Cook, our pilot, and Joe MacInnis was onboard the *Sea Diver* as physician and dive coordinator.

Once we reached the bottom, Roger maneuvered the *Deep Diver* to 120 feet and then searched for a safe and interesting site, from a scientific viewpoint, to set the sub down and start our adventure. At this depth off Great Stirrup Cay, we were very close to the drop-off and had to find a spot that was reasonably level and where there was no danger of the sub slipping over the ledge. Once in place, Roger added ballast water to the *Deep Diver* to make it heavy on the ocean bottom. Rick and I then proceeded to test the diving equipment including the breathing system, helmet, communications, and mix of helium and oxygen. We also ran a check on the chamber life-support system to make sure the scrubber was loaded with adequate chemicals to remove excessive CO_2 from the atmosphere and the oxygen was flowing at 1.5 liters per minute per person.

Rick and I unlatched the bottom hatch and grabbed our noses to ready for a rapid compression. We would constantly blow out to compensate for the increased pressure on our ears. On signal from Joe, we began our dive by opening the valve that released gas into the sub's chamber; the clock was now running. The mixture of helium and oxygen flowed into the chamber with a deafening scream. I couldn't even hear my ears popping as I blew out hard. The temperature rose rapidly, and we were soon in a sauna of hot breathing gas. Within a minute the pressure inside the chamber reached the ambient 120 feet and the hatch dropped open. A belch of bubbles released through the open hatch flowed along the outside hull, signaling that we should shut down the pressure valve. Helium is very expensive, and we were warned not to waste any by over-pressurizing the chamber. Joe radioed asking for a status report and I answered, "Everything's okay; we reached ambient pressure."

Even though I knew the effect that helium had on a person's vocal cords, I was shocked to hear myself talking with a silly Donald Duck voice. Soon Rick and I were talking away in squeaky, wimpy little voices and laughing our asses off.

"Okay guys, let's get back to reality," interjected Joe.

He was right—time to shut up and get back to business. The temperature in the chamber was now well over 100°F and we were eager to jump though the hatchway to cool off. For the moment we were very uncomfortable, but the whole experience was exhilarating. The ear-splitting sounds, heat, rapid pressure changes, and dim light inside the cramped chamber felt like a proper way to pass from one world to another. It wasn't like sitting in the nose of a rocket blasting off into space, but it was a big rush, nevertheless.

We took turns making 1- to 1½-hour excursions outside the sub over the next 24 hours. One of us remained in the chamber as backup and safety diver. Each excursion outside the sub was limited by the 200 feet of life-support hose and communications wire. During the 24-hour dive period we observed and

PHOTO COURTESY DENNY BREESE

Author feeding a peanut butter and jelly sandwich to a black grouper during a record saturation dive from the Deep Diver *lockout sub—120 feet for 42 hours.*

photographed the deep reef. It was primarily an experimental dive, but we used the opportunity to acquaint ourselves with the reef residents and their day and night behaviors. It was during the first couple of dives that I encountered the friendly, but aggressive, peanut butter sandwich-eating black grouper described in another section of this book.

Part of the mission during this dive was to test our ability to switch to breathing air during excursions and back to a helium-oxygen gas inside the chamber. It would save a lot of money if it proved to be feasible. Helium, especially breathing quality, is expensive. A hose delivering straight air was lowered from the *Sea Diver* so we could exchange the sub's breathing supply with the air by simply changing hoses to our dive helmets. On my first excursion breathing air, I could feel the effects of narcosis for a few minutes, and then it seemed to wear off. Because I was now attached to the surface ship, it was important to not wander too far from the sub. Although the ship was on a two-point mooring system, it would still swing at least 50 feet or more depending on currents and wind patterns. Instead of a direct communication link to the *Deep Diver*, it was now to the surface and back down to the sub.

During the several one-hour experimental excursions on air, both Rick and I relayed our status to Joe. Were we comfortable, feeling heady, could we perform simple and complicated tasks without any problems? Although not very scientific, the tests seemed to indicate that, at least to 120 feet, we could safely and effectively conduct our saturation dive partially on straight air. However, the amount of time that we could do this was restricted by the partial pressure of oxygen we breathed. At 120 feet the partial pressure of oxygen in a straight-air breathing gas is about four times that at the surface. Breathing this high partial pressure of oxygen over long periods would literally burn out our lungs or possibly cause us to go into convulsions. Further, more scientific, experiments would have to be conducted to determine the safe time limits on breathing straight air at different depths before we did much more of this switching back and forth between an oxygen/helium mix and straight air.

The dive, although uncomfortable when resting in the cramped quarters of the *Deep Diver's* chamber, was a complete success, and we were sorry to reach the 24-hour mark. We demonstrated the feasibility of using a lockout sub for extended and saturation diving, took the first steps toward switching breathing gases during the dives, and we had a chance to see some new biology. We had the opportunity to observe the night and day activities that make up a deep coral reef. Never before had anyone had the ability to watch marine animals over a day's length at this extended depth.

At the moment of the 24th hour, we closed the hatch and put ourselves in Joe's hands. He would oversee the 18-hour decompression. The countdown started when the hatch was closed and Roger started to blow ballast from the sub. About 20 minutes later we were lifted onboard the *Sea Diver*. The crew immediately shaded the sub from the blazing West Indies' sun. About every 15 minutes the crew would flow seawater down the sides of the sub's chamber to further cool us down. Even so, the heat inside was tough and we were instructed to drink a lot of water. It is critical during a long decompression to keep the diver's blood volume up. Low blood volume increases the chances for the bends.

Eighteen hours later we emerged from the sub's dive chamber and realized that we had made history with the first saturation dive from a submarine.

13

DIVING THE BAHAMIAN SLOPE

Some months later, I was once again aboard the *Sea Diver* to conduct a series of lockout dives. One in particular peaked my interest. Ed Link was interested in demonstrating the full capability of the *Deep Diver* for scientific exploration, and I was interested in collecting fish species from the deep drop-off. This region of the ocean is still virtually untouched by science, even though it is a common habitat from 30 to 600 feet deep in the Caribbean region. Its almost vertical slope and average depth is not hospitable to common fishing techniques that use traps and nets, and it is too deep for any serious diving, so little is known about the marine life in this environment. Small research submersibles and ROVs have been used to study these regions of the tropical oceans, but they are not very efficient at capturing mobile species.

On a previous one-atmosphere sub dive in the Tongue of the Ocean, a very deep region of the West Indies surrounded by the shallows of the Great Bahama Bank and loosely resembling a tongue, a relatively flat terrace large enough to land the *Deep Diver* was sighted just off the coast of Andros Island, Bahamas. Some others, not as flat, were found about 200 feet deep with just enough room to place the sub, affording a little extra margin for safety. But these were thought to be too sloped with the danger that the sub could slip off. With the good possibility of finding the right terrace to stage our dive, we excitedly prepared to steam to the Tongue of the Ocean and the area where the site was previously found. Our plan was to set the sub on a terrace, blow down the chamber, and make a downward excursion to the length of the diving hose, which was about 150 feet long. Of course, the resultant decompression could be extreme, so we had to be prepared to compromise if the depths of the terraces were any more than 200 feet or so.

After leaving Nassau Harbor, we sailed part of the day and through the night, arriving in the general vicinity of Fresh Creek, Andros Island, the next morning. Andros Island is also the site of the U.S. Navy AUTEC base, which tracks military submarines brought into the Tongue of the Ocean for signature identification. Each sub can then be identified by the unique sounds it emits while running underwater.

Since we would be operating in this same area, we had to get clearance from the Navy. They obviously would not be too happy if we came unannounced and were possibly mistaken for a Soviet spy sub.

When we arrived, Captain Link ordered the launching of the *Deep Diver* to survey the deep drop-off about one mile offshore of the island. It took many hours of searching before anything useful was found. To make matters worse, it was during the winter months and cold, denser water from the Andros Island shallows was running out along the ocean bottom and spilling over the cliffs. At times the pilot brought the sub close to the deep ledge and we were dragged downward an extra 100 feet before he could recover our buoyancy. The underwater waterfall was also dragging large amounts of sand over the cliff and into the deep. It was fascinating and pointed out the value of putting eyes underwater. On the surface all was quiet, but just below a very dynamic event was occurring.

We were starting to get somewhat discouraged in our search for a terrace. Finally, after the second day, a likely candidate was found. Pilot George Bezak set the sub on the terrace and added ballast water to test for stability. This was an important exercise; if the sub could possibly move and slip off the terrace, it was best if it happened when the chamber hatch was closed and secure. Once the hatch was opened as the divers got out, a sinking sub would take on considerable water and weight. The sub would then quickly go into an uncontrolled descent with little chance of recovering its buoyancy; the result, of course, would be fatal for the divers and most likely for the people in the forward pilot's chamber as well. The continuing amount of weight added by the flooding would far exceed the ability of the pilot to compensate by blowing the ballast tanks. The sub could thus possibly be carried beyond its crush depth. The second job of the pilot was to take the exact depth measurement, which was necessary to predetermine total depth reached and the decompression schedule that followed the excursion.

George found a terrace at 210 feet. It allowed the sub to sit fairly level with an extra five feet, or so, to the ledge. We followed with a meeting to determine the feasibility of working the dive from this terrace, and it looked good. We could make the excursion to just about 300 feet deep, although the hose length would limit the diver's movement horizontally. The tables were set for a one-hour, 300-foot dive. Roger Cook and I would make the dive, and I would make the deep excursion. I don't quite know how I got the nod to do the excursion dive, but I sure was happy. It would allow me to spend an hour at depth and in a habitat that I would never otherwise see. My plan was to collect as many fish as I could from as deep as possible along the drop-off.

The following day we gathered a squeeze bottle filled with the fish poison Rotenone, a nylon collection bag, and a small net on a handle that resembled a miniature butterfly net. At the end of the dive, I would place the catch in an enclosed tray on the outside of the sub just before going back into the chamber. Walter Stark, a renowned fish biologist from the University of Miami, would remove the fish when the sub was brought aboard the *Sea Diver* and place them in a preservative solution. Walter had made an earlier survey dive on the terrace and had collected some fish at 210 feet.

My heart was racing with anticipation and excitement. Soon I was going to be swimming freely in a world never touched like this before.

Late in the afternoon, Roger Cook and I climbed into the *Deep Diver* chamber and locked the hatch. The support ship's powerful crane lifted us off the deck and gently placed us in the water just off the transom. A swimmer unhooked the sub from the crane's cable and we were on our way. My heart was racing with anticipation and excitement. Soon I was going to be swimming freely in a world never touched like this before.

Within 20 minutes the pilot located the targeted terrace, slowly put the sub in position, and took on ballast water. Once stable and confident that the sub would not move, we started our safety checks. I glanced out one of the small portholes and could only see down into the abyss. We were so close to the edge of the terrace ledge that I could not see it at all. I remember trying to rock the sub to test its solid connection to the bottom of the terrace. Of course, we had hundreds of pounds of negative buoyancy and the sub did not move.

"Oxygen flow in the chamber is three liters per minute. CO_2 scrubbers loaded and working," went the checks.

"Dive helmet in good working order. Communications clear," they continued.

We were still at one-atmosphere pressure in the sub's dive chamber and we wanted to get all checks out of the way before opening the pressure valves and starting the dive clock ticking. We had one hour total, so every second was precious. It was five o'clock in the afternoon and the sun was dipping rapidly. The blue color of the water was changing to gray. We needed to get the dive under way before darkness set in; it was winter and the day length was short.

Once assured that we had checked all systems, we set our watches and Roger opened the blow-down valve. With a deafening scream from the incoming helium/oxygen mix, the dive began. The sound was different than other blow-down events. Helium is a different density than nitrogen so the sound was a lower pitch. Helium also conducts heat about four times faster than nitrogen so the heat-up from rapid pressurization was a little less.

Nevertheless, it got stifling hot inside the chamber before we reached 210 feet, or roughly 108 pounds per square inch. We opened the valves all the way to decrease our descent time. Every minute pressurizing was a minute used against the one-hour dive limit. When the hatch fell open exposing the great ocean to us, we quickly took turns ducking outside to cool off. It was exhilarating to swim around over 200 feet deep on just a breath of air.

No time to waste, I reentered the chamber and gathered the collection gear, donned the helmet, strapped on the small bail-out breathing tank, checked my watch, and left. Roger paid out the hose as I descended down the cliff. I was by myself except for the voices communicated from the *Deep Diver*. I could see many small fish and invertebrates hovering or attached to the almost vertical cliff. It was like flying along a mountainside. The helium/oxygen breathing gas kept my head clear and the water temperature was comfortable even at these depths. The spill of dense water over the side of the cliff had ended with an incoming tide. Although I was only minutes into the dive, I kept thinking that I never wanted it to end—it was fantastic.

Within a few minutes I reached the limits of the umbilical cord and was just able to touch 300 feet; I peered into the blackness below. Looking up, I could see the umbilical leading straight to the tiny sub, now barely visible. It appeared to hang precariously on the terrace. One of my favorite cartoons was of a hard-hat diver holding onto his hose leading to his support ship that had just sunk next to him. It was entitled "Feeling a little vulnerable" or something like that. I was thinking of that cartoon while looking up toward the sub and wondered, for just a moment, could it happen? It would be the ultimate bad joke for me to watch the *Deep Diver* slip by on its way down to the depths of the Tongue of the Ocean.

But, there was no time for fantasy here. I had to catch some fish, so I set out for a rocky ledge with many crevices and holes. I spent the rest of the hour exploring places where fish might hide and releasing small amounts of Rotenone in holes. Occasionally, a fish floated out of the hole stunned by the poison; I caught and placed it in the bag. The sub's crew kept in constant contact with me.

Toward the end of the dive, I told them that I wanted to stay longer.

"Bet he'd be back in a hurry if we shut down his breathing gas," I heard one say.

"Yeah, we could get Roger to reel him in like a fat mackerel," said the other.

"Okay, I'm only kidding, but this is another magic place, and it will be hard to leave," I added in my squeaky little Donald Duck voice.

Fifteen minutes before the end of the hour, I had collected about ten fish or so. The setting sun made the depths and visibility fuzzy. "Time to come up and start the decompression schedule," said the voice that filled my helmet. It took just a few minutes to reach the sub, and I placed the catch on the outside tray. Roger came out on a breath to help gather the umbilical and popped right back into the chamber. While I was standing next to the sub to secure the bag onto the tray, a loud crack seemed to hit the side of the sub. A moment later it happened again with the intensity of a sledge hammer hitting the steel hull. It was startling and I feared the sound was of the sub's integrity failing.

"What the hell was that?" I heard myself yell into the helmet microphone.

"I don't know, but everything seems to be okay with the sub," said the pilot.

We were getting very close to the end of the dive and decompression had to start immediately. We had no choice but to secure the sub and begin the decompression. The sub had to reach a shallower depth in order to vent the pressure inside the chamber, so once we were inside and the hatch was closed, the pilot began to blow ballast water, and we started our ascent and decompression An hour later we were on deck and settled down to finishing over a six-hour decompression, which went off without a hitch.

The next morning, Walter and I consolidated our catches and found that we collectively had fifteen species, seven of which were new to science. We couldn't believe our eyes; it was astounding that two hours of simple fish collection could result in almost half of the species having never been seen before. All were sent to taxonomists, who Walter knew had been working on specific families of the fish we caught, to be added to their collections and species descriptions.

For the rest of the day I couldn't help but to reflect on the dive. Only a short distance from shore and in relatively shallow water (the Tongue of the Ocean itself is over 4,000 feet deep), there was another world of marine life. It was possible that in the Bahamas alone, thousands of undescribed organisms inhabited its vertical slopes. What about the rest of the West Indies and Caribbean with similar habitats? It was mind boggling. Not only was the biodiversity interesting along the vertical cliffs, but I thought about the spawning. Did the eggs and larvae drift up to the surface like many other species that live on a shallow reef, or did they just move along in deep currents? There was so much to learn and understand.

These experiences and experimental dives that spanned two years were like a dream to me. The adventure was one thing, but it gave us the opportunity to touch the sea as in no other way.

The other part of the dive that had us guessing was the sound of something hitting the side of the sub. We figured the Navy, knowing exactly where we were located, used the *Deep Diver* for target practice and sent down a couple of sonar pings. But this was far from a ping, and I was surprised that something so intense didn't affect me very much, even though I was right next to the sub while it was sitting on the terrace. I later learned that sonar is not all that directional and I should have been hit by it.

In later years, the U.S. Navy became the center of growing controversy regarding the effects of very powerful sonar on the health of marine animals, especially whales. Recent incidents in the Bahamas and elsewhere linked Navy exercises with the beaching of large numbers of whales. Similar operations have been suspected of causing high mortalities of giant squid. Considering my firsthand experience and that today sonar systems are so much more sophisticated and powerful, it would not surprise me if many marine animals were harmed by these Navy war games.

These experiences and experimental dives that spanned two years were like a dream to me. The adventure was one thing, but it gave us the opportunity to touch the sea as in no other way. I thought the lockout sub was the wave of the future. It gave the scientist or undersea explorer great freedom with its capability of moving from place-to-place and from depth-to-depth. It allowed us to spend precious time in this near, but also remote, habitat down the vertical undersea walls of the Caribbean, which was of such great scientific value. I couldn't wait to go back.

Unfortunately, after a short period of lockout expeditions by the next-generation *Johnson Sea-Link* in the early seventies, all such dives were cancelled and never resumed. I can only speculate on the reasons. Only a few of us had the opportunity to experience the lockout capability, so there was no real constituency to support more such operations. This and a couple of mishaps in later years, one of which resulted in the deaths of two men, including Ed Link's son, and the other a near death during Project SCORE, combined to sink lockout diving's future.

Nevertheless, the technology is as fresh today as it was back in the sixties, and one can only hope that it will be revived to support scientific studies.

14

DIVING BELIZE—LIMITATIONS OF FISH MOVEMENT

Although the lockout and experimental phase of diving was over for the time being, Ed Link, his wife Marion, and Seward Johnson arranged for a diving expedition to the outer islands off the coast of Belize, Central America. It was 1969 and Belize was then British Honduras, still under the Commonwealth of the United Kingdom. I was again invited to participate, along with Dr. Perry Gilbert, a shark expert, Al Giddings, one of the world's foremost underwater cinematographers, Dr. Joe MacInnis, Denny Breese, and others. The intent was to place a modified diving chamber on the bottom to use as an observation chamber to study sharks.

Additionally, I designed an experiment to study the effects of increased pressure on reef fish with closed swim bladders. Fish use a gas-filled bladder to compensate for buoyancy; I was interested in the effects of rapid increases in depth, and therefore pressure, on the bladder and the possible effects on the health of the fish. Most of the fish found around a coral reef have closed bladders and can only exchange gasses very slowly through thin membranes. When fish with closed systems are quickly brought to the surface from the bottom of the ocean, they cannot compensate fast enough and their swim bladders will extend dramatically, as most fishermen can verify from personal experiences. There was little known about the effects on a fish experiencing a rapid increase in depth, and this was my goal.

We met the *Sea Diver* in Belize City and sailed the 60 miles offshore to Lighthouse Reef, the outermost atoll off the coast of British Honduras. Onboard was a modified commercial diving chamber that we would use as a base of operations once it was placed on the ocean bottom. Perry Gilbert proposed to use it to film the behavior of local sharks. When we arrived on site, Captain Link positioned the *Sea Diver* near the western edge of the large atoll and anchored in an adjacent sandy bottom.

Not far from the ship's position were rich coral heads leading to an abrupt drop-off into the abyss. The drop-off started in only 35 feet of water in some places and deeper in others. For the next 19 days, I was going to do some of the heaviest and most exciting diving of my life. The clear water and healthy coral reef system was teeming with marine life of all sizes. Large grouper and lobster were everywhere. The sandy regions and grass beds were full of queen conch. It was, in my opinion, paradise. The only other people we saw in and around the islands during the whole trip were conch fishermen in dugout canoes. They would sail the 60 miles from Belize City in a small motorboat with the canoes on deck, then spread out along the shallows of the atoll, skin dive for conch for a number of days, and sail back. It was an extremely rugged lifestyle, but it worked for them.

The second day, we launched the chamber into 60 feet of water onto a sand bottom and weighted it down with several tons of lead. It was then pressurized to the ambient depth and left in place with an open hatch to allow divers to come and go as they pleased. It was fun to have as a way station, but in the end it proved not very useful as a scientific or photographic tool.

As all of this was taking place, Seward Johnson arrived on his magnificent sailing schooner *Ocean Pearl*, a 60-foot yacht built entirely out of teakwood and one of the most beautiful schooners I had ever seen. It was not ostentatious as many yachts are, but elegant in its simple lines and obvious seaworthiness. Seward, a pleasant man in his seventies, was small in stature and wore a salty Captain Ahab beard. He was also one of the richest people in the world, which he never flaunted in any way.

Soon after, an old friend and diving buddy, Al Giddings, arrived in a small Mexican boat he hired for a week of filming and photographing the operation. Each of the boats anchored in the area, but at least a half mile apart to allow plenty of room to swing on its moorings as currents and wind patterns changed. Perry Gilbert soon set out to study the local shark population, and I prepared traps and containers to capture and carry the reef fish to deeper depths and observe their behavior and possible depth limitations.

I set the traps on a coral head at 50 feet and soon captured two white grunts, a common species that frequents the shallow reefs of the Caribbean. Grunts have closed swim bladders and would be perfect for my study. The fish were transferred to the specially built containers consisting of two round, clear hemispheres separated by one-inch spacers, which allowed a good flow of water along its equator.

> The experiment demonstrated that at least some closed-bladder reef fish were very limited in their short-term depth range, both up and down. It was interesting that human divers could move up and down through the water column with ease, but the fish could not.

To reduce the trauma on the fish, I had to transfer each one at the 50-foot depth which was difficult at best. After several tries, the grunts were safely in their containers, and I let them stay at depth for several hours before beginning the experiment. I made a planned dive to 200 feet accompanied by Al Giddings. We had but a few minutes at that depth before getting into a serious decompression situation, so when we left the surface and the clock started ticking, it was prudent for us to pick up the two containers and head offshore to the drop-off as quickly as possible.

It was not long after we passed the 80-foot depth that I noticed the grunts becoming more agitated than usual. By the time we reached 200 feet, the fish were sinking to the bottom and trying to swim up, only to sink to the bottom of the containers once again. The depth increase had compressed their swim bladders, and the fish could not compensate quickly enough to maintain buoyancy. Our dive lasted for 10 minutes, after which I left one of the containers on the bottom and retrieved the other. On the way up I placed the one container back at 50 feet and we surfaced after a short decompression.

The next morning, we retrieved the grunt left at 200 feet and brought it back to 50 feet. To our amazement, the fish's swim bladder was permanently damaged; it could not rise off the bottom of the container and later died. On the other hand, the fish brought back to 50 feet, after spending only 10 minutes at 200 feet, fully recovered. Over a 19-day period we repeated the experiment with the same results. The experiment demonstrated that at least some closed-bladder reef fish were very limited in their short-term depth range, both up and down. It was interesting that human divers could move up and down through the water column with ease, but the fish could not.

Later observations on a number of reef grunts and snapper species revealed that they schooled around a shallow reef during the day and moved out in columns toward their sand bottom feeding grounds at dusk, some going a little shallower and some going deeper. The fish that went offshore did not go any deeper than about an additional 20 feet.

When the deeper-water fish returned, some were observed slightly buoyant and pointing at a reference, such as the tip of a gorgonian (a fan-shaped, branching soft coral), until their swim bladders slowly compensated for the shallower depth. The implications for these depth limitations may apply to the release of young fish for stocking purposes. Rather than release them from the surface with the expectation that they will seek the bottom, and possibly damage their ability to quickly compensate for buoyancy, they may have to be slowly lowered in stages.

On one occasion, I was carrying a container with a dead grunt to the surface. The container had a short rope attached to allow me to drag it behind. Just before we finished a decompression stop at ten feet, a small, about five-foot, silky shark appeared and was trying to attack the fish in the chamber. It continued to bump the chamber for several minutes. When we finished the decompression and climbed aboard the boat, I let the chamber dangle in the water to see what the shark would do. In the process, I lost a depth gauge from my wrist, and it fell to the reef about 35 feet below.

After we pulled the chamber and dead fish onboard, the shark swam around the boat for a few minutes and appeared to leave. I wanted my gauge back and poked my head overboard to see if the shark was gone. Convinced that it was, I quickly made a breath-hold dive to the bottom to retrieve the gauge and found it right away. While picking it up with my legs dangling above me, the shark made an attack on my legs. Just before it reached me, I turned my body upward still unaware of its intent and by doing so presented a bigger object to the shark, which then aborted the attack. By this time it rushed by my head so closely that its wash moved me back a few inches. Now knowing the situation, I hightailed it to the surface and the boat. Perry Gilbert, who was on the boat and saw the whole thing, said it was definitely an attack and I was lucky. Although it was a small shark, it could have done some damage. In all my years of diving, that incident was my closest call with a shark.

Although it was a small shark, it could have done some damage. In all my years of diving, that incident was my closest call with a shark.

I learned a lot on the Belize trip by observing fish and other marine organisms on a relatively pristine reef. Each morning, Seward Johnson picked me up in a small boat and we would dive together studying the reefs, while other activities continued with the shark project.

One night we all dove on the reef to observe the behavior of nocturnal creatures. Most of the daytime fish were hiding in crevices or just staying close to the reef. Lobster and other invertebrates were now active. We all had a chance to photograph and play with a huge green moray eel that had come halfway out of its hole. While some of us were watching the eel, Dewey Bergman, who came with Al, spotted a nice size octopus moving in the open. We didn't know, at the time, that Dewey loved to eat octopus and to our amazement attacked the creature. His light must have blinded the octopus, for Dewey easily grabbed it with his bare hands and started to swim over to show us his catch.

It must have been a distress sound from the octopus that attracted the moray, which quickly left its den and went after it. We could now see that the moray eel was huge, maybe five feet long and looking nasty as it went after Dewey's prize. Dewey started swimming backwards toward the surface. It was obvious that he wasn't going to give in to the eel without a fight. We watched helplessly as Dewey kicked at the moray and then, to our disbelief, he opened the zipper on his wet suit jacket and stuffed the struggling octopus into his suit and closed the zipper. The eel was now homing in on Dewey's chest, but he was relentless and fought the moray all the way to the surface, successfully getting into the boat without being bitten. Late that evening, with a chest full of suction marks, Dewey cooked up his octopus dinner and the rest of us didn't even ask for a taste. We figured he earned the whole thing.

Into the second week a few of us were getting a little restless. If we were not conducting night dives, there was little to do aboard the *Sea Diver*. Ed Link was a stickler for everyone turning in early and no alcohol aboard his ship. One night when Ed and Marion retired and all was quiet, we could hear laughter coming from Al Giddings' Mexican boat a half mile away. Joe MacInnis, Denny Breese, and I all thought the same thing at once—those guys are having a party and we're stuck here.

Within minutes we unhitched a rubber dinghy and very quietly lowered it overboard so as not to wake the captain, and off we paddled toward the party boat. When we arrived, Al, his partner Dewey, and the Mexican captain were just talking and telling sea stories, but once we jumped onboard, the captain saw an opportunity to ratchet up the evenings activities and went to the bilge area of his boat to pull out a bottle of tequila. Now the sea stories were coming like wildfire as the bottle was passed from man to man. When that one was finished, another bottle magically appeared and then another.

As the evening wore on, most of us were more than three sheets to the wind and having a good time. Around midnight, Joe and Denny decided that they were staying rather than try to paddle back to the *Sea Diver.* I, on the other hand, was so wasted that I climbed up on the boat's mast and jumped into the ocean, intent on swimming back.

From that moment, and after many years, I still have no recollection of what happened next, but Al claims that after jumping off the mast, I was next to the Mexican boat floating on my back and he stuck a lit cigar in my mouth and off I swam. I swam the half mile in darkness where Perry Gilbert had caught a 10-foot tiger shark the previous night, climbed up the side of the *Sea Diver,* and got myself into my bunk. How, I don't know. If I were a religious man, I might embrace the old saying that God protects children and drunks.

The next morning, Seward Johnson arrived early, and I was a wreck. We still went on our dive, but instead of me looking after Seward, he took care of me. It was embarrassing. This 70-something-year-old man even helped me get my dive tank into the boat. A lesson learned? Still deciding.

15

FIRE ISLAND NIGHT LIFE

During the summer of 1968, Bori, Stu Wilk, and I initiated a study on the behavior of winter flounder, an important commercial and recreational fish common to northeastern coastal waters. We chose Fire Island Inlet near the Coast Guard station, a short distance from Great South Bay, New York, where we knew the flounder were abundant and which offered protected waters for our dives day and night. The first of four trips from Sandy Hook to Fire Island Inlet on the *Challenger* was only a couple of hours, but rough seas forced Bori and me to the aft deck with typically queasy stomachs, especially mine. Heavy rains prompted us to place buckets over our heads. This worked well for me when my stomach gave out. With my head already in the bucket, it was a simple task to just lean over and vomit my guts out into the container. In the meantime, Bori was telling jokes from under his bucket with a tinny resonance that was funnier than the punch lines. In spite of my misery, I started laughing and puking at the same time, and it was no picnic.

Surviving the trip, we set up a diving schedule that allowed us to observe the flounder's feeding behavior throughout a 24-hour day and to collect specimens to determine stomach contents. Over the summer we learned a lot about the winter flounder, how and when they feed, their day and night behavior, and their activity levels. The flounder slept, or were at least dormant, all night and much smarter than us. We, on the other hand, headed out each night in a small boat to the Fire Island hot spots in between our dives.

On one infamous foray Bori, friend Ralph Sheprow, and I were at one of our favorite spots about three miles down the Great South Bay. We overstayed our time and had only 45 minutes to make our next appointed night dive. It was about one in the morning and a pitch black night with no moon, as I recall. We ran to the boat and fired up the 35-hp outboard motor. I was the pilot and Bori used a flashlight to watch for obstacles. We knew that we had to head first to a large NUN buoy that would keep us in the narrow channel. We were late, so I pushed the throttle to full speed and took off into the night.

PHOTO COURTESY ROBERT WICKLUND

Sleeping winter flounder during late night studies of feeding behavior of the species.

The first few minutes were okay, until Bori yelled, "Bob, the buoy is just ahead!" We were on it in an instant. I turned the boat sharply to starboard and would have missed hitting the buoy, but the turn and speed heeled the boat hull almost to its gunwale. The shallow, wooden-hulled boat slid to port as we turned and hit the buoy hard, right along the rounded part of its bottom. I yelled that I thought it was okay and Ralph answered, "Bullshit, we're sinking" and pushed a cushion into the hole that didn't help much. We looked in horror as water flowed into the massive hole in the bottom of our stricken boat. We were sinking quickly and were fortunate to make it to shallow water on the edge of the channel where we sank completely.

There we sat in the flooded boat in several feet of water. We were miles from the *Challenger* and three sorrier souls didn't exist at that moment. Here we were government employees responsible for a government boat, hitting a government buoy and our asses were grass, we thought. "Maybe we'll get lucky and die of exposure or something, and not have to face the music after all" was offered by one of us. However, when your butt is very exposed, as ours were that night, a desperate person is capable of getting it covered pretty fast.

We anchored the boat, which was somewhat of a joke, removed the brand new motor and headed inshore until we reached a depth where we could easily walk. Ahead of us in the darkness a couple sat on a dock smoking pot. They probably thought they were hallucinating. Here were three wet, scrubby guys carrying a motor walking out of the dark bay. "Hey man, where are you coming from?" one said. "Way out there," one of us replied, pointing offshore. "Cool" was the only response we heard. We were lucky to find a phone booth to call the local police. When they arrived, we told them we had hit a submerged object during a scientific survey. We could see on their faces that they knew we were bullshitting. Although the police were unhappy about letting us and the motor into their clean car, they did take us back to the *Challenger*.

We arrived after daybreak, cold, wet, dirty, and beat, having walked for hours in water, mud, and sand. Our desperation pushed us to reach down deep, and we made it. Captain Irv was worried about us, but that soon changed when he heard what happened. He even referred to me, his offspring, as a shithead. Well, at least I was his shithead. Late that morning the boat was recovered, repaired, and nothing more was mentioned about the incident. We lived to dive another day.

All in all, the project was a success. We proved that winter flounder feed only in daylight hours and were dormant at night; information that may be important to future management of the species. We also learned of the day and night behavior of another species, the tautog. These studies led to several years of further work by Bori.

Did we learn anything personally from the flounder, such as the benefits of getting to bed early rather than sniffing out the Fire Island night life? No, but spearing the poor sleeping flounders in the middle of the night, just to check their stomach contents, reminded me that we all have our troubles, whether we go to bed early or not.

16

FIRST *HYDRO-LAB* DIVE

With the increased interest in the oceans, and as more and more people ventured underwater, some of us dreamed about the possibility of actually living on the bottom of the sea. We worked to help design an underwater lab for the Northeast, to be placed somewhere around the Isle of Shoals, off the coast of New Hampshire. That never happened, but following the lockout experiences from the *Deep Diver* submersible, my interest grew keener and I felt in my gut that it would eventually become a reality. In the meantime and throughout the sixties, a number of countries, including the U.S., dabbled in the concept of undersea living.

Early in 1962, Ed Link's "Man in the Sea" project was launched. That same year Jacques Cousteau built and briefly operated the *Conshelf I* undersea habitat in shallow water and later the *Conshelf II*. In 1963, the U.S. Navy experimented with a series of deepwater habitats designated *SeaLab I, II,* and *III* from 1964 to 1969. The Navy project was terminated after a diver, Barry Cannon, was killed making an excursion from the *SeaLab III* habitat in 600 feet of water.

During the late sixties and into the early seventies, over forty undersea laboratories were built in at least fifteen countries. The majority of these were only demonstrations and not for any serious scientific studies. By 1977, the only one left operational was the *Hydro-Lab.*

Hydro-Lab was constructed around 1966 from half of a discarded pressure chamber, previously used by Perry Oceanographics to test the integrity of manned submersibles slated for offshore oil exploration. It measured 16 feet long and 8 feet in diameter with a 42-inch diameter window on one end and several 12-inch windows on both sides of the hull. A lockout trunk constructed inside the *Hydro-Lab* enabled pass-through of divers when the habitat was not at ambient pressure. This allowed the habitat to operate as a saturation system with free movement in and out of the habitat, as well as a one-atmosphere system serving both as a decompression chamber and for overnight stays without the problem of accumulating a nitrogen debt.

The original *Hydro-Lab* did not have windows and was attached to a weight by four chains. It was first launched off the coast of Palm Beach, Florida, but was soon found to sway violently on the chains causing frequent seasickness of its occupants. Once it even broke loose from its moorings and floated to the surface; the Gulf Stream carried it 25 miles north before it was recovered. Soon after, it was brought ashore and fitted with legs permanently attached to a cement base which served as part of its ballast system. Two ballast tanks that could be filled with water or air were added to the lab's hull, and later the windows and lockout trunk completed this phase of the habitat.

The *Hydro-Lab* was again set one mile off the east coast of Florida and was used by Florida Atlantic University as an underwater engineering platform for a couple of years. John Perry wanted to see more done with the lab. So in 1968, Joe MacInnis, who at that time was a medical hyperbaric consultant to the Perry companies, and Denny Breese contacted me to ask if I would be interested in conducting a demonstration saturation dive in the *Hydro-Lab*. Of course, I jumped at the chance and immediately started to plan for some studies during the dive.

Seward Johnson became interested in the project, offering his yacht *Ocean Pearl* as a surface-support boat. This was the only amenity that we received on this project. Joe, an FAU student, and I conducted a two-day saturation dive at 50 feet using only scuba tanks for our life-support system. Surface divers aboard the *Ocean Pearl* brought us a steady supply of tanks to be used for our excursions outside the *Hydro-Lab* and also to maintain a healthy level of air inside by purging the contents of tanks when needed. There were no scrubbers to remove CO_2 from the atmosphere, and since the partial pressure of oxygen was going to be high to start with, we only needed to add air from the tanks when we detected that our breathing was being affected by increased CO_2 levels. With no air conditioning, the level of humidity inside the habitat would be just about 100 percent. A light bulb powered by a battery was our light at night and a CB radio with a wire leading to the surface marker buoy kept us in communication with the support divers aboard Seward's boat. Toilet facilities were "outside" and divers brought simple food and somewhat dry clothes to us in pressurized pots. It was, without a doubt, very Spartan living, but we couldn't have been happier. The dream of living on the bottom of the ocean was becoming reality.

It was, without a doubt, very Spartan living, but we couldn't have been happier. The dream of living on the bottom of the ocean was becoming reality.

The *Hydro-Lab* sat on a sandy bottom on the inner edge of the Gulf Stream. A steady but fairly mild current moved water by us from south to north. Over the two years that the lab was in place it became a pretty effective artificial reef. It was home to schools of fish and a large number of spiny lobsters. Large barnacles, hydroids, and other invertebrates attached to its hull. Mobile invertebrates such as crab, shrimp, and tiny octopi moved among the heavy growth of algae also attached

PHOTO COURTESY ROBERT WICKLUND

False albacore preparing to make an attack on a school of scad off the Florida coast. Photographed during the first Hydro-Lab *saturation dive.*

to the hull. Juvenile fish used the habitat as a home, occupying any nook or cranny they could find.

Joe was leader on this expedition, not only planning the logistics, but also developing the decompression tables we would use after the two-day dive. He also served as our medical backup. Denny was the topside project director. When we entered the *Hydro-Lab*, it was immediately obvious that our stay was going to be a challenge. The humidity made the pressurized air thick with moisture. At first the air inside was pleasant, containing adequate oxygen and little CO_2. Later, the smell from three sweating divers and the moisture dripping off the inner walls of the habitat would become an issue. But, in the beginning, we were fresh and eager to start our dive, and I excitedly prepared to enter the water with a camera to record anything that was new to me in terms of the behavior of fish and other organisms in the vicinity. We made it a rule to stay within sight of the lab when making excursions and to make our longest swims against the current, so it would be easy to swim back if a problem occurred.

The FAU student and I left the *Hydro-Lab* through the hatch and donned the scuba tanks that were waiting outside. The surface divers brought us a number of tanks for inside the lab, and three sets each of tanks with regulators were left on the lab's platform so we could continue our dive for several hours without interruption. I was in heaven. I couldn't believe that we could just stay underwater for as long as we wanted and not be restricted by a very limited decompression schedule. The clear water moved past us at about one-third knot and the water column was full of small scad feeding on the plankton brought in by the current. Thousands of fish were scattered from just off the bottom up to the surface. The *Hydro-Lab* was clearly their reference point. As described in another section of this book, the scad were repeatedly attacked by small schools of false albacore, a member of the tuna family. It was an exhilarating experience to be smack in the middle of the attacks; the power and efficiency of the tuna were impressive and somewhat scary. The long hours that the saturation dive provided allowed us to carefully study the behavior of the scad.

It was an exhilarating experience to be smack in the middle of the attacks; the power and efficiency of the tuna was impressive and somewhat scary.

Over the 50 hours, we spent more than 20 in the water, day and night, coming back to the lab to eat, sleep, and just rest. Some of our excursions lasted over three hours at a time. The water temperature was about 82°F, so with a minimal wet suit we could stay as long as needed without worrying about hypothermia. The two nights that we spent underwater were used to watch the nocturnal activities of the species that were close by. A dozen or more spiny lobster, which hid under the platform during the day, emerged in the evening and crawled up and over the lab and out into the flat sandy bottom to look for food.

On both nights we observed, for the first time, lane snapper displaying a courtship and spawning ritual. The snapper that hung close to the lab during the day now gathered in groups at dusk and were milling about close to the bottom. Unlike other species of snapper, we didn't see them rise off the bottom to release their milt and eggs. To this day, we may still be the only witnesses to the lane snapper's courtship and spawning behavior.

By the second day, all of our clothes were soaking wet from the heat and humidity; we needed to empty tanks of air into the lab more frequently to cut down the increasing CO_2 levels. At times our breathing became heavy from the creeping CO_2 buildup and occasionally we developed slight headaches, but nothing serious enough to cause concern.

On the second night's dive a rather amusing trick of perception was played on me. While outside the lab on an excursion, I spotted two bright lights off in the distance and at the same time I picked up throbbing sounds of a propeller. As I watched the lights, the sound was becoming louder and closer. The lights also appeared to be moving and heading straight for the lab and me.

Startled, I quickly returned to the lab and told Joe that it looked like a submarine was heading right for us. Joe called our surface crew and asked them to check it out. I went back outside and the throbbing was now much louder; I could see the light still moving in my direction.

Back inside again. "It's still coming, Joe," I yelled.

Several minutes later, the surface crew reported that a ship was passing by us a short distance offshore. They also told us that they had put the lights on the bottom and that they were fixed. The lights in the distance with the sound of the approaching ship tricked me into believing the lights were moving toward me. It was an embarrassing lesson and it took a while to remove the egg on my face, but it also taught me that some things are not always what they seem. I used that experience to hone my skills in future underwater observations.

By the end of the dive, we prepared for a much shortened decompression that included 3½ hours in the water, a ½-hour surface interval while a boat brought us back to shore, and then several hours intermittingly breathing 100 percent oxygen in the aft chamber of the *Deep Diver* sub in the Perry Oceanographics warehouse. We were all young and fit and suffered no adverse affects from the abbreviated decompression. They were Joe's tables that we followed, and he put himself on the line with the rest of us.

Although under relatively primitive conditions, the dive was an enormous success and led the way to many years of scientific saturation diving and to many discoveries. We not only demonstrated that saturation diving could be done without expensive support, but that living on the bottom of the ocean could be a productive means of conducting scientific projects.

17

HYDRO-LAB UNDERSEA RESEARCH PROGRAM

FOLLOWING THE SUCCESS of the 50-hour dive in the *Hydro-Lab*, John Perry decided that he would sever the association with Florida Atlantic University and move the lab somewhere it could be more useful. Sometime after our dive off Palm Beach, I received a call from Denny Breese asking me to come down to Florida for a meeting. It seemed that Denny and Joe MacInnis were asked to find a candidate to oversee a program that would best use the *Hydro-Lab*, and they recommended me.

The meeting with Denny, Joe, John Perry, and a few others lasted about a half hour followed by an offer to head up a program based in Freeport, Bahamas, with no specific agenda. Not only were the offshore conditions perfect for a habitat-based program but John owned two of the three newspapers in the Bahamas which could be tapped for publicity and some logistical support. Freeport was only 70 miles from West Palm Beach, Florida, so plane flights and shipping were convenient.

The decision to take the job was more difficult than I could imagine. I had been at the Sandy Hook lab for eight years and was now a permanent employee, although without a formal higher education getting beyond a GS-11 would take a long time. I also had four children to support and this offer would increase my salary a little bit. My gut told me that this was an opportunity to not only advance my career but also to help demonstrate the importance of diving science to the world. With much soul-searching, I finally accepted the position as director of what we would eventually call the *Hydro-Lab* Undersea Research Program. Leaving Sandy Hook was difficult, but I was looking forward to the challenges of the undersea program.

In October 1970, Gerri Wenz, a colleague and biologist, and I moved to Florida to begin the design and construction of a system for the lab that would allow at least three, and occasionally four, occupants to live comfortably under saturation conditions for up to a week at a time. Experience with the lab off the coast of Florida showed us that the life-support and general comfort system needed vast improvements to make it work. Most undersea laboratories depended on surface ships to provide safety, air, power, and support divers and were very expensive to maintain.

Often the surface ship and crew were more expensive to operate than the lab itself. We wanted to develop a semi-autonomous system that eliminated the onsite surface crew altogether. This would require an unmanned surface buoy that could provide 110v AC and 12v DC continuous power, low-pressure air flow, fresh water for showers, a base for communications from the subsurface lab, and enough fuel to last a month. The buoy would also have to withstand heavy seas, be easily removed from the site, and towable to safe harbor in the event of a hurricane.

The answer was to build a support buoy into a boat hull. We bought two 23-foot-long, wide-beam T-Crafts, one of which would become the buoy, designed by Denny and the Perry company, and the other would serve as the surface-support boat. The buoy was a brilliant design, completely enclosed with the exception of a self-bailing tower that allowed air into the engine room, and could take solid waves over the top without water entering. The lab had already been used to house several people at surface pressure. It had a small lockout trunk just above the hatch that allowed people to pass from one-atmosphere to ambient pressure without pressurizing the whole interior of the lab. We used that capability to build in a system that allowed divers to decompress, without leaving the lab, by adding a simple hose system to vent pressure to the surface.

The addition of needle valves allowed us to manually fine-tune the rate of pressure changes and, therefore, we could follow a decompression schedule closely. The four-foot-diameter, four-inch-thick main window was machined and polished, and the hull was sandblasted and painted. The life-support and operational design of the *Hydro-Lab* later became the basis for a new advanced saturation system, *Aquarius*, which to this day is still supported by NOAA and operated by the University of North Carolina Wilmington off the Florida Keys.

During the four-month building phase, Denny, Gerri, and I surveyed the waters off Freeport to select a site for the *Hydro-Lab* and decided on a location 50 feet deep, on a sand bottom and surrounded by coral heads. The potential site was just over one mile from the Bell Channel inlet in Lucaya on Grand Bahama Island, where our base of operations was to be located.

We formed a partnership with the International Underwater Explorers Society (UNEXSO), a tourist dive operation that would provide us a home base. UNEXSO was located just inside the Channel and had complete dive operations, personnel, equipment, office space, and boats that would help support our program. We in return offered to pay a reasonable rental fee and to set up a complete decompression chamber system at the Society's base. The chamber was to be a backup system for the *Hydro-Lab* divers but also would be a safety system for all divers in the region.

Additionally, Perry bought a 65-foot-long ferro-cement houseboat that was originally designed to be part of a floating hotel complex. The company building the boats went bust and sold this one to us. It was later towed from Florida to Freeport and docked at the Explorer's club to serve as our home and office. About a year later, a nail plastered into the cement on the hull bottom rusted out and, while we were away over the Christmas holiday, the boat developed a leak and sank in the middle of the night.

Although only sinking in 15 feet of water next to the dock, the collapsing 40-ton cement roof caused the house section to literally blow up. When we later dove on the wreckage, we saw almost total destruction—shattered glass and twisted metal. Apparently the weight of the roof forced the boat down rapidly when the water level in the hull reached a critical point. If we had been sleeping, and not aware of what was happening, the final sinking would have killed everyone onboard. As it was, we lost a few pets and lots of personal belongings.

After completing the refurbishment and all systems tested, the 60-ton *Hydro-Lab* was placed on a barge at the Port of Palm Beach and carried to the Bahamas. Official launching on the pre-selected site was in choppy seas on the morning of February 19, 1971. It was the first of many times over the next five years getting battered about while working on the lab in a choppy or heavy sea state. Once in place, a baseline survey of the site's flora and fauna, and setup of a grid pattern on the bottom, was conducted by scientists at the Rosenstiel School of Marine

Scientists preparing to study oxygen consumption by different species of coral outside the Hydro-Lab.

and Atmospheric Sciences, University of Miami. With the exception of an air conditioning system, the lab was tested and retested over the next month, followed by a short saturation dive by a few of us.

One important and hard lesson we learned during the test is that portable toilet facilities are unsuitable for an underwater lab. The *Hydro-Lab* was equipped with a trunk that was originally used to demonstrate the ability to transfer people back and forth between the lab and a submarine. The trunk could be accessed by a ladder from the main living quarters down to a submarine locking system. No longer in use for that purpose, we thought it was the perfect place to place a portable toilet system, away from the main living quarters with privacy and less odor. It was in this trunk that we placed a porta-potty, a simple system where the user opened a seal on a small plastic tank for the waste to flush. After the first dive, the tank was almost full but with some airspace.

During decompression inside the lab, the decreasing pressure caused the internal air in the porta-potty's tank to expand and it finally burst wide open, splattering the contents all over the trunk—a disgusting mess that took a long time to clean up. Following that fiasco, we decided that the ocean outside the lab was perfectly okay to use as a toilet facility.

Our first official mission was conducted by scientists from the University of Miami. Dr. John Bunt, Dr. Mike Heeb, and I entered the *Hydro-Lab* on a March morning. Hours before, we had transferred a very fragile, experimental, miniaturized mass spectrometer developed by NASA, to be eventually sent to Mars, into the lab. The intent was to measure the gas exchange of some algae found around the lab. The instrument, worth over $500,000, was transferred through the water column in a homemade plastic case designed by Denny. We had to swim it down very slowly and manually change its internal pressure with a scuba tank, thus preventing the case from imploding with the increased pressure. This was, in itself, a test of our ability to support scientific experiments by demonstrating the transfer through 50 feet of water column and almost two atmospheres of pressure.

The mass spec was transferred successfully, but once inside the lab and exposed to the high internal humidity, it did not function well. This first saturation dive had no air conditioning or humidity control, except for a pathetic attempt to cut down on the moisture by tying a rag to the air intake. It was something we needed to rectify before other dives were scheduled.

The high humidity not only took a toll on equipment and scientific instrumentation but caused some serious skin and ear infections as well. The dive was to last five days, but because of the mass spec failure, we aborted the dive after 28 hours. Even so, John Bunt was able to spend many hours outside on the coral reef conducting his research.

PHOTO COURTESY GERRI WENZ

School of large green parrotfish preparing for their evening sleep. The school swims in large circles expelling the contents of their guts, most of which is fine coral scraped from the dead sections of reefs as they feed on algae.

This was now my third saturation dive, and I was getting quite comfortable as an undersea dweller. Save for the humidity and heat, I was starting to feel that this was where I belonged and perhaps should spend much of my time, just living on the ocean bottom. Not a very practical concept, but a strong feeling nevertheless.

Following the operational part of the dive, we started the decompression phase using new tables that required 13½ hours, including several periods of breathing pure oxygen. This was a far cry from the little over three-hour decompression period during the last saturation dive in the *Hydro-Lab* off the coast of Florida. Following the decompression and still inside the *Hydro-Lab,* but now at one-atmosphere surface pressure, we had to enter the lockout chamber one at a time with mask and fins, blow it down to ambient pressure, and leave the lab. A support diver met each of us with a scuba tank, which we simply held in our arms while we swam to the surface. Once ashore, we were required to stay within reach and in communication with the medical team for 48 hours in the event a latent case of the bends or other emergency occurred from the rigorous dive.

Our first official scientific saturation dive went as well as expected. We learned some things from the scientific phase of the dive, but more importantly at this juncture, we needed to know how to make the system more efficient, safer, and comfortable for future scientists and other users of the lab. It was clear that the decompression went well except for the uncomfortable masks during the oxygen-breathing periods.

The humidity and heat were a big problem and living under those conditions over a week's period had the effect of seriously draining the energy and enthusiasm of the inhabitants of the lab, not to mention the effects on sensitive equipment and instrumentation. Another big problem was the requirement of the surface crew to be constantly running back and forth to the shore station to fill tanks for us. Spending hours in the water burned up many tanks daily. It was an inefficient system that would have to be rectified by finding a way to fill tanks on site, without the assistance of a support team.

I took an immediate liking to John Bunt. Although he was the director of functional biology at the University of Miami and a good scientist, he was also a big rough and tough character from the wilds of Australia. Sporting a black beard, John was a no-nonsense man who could also drink all of us under the table. He demanded that in all future saturation dives a bottle of Scotch be added to his life-support supplies. He insisted that one drink in the evening would keep him lean and mean. This, of course, was taboo, but I often suspected that he found a way to smuggle some Scotch down to the *Hydro-Lab,* and we didn't go out of our way to conduct a search.

Without any solid funding, we used the next few months to upgrade the system's safety, comfort, and operational capabilities. We also made the lab available

Green parrotfish sleeping in a coral crevice at night off Freeport, Bahamas.

PHOTO COURTESY GERRI WENZ

for various uses to bring funding to the project. It was about this time that Dick Clarke, a young man working for UNEXSO as a diving guide, expressed interest in our project.

Dick was a likable fellow, born and raised in rural England. He joined the British Navy for a 10-year period and while on a tour of the Bahamas, still a Commonwealth member of the United Kingdom at that time, he decided that the Navy was not his cup of tea and wanted to stay in Freeport. He bought his way out of the British Navy, which was a common practice back then, and signed on with UNEXSO.

With the Society's approval we hired Dick, who turned out to be an extremely valuable member of the team. With no formal education, Dick nevertheless showed that he was a solid student of diving physiology and hyperbaric medicine, as well as a fit and capable diver. Gerri Wenz, Dick Clarke, and I were the entire full-time complement of the *Hydro-Lab* Undersea Research Program and would remain so for the next five years. Denny Breese's expertise and engineering skills provided the backup to the project that made it all work. Gerri quickly became a proficient diver and took over the day-to-day administration of the program.

The next month or so saw a stream of visitors including media, industry representatives, and academia. George Bond, the recognized father of saturation diving, along with 35 medical doctors also visited and dove on the lab. Ed Link, at the request of the Smithsonian Institution, inspected the lab and our operation in May. We finally made a few dollars when we hosted the late Peter Benchley, author of *Jaws*, and two others for a night in the *Hydro-Lab* at one-atmosphere pressure. Peter wrote for *Signature* magazine of the Diner's Club at that time and wanted to write an article about his experiences living under the sea. The stay included dinner, consisting of freeze-dried delights, and two half-hour night lockout dives.

By this time we had added a freshwater shower and an air-conditioning system that kept the lab very comfortable. At the end of the dive the next morning, we simply locked the occupants out with no decompression necessary and guided them to the surface. The dive went well and Peter and gang emerged energized by their experience. It is interesting to note that a few years later, Peter's book and movie about a killer great white shark spooked a lot of divers, including some that used the *Hydro-Lab* in later years.

The program was going to take time to become a viable self-supporting entity. We were determined to make it work, even if we needed to do some projects that were not necessarily mainstream, such as hosting a honeymoon couple for an overnight one-atmosphere stay in the lab. We also participated in an actual undersea wedding with a diving preacher and a glass-bottom boat for the non-diving guests. The preacher stood in a tiny Plexiglas hemisphere placed in 50 feet of clear water that we used as an undersea talking station. The bride and groom were diving guides for UNEXSO and also had a commercial fishing business, mainly diving for lobster and grouper. The bridal party, including Gerri as maid of honor, and the diving guests all stood, knelt, or floated on the bottom alongside the couple. Several people had their scuba gear on over their tuxedos and dresses. We didn't make any money with this, but it was certainly a lot of fun.

Through November 1971 we conducted five saturation, scientific missions—including Westinghouse Ocean Research Laboratory, Texas A&M, University of Miami, University of Southern California, and one in-house dive. Additionally, four educational, one-atmosphere dives were conducted, and the lab was used as a set for several television and movie projects. This gave us a lot of experience, but it wasn't enough to pay all of the bills.

During this period I had some time to dive on and learn about the coral reef ecosystem off Freeport. I would spend hours just lying motionless or swimming slowly in the warm, crystal-clear waters, with only the sounds of my breathing and the bubbles escaping from my regulator and heading for the surface.

On one April morning, I witnessed an intricate and elegant courtship and mating behavior of the peacock flounder. Not far from the *Hydro-Lab* site, a female flounder had just set down in the sandy bottom. It was almost invisible as it quickly changed color to match the sand. Shortly afterward, two males did the same thing not far from the female. As I watched, the two males started to swim up off the bottom while the female remained stationary on the bottom. The males then approached each other until about one foot apart and raised their elongated pectoral fins, which is unique to the males of this species.

As they rose off the bottom their bodies took on an "s" or cobra-like shape. About six feet from the bottom, the fish stopped and began striking at each other for several seconds, again like a cobra, but not actually touching. This was followed by the two males coming together spinning horizontally, one over the other for six to eight seconds followed by a rapid looping chase in tight circles. The whole thing lasted about a minute. They parted and rested on the bottom for three minutes and repeated the ritual.

Whatever determined the winner in this mock battle for the female's attention was not obvious. Soon the victor approached the female and the two swam upward where the male pressed closely on top of the female and started to quiver, which was the actual mating. This was repeated a number of times over a 10-minute period, with the losing male remaining quietly on the bottom about 50 feet away.

As exciting and adventurous as the *Hydro-Lab* project proved to be over the next years, it was being witness to the coral reef dance of life that thrilled me the most. Previously unknown behaviors of fish and the marine critters that make their lives possible were being played out on the ocean stage, and I was in the audience.

Grunts and a Nassau grouper on a shallow reef off Freeport, Bahamas.

Just before we set up shop in the Bahamas, the Stratton Commission report to the President on ocean policy led to the formation of the National Oceanic and Atmospheric Administration (NOAA), which included a new office named the Manned Undersea Science and Technology Program (MUST). The office was charged with advancing the development of techniques to study the oceans from an undersea vantage point. MUST began by funding a few short-term projects in 1971. By December the office, headed by Don Beaumariage, had discovered our project and decided to fund a five-day dive in the *Hydro-Lab* using researchers from NOAA's National Marine Fisheries Service to basically test its capabilities as a scientific support system.

The dive included scientists Bill High and Ian Ellis, from the Seattle Exploratory Fishing and Gear Research Base, and Bill Schroeder, from Texas A&M. Their project studied the effects of different fish traps on the behavior of several reef species. Although the seas reached eight to ten feet high for several days, the mission was not hampered, finishing safely and efficiently right through decompression.

NOAA personal were so pleased with the results of the dive, the MUST office set up a contract with us for the next four years. In 1972, with just the three of us as the base crew, and using a few surface divers and watch-standers from the visiting teams of scientists, we ran 17 saturation dives and a one-atmosphere scientific dive. The MUST contract reimbursed the project $500 per day, including a few days for training and orientation before the dive and a couple more following decompression. As hard as it is to believe today, we operated the *Hydro-Lab* program over the next four-year period on a meager $90–100,000 per year at an average saturation rate of over 60 individuals annually.

PHOTO COURTESY DICK CLARKE

Grunts swimming along trails toward their evening feeding grounds. The same group returns to their daytime resting area along the same trails.

Once the NOAA-funded program began in 1972, Gerri, Dick, and I found little time for anything else. It was a grueling schedule requiring year-round diving, night and day for Dick and me, while Gerri manned the shore base and dealt with the unenviable task of ordering supplies and parts, arranging for shipping and seeing the visiting teams through Bahamian Customs and Immigration, a painful drill when the scientists brought large amounts of equipment. Often there were hours-long arguments with customs officials over our duty-free permit. Although we had a written agreement with the Bahamian government to bring scientific equipment into the country on a temporary basis without duty, individual agents often flexed their muscles, and we sometimes had to capitulate.

Because of the rigors of saturation diving, physical examinations were required of all potential inhabitants of the *Hydro-Lab*. Gerri would set this up with the island's government doctor, John Clement, at his local medical clinic. Additionally, an open-water, pre-saturation diving test of all new users of the *Hydro-Lab* was conducted by Dick or me. Although we didn't have an on-site hyperbaric physician, John Clement, a diver himself, was on call at all times. We soon realized that Dick had an extraordinary gift for understanding diving medicine, and he became a real asset to the program as its paramedical person. Even with all this, Dick and I found time to join the island British rugby team. The diving, moving equipment back and forth from the lab, and rugby kept us pretty fit, save the occasional injury.

The march of researchers and visitors was constant. The Prime Minister of the Bahamas, Lynden O. Pindling, was a diver and joined John Perry and me on a dive to the *Hydro-Lab* one summer day. It was interesting that the Prime Minister arrived onboard our boat with two bodyguards dressed in suits and ties, obviously not divers. Denny Breese, who was operating the boat, told us later that after the three of us entered the water and disappeared beneath the surface, it dawned on the bodyguards that they had just lost control of their charge.

Denny said they went, as he put it, "batshit" and paced frantically up and down the boat deck, extremely nervous about the situation. By the time we returned, the bodyguards were a wreck, and I'll bet one or both of them soon learned to swim and dive. During the dive John Perry scraped his leg on something and joked to the Prime Minister that he had bled for him. Mr. Pindling came back with the quip, "But aren't you glad it wasn't my blood?"

Other visitors included Wernher Von Braun, the father of rocket science, Prince Charles of the UK, and Secretary of Commerce Pete Peterson, to name a few. During the Undersea Medical Society Symposium in Freeport, over 75 physicians and scientists visited the *Hydro-Lab.*

An example of the tight mission schedule we kept, aside from hosting all the visitors, is reflected in 1972. Starting May 11–16, we supported a *Hydro-Lab* mission with the University of Michigan, followed by the University of Miami May 18–25 and again on June 1–6; University of Southern California June 11–17; University of Miami July 11–18 and again August 1–8; Texas A&M August 11–16; University of Miami August 31–September 7; UNCW September 11–15; University of Miami October 1–7; University of Alabama October 24–25; Texas A&M October 27–November 2; University of Miami November 14–21; American Institutes for Research (one-atmosphere) November 28–29; University of Miami December 1–7; and the University of Central Michigan December 12–19.

Dick, Gerri, and I fell into a rhythm. One mission after another kept us working day and night including most weekends. The schedule was exhausting for just the three of us, and exhilarating at the same time. In 1973 it was even busier with 19 missions and that continued right to the end in 1975. Sometimes we would have to work straight though several nights after a mission just to get the system ready for the next one. There were even times when two teams of scientists overlapped, with one team just finishing a decompression schedule and the other preparing to enter the *Hydro-Lab* for the next mission.

During one of the missions, a scientist from Columbia University's Lamont Geological Observatory demonstrated how even shallow, direct observations can be valuable to science. He had tagged along with a team of scientists scheduled to dive

PHOTO COURTESY DICK CLARKE

Scientists entering the wet submersible Shark Hunter *to move to a new area of a Bahamian reef to study fish behavior at dusk.*

the *Hydro-Lab*. He was interested in collecting tropical Foraminifera, his specialty. He was not a diver and, in fact, could barely swim. On one trip to work on the lab, the scientist came with us and collected water samples from the boat. He asked us if we could see forams while we were diving. I described a tiny spherical one with many strands of cytoplasm, looking something like a WWII floating mine. He was puzzled by this and had no idea which species it could be, particularly when I told him they were very abundant. What made it more confusing was that his sampling showed no such animal.

We convinced the scientist to don a mask and snorkel, enter the water, and hang on the side of the boat with one of us holding a rope around his waist, so he could have a look for himself. With some trepidation he got in the water and within moments started to yell in his snorkel. Just as we had described to him, the somewhat spherical forams were everywhere. His first impression was a new species, but how could it be possible that one so abundant had never been found in these waters? Well, it turned out that the forams he was seeing underwater were the same as those he was capturing, and he was the scientist that originally described the species. His description did not include the appendages that would retract into the body of the animal when brought out of the water. They were totally different in appearance. So, with just a few glances with his own eyes underwater, he was able to redescribe, correctly, this very common foraminifer.

Many of the repeat participants in our program were becoming proficient saturation divers. Sometimes called "aquanauts," scientists were soon requesting longer and longer excursions from the *Hydro-Lab*. To reach a depth of 90 feet, the divers would have to swim about 500 feet straight offshore from the *Hydro-Lab*. A depth of 200 feet was only 300 feet further at the drop-off. These excursions were limited by the availability of breathing air, as well as the additional uptake of nitrogen in the blood and tissues that could lead to the bends.

To expand the ability of the scientists to work further away and out of sight of their home base, we established a string grid highway along the bottom. Additionally, any excursion that would take the scientists out of sight of the *Hydro-Lab* required an accompanying surface boat with rescue divers. This also allowed us to supply extra tanks to them for longer dives.

During their first excursions, several of the scientists got nervous on the way out and displayed telltale signs by the way they were swimming, often erratically or frequently stopping to check gear or look around as if lost. Watching this from the surface, we would quickly send down a rescue diver to communicate with the scientist and to escort him or her back if necessary. If there were only two scientists making the excursion then, of course, both would have to return if one was having trouble. It was often unnerving for scientists to know that in the big ocean, their only sanctuary was the two-foot-wide opening in the bottom of the *Hydro-Lab*. When a diver was a thousand feet away and completely out of sight of the lab, that two-foot hole seemed like the size of a pinhead.

By the second year the program had progressed nicely, but it still was a big challenge to us. Dick, Gerri, and I would be on duty for months at a time. We would take turns manning the radio to the lab throughout the night. On one very stormy night there were three scientists in the *Hydro-Lab* reporting back to us that the lab was rocking slightly, but all seemed to be okay. By about one in the morning, the wind had increased and the seas grew to eight to ten feet high. At two o'clock, we didn't get the radio check required from the scientists. We called back for 10 minutes without any response.

Suspecting that the heavy seas had damaged the radio cable from the lab to the surface buoy, I had no choice but to go out to the site to first make sure everyone was okay and then to repair the problem. With Gerri manning the onshore radio, I fired up the *Bahama Hunter's* diesel engine and set out for the *Hydro-Lab*. The *Bahama Hunter* was 23 feet long and very wide with a shallow draft. It had a small cabin forward and a windshield protecting the steering console.

Exiting Bell Channel, I was a little over a half mile from the outer reef. Even so, the waves were six feet high and pounding the *Bahama Hunter* relentlessly. I needed to get out as quickly as possible and to save time I could not take the longer and safer route around the reef; I decided to head straight for a narrow opening in the reef that led right to the lab site some half mile beyond. The visibility was poor and I could just see the lights that flashed on the end of the channel's jetties. I had to set the lights perfectly on a specific course to find the opening of the reef.

Several minutes before reaching sight of the reef, I could hear the distinct roar of the waves crashing over its shallow top. It sounded like a freight train running in place. When I could finally see the reef through the darkness, rain, and mist, I was shocked. There was a continuous high wall of white breaking waves marking the length of the reef. The opening was covered as well. At first I thought that I had missed it, but after checking my compass and sighting the shore lights again, I was sure it was the right place. The waves were breaking so high and hard that they covered over the narrow opening in the reef.

Holding off for a moment, I called back to Gerri to see if she had made contact with the *Hydro-Lab.* She had not and I knew that time was critical; I needed to move quickly. Deciding that I was in the right position relative to the reef opening, I gunned the *Bahama Hunter* engine and headed straight for the wall of breaking water. I needed all of the power possible to break through. There was no going over it. I almost expected to hear the ripping of the hull hitting the reef. Just as the boat hit the wall of white water, I ducked and a mass of water crashed over me, partially filling the cockpit. The boat lurched with a bone-crunching crash into the foaming wall of water. Then another wave hit—more water in the boat. The small drain

PHOTO COURTESY DICK CLARKE

Scientist photographing reef organisms during a saturation dive from the Hydro-Lab, *in backgound.*

Life-support buoy for the Hydro-Lab.

scuppers and bilge pump could not handle the large amount of water, but I could not leave the wheel to man the pump for fear the boat would turn sideways into the sea and flip over. I was now very sorry that I couldn't wait for someone to come with me, but my sense of responsibility for the safety of the people in the *Hydro-Lab* was too strong, so I went out by myself.

After the second wave hit, the boat moved out into clearer but still wild seas. The engines kept running and the boat eventually drained. By this time, I was only a few hundred yards from the surface buoy and life-support system. I was relieved to hear the Lister diesel running and to see light and bursts of bubbles coming from the habitat, meaning that all systems appeared to be working. Losing communications with the scientists most likely was due to a damaged cable from the heavy seas.

Tying up to the surface buoy was going to be the next challenge. Several attempts to negotiate near enough for me to jump onto the buoy system with the *Bahama Hunter* bow line in hand failed. The heavy seas made it too perilous to move close enough without crashing. I finally paid out a long length of line, put on my mask and swim fins, maneuvered the boat as close as possible, and jumped overboard swimming as fast as possible to tie the line onto the aft cleat of the buoy. It worked, and after returning to the boat and taking a few seconds to rest, I grabbed a tank and regulator in my arms and jumped back overboard.

The swim down to the *Hydro-Lab* took only about 30 seconds. Entering the hatch, I climbed up into the lab. The sound of snoring punctuated the almost rhythmic belching of air through the hatch. When I looked around the lab everyone was sleeping, including the person that was supposed to be on watch. I could see immediately that the radio volume had been turned all the way down so that it made no noise. The so-called watch person had obviously turned down the sound, so that it would not interfere with his sleeping.

There is little I can say about my feelings at that moment. I had made a difficult and dangerous trip only to find out that this yo-yo had turned the communication radio down and had gone to sleep. That I saw red is a vast understatement. The culprit was still asleep, lying on the deck. I made a point of standing right over him, dripping water on his face, as I readjusted the radio's volume. He woke up with a yell, waking his buddies. I called Gerri and got her immediately. She was relieved to hear my voice and told me that Dick was on his way out. I told Gerri that everything was working fine, except for the idiot on watch, and to tell Dick to turn around and go home.

Since I was in the lab, I made it a point to keep everyone up for the next half hour for a brusque lecture on safety, and how I didn't appreciate getting my ass kicked by the sea for no good reason. I told them that falling asleep on watch was pretty much a hanging offense. Needless to say, the guy that was on watch was very unpopular for the rest of the mission. It was soon after this episode that we installed a new communication system, which allowed us to key open a microphone inside the lab from the shore watch station. With this system we could, at any time, listen to sounds inside and get a response from the scientists without their needing to be physically by the radio. We also made the decision that in heavy seas and at night we would always have at least two people onboard the boat, even if it meant a short delay.

During the years of the *Hydro-Lab* program, I continued to observe the rich marine life within the waters off the western side of Grand Bahama Island. One day following some repairs on the *Hydro-Lab*, I set out to collect a few jacks that were schooling nearby and displaying courtship behavior. Some of the fish in the school were changing from their normal silver and blue color to a deep copper hue. I suspected that these were the males and they seemed to be somewhat aggressive within the school. I had a Hawaiian sling with a five-foot stainless steel shaft and a strong poly net bag to hold the collected fish. It was luck that the school was swimming in a circle, so I could get close enough to make an accurate shot.

I collected two of the fish displaying the copper color, and stuffed them into the net bag. They were about five pounds in weight and almost filled the bag. I placed the bag on the bottom and set out to collect one more specimen. By this time the school had disappeared, and when I returned to the bag, a small reef shark was swimming rapidly around the dead fish.

The shark looked too agitated to confront and I was forced to watch it attack the bag, violently twisting and turning. Within a short time the shark and two fish were

PHOTO COURTESY DICK CLARKE

Support diver repairing the Hydro-Lab *umbilical from the life-support buoy.*

gone, leaving behind just threads of the poly bag hanging from its metal handles. It was an incredible feat. This relatively small shark had cut through the very tough material with its razor sharp teeth and, with no way of holding it down, had ripped it apart. The teeth had cut through the tough poly material like a mechanical scissor.

I was curious to see how difficult it would be to cut the poly with a good pair of scissors, without holding or stretching the bag. I bought another similar bag and cut it in half, but I took much longer than the shark. Even though the scissors were new and sharp, it took some time and my respect for a shark's biting capability, regardless of its size and species, went way up. The combination of incredibly sharp teeth and the ability of some species to create torque by twisting their bodies after grabbing prey, make these sharks ocean-going buzz saws.

As the years passed quickly, we came in contact with hundreds of divers with all levels of expertise. After a while we developed almost a sixth sense that allowed us to anticipate trouble and take preventive action. No matter what the experience level, certain subtle movements or preoccupation with equipment told us that a diver was not functioning well underwater.

We often guided divers away from trouble without them even knowing it. Even mild currents could panic a weak swimmer, especially when they first entered the water and were still on the surface. If a diver were not attempting to swim against a current, we would quickly pull him or her back to the boat. Over a five-year period, we prevented dozens of potential disasters, almost all involving visitors to the *Hydro-Lab* site.

By the end of the first year of the project, I was pretty confident of my ability to see trouble coming. During the third year, however, I met my match. He was a freelance writer who wanted to see the *Hydro-Lab* firsthand for an article he was writing about living in the sea. Although I have long forgotten his name and the magazine that commissioned him to write the article, I will always remember the dive. He was a certified diver with limited experience, and since it was a beautiful summer day with calm seas, I did not anticipate any trouble. We would dive to a 50-foot depth, go inside the lab for a few minutes, and then explore and photograph the reefs in the area.

Following about a 10-minute visit to the lab, we began a swim around the small coral heads a short distance away. About 30 minutes into our dive, I checked his air gauge which showed about 1,000 psi. He was using more air than normal, but he seemed very relaxed and swam easily around the reefs. About 15 minutes later, he turned and slowly swam toward me without any sign of a problem.

Thinking that he was going to signal me to return to the surface or to move somewhere else, I watched him approach. When he got close, he very nonchalantly reached out and ripped my regulator out of my mouth and started to breathe off my tank of air. I didn't have an octopus rig on my tank so he had my only source of air. I signaled to him asking if he were out of air. There was no response, but he still appeared very calm. I let him breathe off my supply for about 10 seconds and signaled that we should start buddy-breathing the regulator, but he wouldn't give it back. More seconds passed and I signaled that we should start swimming to the surface, again with no response and with no indication he was giving up the regulator.

Now the alarm bells went off—this guy was in a panic, but without the usual signs. Forcing the regulator away from him would probably cause him to go berserk. I was baffled by his behavior. I thought it prudent to let him calm down before making a move but I also needed some air for myself. Funny how quickly priorities can change when you're sitting at 50 feet with no air to breathe. I grabbed the writer by his tank strap and started hauling him to the surface. The man swam with me, but in no apparent hurry. I basically had to drag him along. When we reached the surface, I took a few seconds to catch my breath and then motioned to him to swim to the boat. He handed the regulator back to me. Although I was pissed, we were still in the water and I thought he may still be in trouble. Back in the boat, I asked him what was going on, but he had no answer. Here was a man in an absolute panic and I couldn't see it. Luckily we were only at a 50-foot depth. If it were deeper, say 100 feet, it would have been a much tougher problem. My self-assured attitude about detecting divers in trouble was tested that afternoon, and I never dove again without an octopus regulator.

By the second year of the program, NOAA's Manned Undersea Science and Technology Office was funding most of the *Hydro-Lab* missions. Our direct contact with the office was Dr. Morgan Wells, a character of the first order and definitely not in the mold of a federal bureaucrat. Morgan was a diving scientist who had participated in the Navy Sea Lab project. He moved to the DC area to take over as project manager of our program. His job was to make sure we were conducting good science and doing it safely. Since we were an unconventional program, Morgan's unconventional ways made it easy for us to deal with him.

On several occasions, Morgan filled in as a scientist on a saturation dive. On one such mission during a supply run, Dick and I were transferring equipment down to the scientists in the *Hydro-Lab*. At the same time, we made a check of all systems in and outside the lab. A few feet away was another small structure we called the *PUTS (Personnel Undersea Transfer System)*. The *PUTS* was a simple steel structure that held an airspace for divers to come into and talk. We also set it up as a high-pressure filling station that allowed divers to fill their tanks on the bottom of the ocean. A high-pressure compressor in the surface buoy could be turned on from inside the lab, sending air to the *PUTS* through a hose that was part of the umbilical. The structure also served as a quick sanctuary for a diver in trouble.

PHOTO COURTESY DICK CLARKE

Author setting up reef fish depth experiments at 200 feet.

During the routine safety check, I swam to the *PUTS* to make sure the air quality was okay and the filling hoses were in good shape. When I popped my head into the airspace and removed my regulator, I almost choked on the putrid stench of stale, wet cigarette smoke. I couldn't believe it. Smoking in the lab or any enclosed space under pressure is a real problem. The partial pressure of oxygen, even at the shallow depth of 50 feet, is high enough to be a fire hazard, not to mention the effect of the smoke and smell on air quality, which would take a long time to clear.

Dick was nearby and I motioned to him to come inside the *PUTS*. He too could not believe what he smelled. It was obvious that someone had brought cigarettes into the airspace, lit up, and then flooded the *PUTS* to remove the smoke. It did get rid of the smoke, but the smell remained and was overwhelming. The wet, rusted ceiling absorbed the smoke and even flooding couldn't remove the smell. Both of us immediately suspected Morgan. He was a smoker and a bit of a wild man who would have no problem pulling off such a stunt, even though he was our official government safety officer. "That son of a bitch—we'll fix his wagon," I, or maybe it was Dick, spit out loud.

Morgan was several hundred yards from the *Hydro-Lab* testing metabolic respiratory rates of corals, and we had to wait several hours to confront him. It was great. We had Morgan cold, and he readily admitted that he got one of the young lady support divers to smuggle a pack of cigarettes and matches down to him in a plastic bag. We insisted that he give up the rest of the pack and matches, which he did. We had just gained a bunch of chips, which we could cash in with Morgan whenever we needed help with his office. Morgan was a charmer, and he often got away with murder.

One time he got under my skin over the phone, and I told him that I was coming up to his office in Rockville, Maryland, to personally punch him in the nose. It had to do with my perception that he was interfering with our operations. I was serious and caught the next flight out of Freeport to Washington. Morgan met me outside the airport with a bottle of rum under his coat and poured me a drink as we walked through the parking lot to his car. It wasn't long before I had completely forgotten my mission. A punch in the nose would have been most satisfying, but tying one on with Morgan was a good substitute.

Another character who was a frequent user of our program was Dr. Bill Schroeder from the Dauphin Island Marine Lab in Alabama. After the full porta-potty blew up during a decompression test early in the program, and I had to clean it up, the open ocean became the mission toilet. The occupants of the lab would go behind a coral head or, if just to urinate, they would simply stand in the water in the open hatch.

It was also lab entertainment to feed left-over food to the fish around the hatch. A population of yellowtail snapper took up residence and would attack the food as it hit the water in the hatchway. One day Bill, who was spending a week in the lab, jumped into the hatch to stand on the bottom and go. Well, you probably guessed it, our ol' friend was buck-naked and the dangling thing coming into the water was too much for a yellowtail to resist, so, with very sharp needlelike teeth, it did a job on poor Bill's peepee. I got a call on the radio that he needed some assistance. When we found out what the problem was, all the guys near the radio disappeared in a flash, leaving me holding the bag, so to speak. This was definitely not in my job description. I quickly remembered that his wife was on the island and was a diver. What a lucky break!

The *Hydro-Lab* proved to be a workhorse. By the second year most of the serious bugs had been worked out, including installation of an air conditioning and dehumidifying system that kept the interior of the lab reasonably comfortable. Denny Breese's ability to make things work in the undersea environment was no less than brilliant. Previously, the high humidity had been responsible not only for general discomfort, but also for serious outbreaks of ear infections that caused us to abort a few missions before they were completed.

The unique, unmanned life-support buoy, which ran continuously day and night except for routine checks, eliminated the need for a large crew to be on-site as was common in other habitat programs. This was particularly important during bad weather. It allowed the divers to stay comfortably on the ocean bottom in the stable lab. It was the surface crew that historically received the beating topside, but they could now safely monitor the dive with frequent radio checks from the onshore station in all weather conditions.

On one beautiful morning, following a successful seven-day saturation dive that ended the day before, we made a routine check of the *Hydro-Lab* before taking the rest of the day off. Another scientific team was already on the island ready to begin their training the next day.

Swimming down to the lab, I passed by the front window and did a double take; I thought I was hallucinating. There, inside the lab, were two dead groupers floating in water. The lab was totally flooded. Almost swallowing my regulator, I discovered that in haste we had not sealed the bottom hatch properly, and by a one-in-a-million coincidence, the valve on the purge hose to the surface used for decompression had failed. How the bottom hatch opened enough to allow the groupers to swim in is still a mystery.

Dick and I immediately closed a backup valve, started the diesel engine on the life-support buoy, engaged the air compressor, and blew the lab dry. Everything inside was completely ruined. The electrical distribution box, air conditioner, radios, sound-powered telephones, and everything else was trashed. In an almost controlled panic, we called Denny in Florida and told him we needed it all back in operation as quickly as possible. Denny and Perry Oceanographics personnel kicked into action to buy new parts and start rebuilding the guts of the lab.

In the meantime, Dick, Gerri, and I did a total cleanout of equipment and washed the inside of the lab thoroughly. We prepared every transfer pot we had, and when Denny flew the equipment to Freeport, we all spent the next three days putting the *Hydro-Lab* back together.

The next mission team was sitting ready on the beach. Unlike Humpty Dumpty, the lab was put back together again, and we only lost two days from the original schedule—much to be said for a simple system.

Prince Charles and a friend viewing the Bahamian reef from the Hydro-Lab.

PHOTO COURTESY DICK CLARKE

18

CAUGHT WITH OUR PANTS DOWN

WE HAD JUST begun a seven-day dive during the late part of the Caribbean hurricane season. The long-range weather and sea state prediction looked perfect with mild seas and clear skies over the next week. Even so, our experience dictated that we keep a close eye on the Caribbean and local weather several times a day. At that time in the early seventies, the Weather Service in the region was not very reliable. Large-scale maps of barometric isobars were the best we could get.

By the third day or so, the three scientists living in the *Hydro-Lab* had settled into their routine schedule of 10-hour days in the water to study the coral reef ecosystem. All was going well, when we received word that a tropical low had suddenly formed just south of us and was predicted to move north. There was no immediate concern. Moderate winds and rain were about all we expected. By the next day the system had been upgraded to a tropical storm and its forward speed had accelerated. We immediately became concerned and started preparing for emergency decompression and retrieval of the three scientists. Within a few more hours the storm was a full but small hurricane and moving quickly. The wind, rain, and seas around Freeport had turned ugly just as we were beginning the decompression schedule. It was too late for an emergency evacuation which was chancy in the first place.

We decided to go through a full 17-hour decompression. The seas had increased to at least 10 feet at the *Hydro-Lab* site, and our dives to the lab to bring supplies for the decompression were becoming difficult. One bit of good news came through late that afternoon from the Weather Service that the projected path of the hurricane would bring it some distance from our position, but we still could expect high winds and sea state throughout the night.

Our main concern was that the seas would damage the communication cables between the surface buoy and the lab, as well as the hose that vented the internal pressure to the surface. If the hose were damaged or ripped from the *Hydro-Lab*, the decompression would end.

We had already doubled the lines to the buoy and were confident that they would hold. The *Hydro-Lab* was equipped with an emergency system in the event the surface buoy with its air, water, and power supply was washed away. Battery powered lights, communications, carbon dioxide scrubbing systems, and a high-pressure emergency air supply could keep the scientists safe for several days.

I knew it was going to be a long and troublesome night, writing in my journal that "the apprehension is great."

When night fell, the decompression procedure was already several hours along and would not end until mid-morning of the next day. The scientists were now locked tight in the lab, and even though the pressure inside had dropped only a few pounds per square inch, it still would take several thousand pounds of energy to open the hatch. I knew it was going to be a long and troublesome night, writing in my journal that "the apprehension is great."

Sometime in the middle of the night the winds peaked, and we guessed that the waves passing over the lab were reaching 12 to 15 feet high. Our radio communications were frequent. We wanted information on the decompression, the condition of the occupants, and how each felt. We also wanted updates on the system. The scientists radioed back that everything remained operational but the water visibility was close to zero. They could see sand and shells swirling around as energy associated with the passing waves reached the bottom. The lab was also rocking and moving slightly along the bottom. I had a knot in my stomach the entire night, fully expecting that we would lose communications at any moment and have to attempt a very hazardous trip to the lab site to repair a cable in the water or at least to ensure that everyone was okay.

The hurricane passed to our east very quickly and by daybreak the wind had cut back considerably. The seas were still high, but at a longer period with much less cresting. Almost a miracle, the surface buoy and communications held and we maintained radio contact throughout the night. Not one of us on shore or, I believe, in the *Hydro-Lab* slept one wink. We were exhausted emotionally, as well as physically.

Only a few hours away from the end of decompression, we prepared to head offshore and recover the lab's occupants. As tired as we were, there was still a lot of work to be done. The wind had died down to a breeze and the seas were still high, but they were manageable even in our small 23-foot support boat. By the time we reached the lab site the sun was shining and the now long-period waves were down to four feet high or so. The water was milky white with almost no visibility.

One at a time, Dick and I swam down to the lab feeling our way along and locked into its interior. The inside pressure was now at sea level and it took about a minute to decompress the lock to get inside. We re-entered the cramped lock with one of the scientists, re-pressurized until the bottom hatch opened, and then slowly swam, with scuba tanks in hand, to the waiting boat.

It took about a half hour to get everyone onboard the surface boat. Standing on the boat deck with the warm sun shining on everyone, an overwhelming wave of relief came over me and the tension in my body melted like butter. Normally we would bring the scientists to shore to clean up, have breakfast, and hang near the decompression chamber in case of a later occurrence of the bends, while we started to remove their equipment from the lab. In this case, we decided to let things go for awhile and take a much needed rest.

The sea, like anything or anyone else we may love, does not always come with wine and roses.

19

SEVEN DAYS UNDER THE SEA

CAPTAIN NEMO HAD nothing on us. After supporting and hand-holding hundreds of scientists and visitors, Gerri, Dick, and I had the opportunity to actually live in the *Hydro-Lab* ourselves and conduct our own research for seven days in October 1973, something like a busman's holiday. The dive would also give us firsthand experiences that we could use to make future missions safer and more effective. Even with all our involvement, we were as excited about our dive as any newcomer. Denny Breese would assume the role of topside supervisor for the dive and a few divers from Florida came over to Freeport to assist him.

By the time this mission was scheduled, the *Hydro-Lab* was in good condition. The troublesome humidity was now under control with the modified air-conditioning and dehumidifier system. Additionally, each person that entered the lab had to first shower with fresh water and dry off inside the lockout trunk. It was very cramped in the trunk, but the system paid off nicely as we were able to keep the humidity at a very comfortable level.

Our research had several goals. We would expand a census of the local fish population and continue to observe the evening and morning migration of several species of grunts. We also planned to test new excursion tables that would allow us to spend extended time at depths up to 200 feet and return to the *Hydro-Lab* with little decompression necessary. If these tables proved to be safe, it would allow scientists to explore and study the deep reefs in a way that had not been available in the past.

In addition, Dick would be taking blood samples from each of us, including himself, over the course of the mission. This was in support of Dr. Richard Philp's (University of Western Ontario) research on the loss of immature platelets due to their adhesion to intravascular bubbles, which could then serve as a marker for decompression stress. If new platelet levels were lower than normal, the hypothesis was that bubbles were being formed and the decompression table was sub-optimal.

Following the normal preparation and stocking the lab with equipment, food, and such, we were ready for our adventure. From the time we entered the lab, Dick,

We worried that he was going into hypothermia and would literally freeze to death in the sunny Bahamas.

Gerri, and I took turns diving two at a time. Except for a one-hour lunch break, two people were in the water all day long and for a few hours each evening after dark. It quickly became a routine that we used effectively. One thing we learned on the first day was that the interior of the lab was very comfortable, and after spending hours in the water it felt really good to come home, drink some hot coffee or tea, and warm up. Even though the seawater temperature was in the low eighties and we wore full wet suits, our body heat was somewhat compromised after many hours in the water.

On another mission conducted by Bob Given and Andy and Vivian Pilmanis of the University of Southern California, we thought that we were going to witness the first person in history to "freeze" to death in the Bahamas. Bob conducted an experiment in which he spent all day in the water, without a wet suit, connected to the *Hydro-Lab* by an umbilical to his helmet that provided air and communications. The goal was to see how his body's core temperature would react to the relatively warm water. Bob came back to the lab frequently to check his temperature and by the end of the day it had cooled down considerably.

Even after he aborted the experiment, his core temperature kept falling for awhile until it could be stabilized. We worried that he was going into hypothermia and would literally freeze to death in the sunny Bahamas. Not a good idea, we later decided, and no more experiments like that were approved. While our situation was not the same, we did learn why some individuals found excuses to stay inside the lab, so they could compile their data, etc. In some cases, we surmised, it was for reasons of comfort.

About 200 yards offshore of the lab was the mid-reef at about 60 feet deep. It was there that large schools, primarily white and blue-striped grunts, stayed throughout the daylight hours before migrating to their feeding grounds in the early evening. The grunt, of which there are a number of species, is a small closed-bladder reef fish, averaging one to two pounds, that feeds on bottom organisms. The feeding grounds for the fish on the mid-reef were sandy areas both offshore and inshore of the reef.

At just about dusk, hundreds of grunts would start an almost single-file migration along the length of the reef. A few at a time would turn off and go to either of the two sandy flats and start to feed by biting into the bottom sediment to capture worms and other invertebrates. All night long the fish would sift through the sand bottom for food and then at dawn gather for a migration back to their daytime habitat on the reef where they would rest.

I was particularly interested in the depth limitations of these closed-bladder fish. The work I had done off the coast of Belize showed that closed-bladder fish could not survive going very deep too quickly. The inflation rate of the swim bladder, to compensate for depth changes and maintain a fish's neutral buoyancy, was slow. I wondered if the grunts' natural migration to deeper feeding grounds was limited by this fact.

For several evenings and early mornings we followed the migrations that appeared to move on trails along the coral reef and observed the grunts' behavior. It was amazing to see these fish use the same trails each night and morning.

Each night the grunts swam along their trails and peeled off to the sandy bottom no deeper than 80 feet, or to the shallow grounds about 40 feet deep. In the morning they returned and hung quietly together among the different species of gorgonians attached to the reef. Some of the grunts appeared buoyant and pointed their snouts at the top end of a gorgonian as a reference point. With their tail ends higher than their noses, they had to continuously move their pectoral fins to maintain position. We believe that these fish had been in deeper water during the evening, their swim bladders having compensated somewhat, and they had returned to their shallower day grounds slightly buoyant.

This study was further evidence that many fish with closed swim bladders were limited in their ability to move about the ocean freely. The grunts stayed in their daytime reef habitat at 60 feet or so and did not migrate any deeper than about 80 feet, or shallower than about 40 feet deep. They were limited to a 40-foot range. Distribution of the species may be partially dictated by the availability of feeding and daytime habitats at the right depths.

During the seven-day mission, Dick and I made 16 experimental excursion dives between us, including several down the offshore wall to almost 200 feet, using the new tables. Before these tables were available, our conservative approach for excursions from the 50-foot depth of the *Hydro-Lab* was to 90 feet deep. This allowed the scientists to move freely to that depth without the need for decompression stops.

The edge of the deep drop-off and wall was almost 1,000 feet offshore of the *Hydro-Lab*. A surface boat lowered fresh tanks of air to us. At the deepest depth it took three sets of double tanks to complete the excursion. We were elated at the ease and feeling of safety that these dives offered. We finally had the capability of extending a working dive to as deep as 200 feet and staying long enough (close to one hour) to accomplish something practical. We felt that science would be well-served by these test dives. On one later mission, the ability to work a little longer at just 100 feet deep produced a new species of coral found by scientist Walt Japp.

After seven days of saturation diving and decompression, Dick, Gerri, and I were tired, but ready to do it again. We learned a lot about the ocean and about extending our diving capabilities. The lab performed well, and our personal experiences gave us a good feeling about future dives.

20

A VIEW OF OUTER SPACE FROM INNER SPACE

ONE OF THE strangest projects we supported involved setting up the *Hydro-Lab* as a subsurface physics lab to measure specific high-energy cosmic particles, such as muons and neutrinos, passing through the earth from somewhere in space. We used a simple cured nuclear emulsion that displays a track in the form of bubbles as the particle passes through.

It is believed that titanic stellar explosions send these high-energy particles whizzing at the speed of light throughout the universe. Some of the particles have energy levels 10 billion times higher than those produced by the world's largest accelerators. Previous studies of high-energy particles coming from space had been conducted underground in deep caves to eliminate the background clutter of more common cosmic rays found on the surface. The problem with the cave system is that rock and soil formations, and therefore densities, vary at depth, creating impure data. A layer of water, on the other hand, not only blocks unwanted background noise but offers a relatively consistent density.

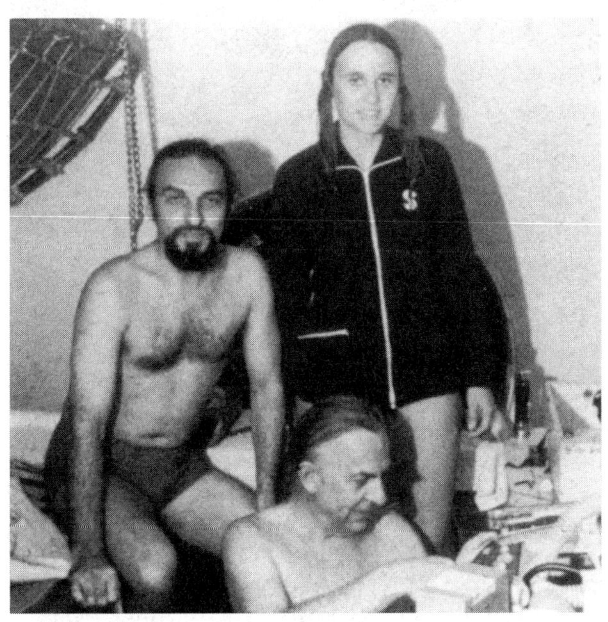

Left to right: Peter Kotzer, Gerri Wenz, Kurt Stehling in the Hydro-Lab *during undersea cosmic ray studies.*

The *Hydro-Lab* was set at one-atmosphere pressure, so we could bring scientists with little diving experience into the lab to work for several hours without getting into a decompression situation. The emulsions were brought down to the lab in a liquid form, poured into a flat tray and allowed to dry for one hour. Once dried, the emulsion

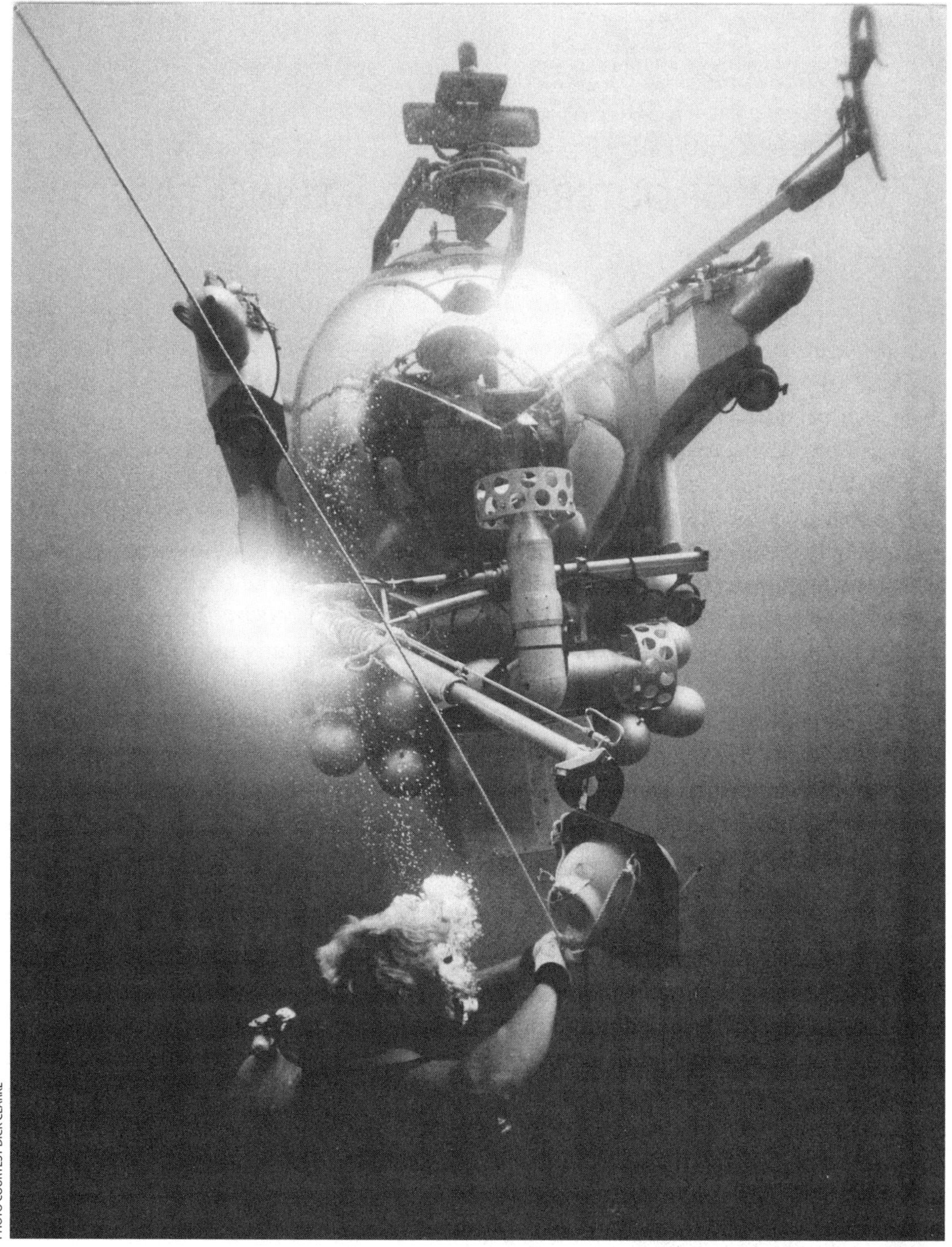

PHOTO COURTESY DICK CLARKE

Diver at 100-foot depth retrieving canister from Johnson Sea-Link *research submersible, which had recovered the canister from 1,000-foot depth. The canister contained emulsion capturing cosmic ray data for one year.*

was cut into four-inch squares, then stacked together and placed in a waterproof container specially built to withstand ocean pressures down to 1,000 feet.

The preparation of the measuring instrument inside the lab at 50 feet eliminated background cosmic rays and produced a pure emulsion ready to capture the elusive high-energy particles as they passed right through the ocean and the entire earth at the speed of light. Once the emulsion was dry and sealed in the pressure-proof canisters, two of us locked out of the lab and carried the canister to the edge of the drop-off, placing it at 200 feet deep. It was left there for nine months, recovered, swum back to the *Hydro-Lab* where it was processed, brought to the surface, and sent off for analysis.

Another experiment placed a canister at 1,000 feet, which we attempted to recover one year later. After it had been brought to the surface by the submersible *Johnson Sea-Link* and before moving it to the *Hydro-Lab,* we hung the canister on a surface buoy. A local fisherman cut the canister off and stole the buoy, and that was that.

The study was conducted by Dr. Peter Kotzer from Fairhaven College in Washington state and Dr. Kurt Stehling from NOAA. Kurt was a wild man who had previously worked on the development of blimps and rigid dirigibles as cargo carriers. He got involved in all kinds of projects and convinced NOAA to support this one. During our several stays in the *Hydro-Lab* to work on the emulsions, Kurt would constantly rag a young assistant about his Russian heritage, and Peter about anything. In the middle of all this, he would emit a loud, almost train-whistling noise, which would startle us all. Kurt was a character and made the project interesting, to say the least. Being stuck for hours at a time in the tiny lab 50 feet underwater with Kurt was an experience.

About a year later, Peter, with great fanfare, invited me to his lab to view the one particle track that was captured on the emulsion instruments. Peter picked me up at the airport and several hours later, following his prerequisite stop at a go-go bar and drinks, we arrived at the lab.

With a few beers under my belt, I finally viewed the event through a microscope and saw a series of bubbles in a straight line where the high-energy particle had passed. This was the stuff of cosmic studies. Peter's excitement was palpable. As for me, I thought counting fish could be pretty mind-numbing—this was beyond that. To each his own.

21

WAS IT A MERMAID?

Saturation diving is not all fun and excitement. After a few days of relative isolation in a small, 16-foot underwater laboratory with two or three other people, life can get a little cramped and trying, especially if it's an all-male team. The thrill of scientific work and the beauty of the underwater sights can keep most people occupied for much of the time, but even so, there is a certain mindset and perception, particularly among young men, that something is missing. And that something usually involves sex.

During the five years of tending saturation dives in the *Hydro-Lab*, we often heard whining about the lack of female companionship, mostly in a joking way, or "Man, living under pressure for a long time sure gets you horny." Most of the saturation dives were no more than seven days long, and a lot of the young guys, I bet, hadn't had a date for the last month or two anyway, so it was mostly, if not all, in the mind. It may have had something to do with their knowledge that they were totally stuck on the bottom of the ocean with a 17-hour decompression ahead of them before coming back to the surface. After years of listening to this, the support crew of the *Hydro-Lab* project pretty much turned a deaf ear to it all.

One evening into the fifth day of a saturation mission in the *Hydro-Lab*, we were in the onshore control room tending radio checks to four male scientists and technicians in the lab. They had completed a full day of research on the reefs, finished dinner, and were relaxing by the four-foot window on the front of the lab. A bright underwater light, fixed above the window, illuminated a large area of the reef and sandy bottom, attracting schools of small scad, blue runners, silversides, and many species of pelagic invertebrates. The small fish were feeding on the invertebrates and silversides, all being viewed by the scientists. An occasional attack by a black grouper or barracuda added to the excitement of the evening. The group was describing the events they were observing over the radio.

During the course of the conversation, one of the men remarked something about how he would like to have his wife visit him right now. Another similar remark came soon after. Here we go again I thought—time to do something about this whining. Right then and there, we hatched a scheme that would give our underwater friends something to chew on.

One of the men in the control room at the time wanted in on our game and fetched his attractive girlfriend who was a diver and eager to participate. With the radio check personnel, support team, and boat in place, the couple and I readied a second boat with two sets of diving gear and set out into the darkness for the *Hydro-Lab* site.

The onshore crew was to keep up the conversation and not let on that we were coming. The radio in our boat was tuned into the *Hydro-Lab,* and we kept tabs on the conversation between the scientists and the shore station as we traveled the little over a mile to the site in calm seas. Passing through the opening of the outer reef, I was anticipating an interesting evening.

About 300 yards from the *Hydro-Lab*, we stopped and set anchor. The lab surface buoy with its flashing strobe light was clearly visible just ahead. The ocean around the buoy glowed green from the underwater light on top of the *Hydro-Lab*. We didn't want to get too close and possibly tip off the scientists that we were there.

After donning our diving gear without wet suits, the young lady and I slipped into the ocean and started swimming on the surface toward the buoy. When we came within a hundred feet of the lab, we dove to the bottom and headed toward the glow from the lab's underwater light. Although our breathing was a bit noisy, we were confident that the occupants of the lab could not hear us over the occasional belching of air out of the lab's hatch and music from their tape player, which we could clearly hear. Reaching our goal, we moved to the side of the *Hydro-Lab* near the big window. They would not be able to see us there due to the refraction of light through the flat window that distorted the peripheral views.

The young lady then proceeded to swim slowly through the lighted area right in front of the window, from one side of the lab to the other, absolutely buck naked.

With everything in place, we went to work. She removed her swim fins first, then slipped out of the scuba harness, handing me her tank but keeping her mouth piece in place. Next was her bathing suit. I gathered each piece in my arms as she continued. The music from inside the lab seemed to be playing for this underwater striptease.

Finally, signaling that all was ready, she removed her mask, took a few deep breaths through her regulator, and handed both to me. I immediately swam up and over the lab to the other side of the window with all her gear, totally out of sight of the group. The young lady then proceeded to swim slowly through the lighted area right in front of the window, from one side of the lab to the other, absolutely buck naked.

The choreography and performance were perfect—a beautiful female form moving gracefully and sensuously through the lighted water with fish all around, long hair streaming. An occasional flash from a bioluminescent organism around her body accentuated the scene. It might have brought tears to Neptune himself.

Although she was holding her breath, she took her time and was careful not to look toward the window, as if on a casual underwater stroll. When she reached the other side, again where no one inside could see us, I immediately gave her the regulator. In a minute she was dressed and we swam off toward the boat.

Inside the *Hydro-Lab* the music stopped and there was silence. Although water carries sound many times more efficiently than air, we only heard the belching of air through the lab's hatch. Seconds passed with no sound from the men. Maybe they weren't looking when she passed by, or was the sight too much for them? Did they pass out? Maybe they were turned into pillars of salt.

Several seconds more and the lab erupted into collective screaming, banging, and foot stomping. Obviously they were stunned, disbelieving what they had seen at first, but now they were venting their excitement. The yelling and banging continued at least until we swam out of earshot and back to our boat. One can imagine the radio chatter coming from the *Hydro-Lab* to the base station that night.

Later, following their 17-hour decompression, we were queried mercilessly by the scientists about the incident, but for many years, we never admitted to any part in the scheme.

22

DISASTER AT 360 FEET

THE NEWS HIT me in the pit of my stomach. While preparing the *Hydro-Lab* for another mission, a call came through from Perry Oceanographics in Florida. The *Johnson Sea-Link* lockout submersible was stuck on the ocean bottom, 360 feet off the coast of Key West, Florida. While not considered particularly deep, a successful rescue would depend on the conditions. Fortunately back then, the U.S. Navy had a major submarine base at Key West, and everyone immediately thought that they would have the means to undertake a rescue, if it came to that.

The *Johnson Sea-Link* was a second-generation research lockout sub designed by Ed Link. Unlike the *Deep Diver,* it was constructed of a thick acrylic sphere that held a pilot and observer forward and an aluminum chamber in the rear that two divers could pressurize for lockout from the sub. Ed's partnership with Seward Johnson created the Harbor Branch Oceanographic Institution, which built and owned the sub, a major facility of the Harbor Branch program.

On the fateful day in June 1973, Ed and his research vessel *Sea Diver* were 20 miles east of Key West conducting a series of survey dives on a shipwreck with the *Sea-Link*. The *Fred T. Berry*, a former destroyer, was purposely sunk to serve as an artificial reef at about 360 feet. The surveys were simply to observe the new reef to see if fish populations were taking up residence around it. The *Sea-Link*'s main job was to recover a trap placed earlier to evaluate the fish population.

That day there was a shifting of currents off the Keys, which apparently brought in cold water from the deep that flowed along the bottom. The currents were strong and reportedly pushed the *Johnson Sea-Link* into the wreck with cables and lost fish nets all over it. The sub immediately got tangled in something that could not be seen by the sub's crew.

The surface crew, including Ed, never lost communications with the sub. In the front sphere were the two pilots, Robert Meek and Archibald Menzies. Ed's son, Clayton Link, and a Perry Oceanographics employee, Al Stover, got into the sub's aft chamber for the dive rather than add lead ballast weights. On every dive a sub has to compensate for buoyancy depending on the weight of its passengers and any additional gear brought aboard. As I heard it, the dive was to be a quick one, so the two men were only in their street clothes and were not prepared for cold conditions.

The call came some hours after the sub became tangled in the wreck. I was asked to be one of two rescue divers using a new commercial dive chamber that the Perry crew was quickly putting together. "Of course," I answered. I knew Al Stover well and I had met Clayton only briefly, but it didn't matter to me. These were people in grave danger, and I would do anything to help. My diving experience by this time was extensive and even though I had not used this system, I was confident that we could make it work. The other diver would be George Bezak, who worked for Perry and was proficient in chamber operations. He would be the operations person and I would leave the chamber to attempt to free the sub from the wreck.

It was late in the evening. After I hung up, my first job was to get from Freeport to Key West as quickly as possible. Knowing I would have to wait until the morning to get a commercial flight, I called a friend living on the island for help. Bob Hempstead, a commercial airline pilot, rallied and prepared his personal single-engine Mooney to fly out of Freeport. We left in the middle of the night, flying across the Gulf Stream to just below Miami and finally following the many islands southward. There were thunderstorms everywhere flashing against the night sky, and Bob deftly maneuvered his plane around these with no incident.

When we arrived at Key West it was early morning, but still dark. George met us and said that the Perry chamber was en route and should arrive in a few hours. By this time the Navy rescue operation had attempted several surface-supplied dives to the stricken sub, but each one had to be aborted because of strong currents that threatened to tangle the divers and their umbilical hoses into the wreck. All of the attempts so far to reach the sub had been by lowering a chamber or platform from a surface ship, making them vulnerable to the currents that were either pushing them away from the sub or into the wreck.

When the Perry chamber arrived, the engineers gave us a quick course on its operation, and we devised a plan of action for our dive. By early afternoon, we received news that the Navy team had not made a dive attempt for over eight hours because of the currents. The Perry chamber was designed to overcome the problems with currents. Rather than being lowered from the surface, the Perry system first placed a very heavy weight on the bottom and a winch would pull the chamber down to it, just like an elevator. We were confident that this system could get us to the bottom and help rescue the sub, overcoming the currents that pushed conventional designs away from the stricken vessel.

More time passed and the situation was becoming desperate. We had not received the call from the Navy.

More time passed and the situation was becoming desperate. We had not received the call from the Navy. All this time, poor Ed Link was on-site but out of control of the situation, and I could only imagine his anxiety and fear for his son and the others. Stories came back that the two in the aft chamber had attempted to pressurize and lock out to assess their problem, but by then they were in a weakened state from cold. The pressurization used a mixed helium gas and further compounded the cold situation, not to mention the efficiency of the aluminum chamber in conducting heat out and into the cold sea. Although the sub was off the Florida coast, the currents brought in 45-degree water that upwelled from the deep.

We waited for what seemed an eternity, but we were never called. The Navy chose to go it alone and, after some time and failure, brought in a research ship, the *A. B. Wood,* equipped with a simple robot with an attached grappling hook. Al and Clay were probably already gone when the remote system hooked a cable onto the sub and a winch onboard the ship tore it away from the wreck.

We learned later that Al Stover and Clayton Link had succumbed to the cold and that the two in the front sphere, Robert Meek and Archibald Menzies, had survived. The sphere, constructed of four-inch thick acrylic, had far more insulating qualities than the aluminum chamber where Al and Clay had died, so they had some protection from the cold sea. I was emotionally drained, and for some time I could not drive out the thought that, by using the Perry system, George and I might have saved our friends.

Later examination indicated that a hook under the sub had probably snarled on a cable, which meant that a diver could likely have pulled it apart and freed the vehicle. That thought brought tears to my eyes, a sour taste for diving, and sadness for Ed and Marilyn Link for the loss of their son. I grieved too for the loss of Al, a hero in his own right. He was a father of seven, and in 1966 he piloted one of the subs that searched for, found, and retrieved one of three hydrogen bombs accidentally dropped by U.S. planes into the sea off the southern coast of Spain.

23

LIVING UNDER THE ARCTIC ICE

In the spring of 1974, Dr. Joe MacInnis, hyperbaric physician and well-known Canadian ocean explorer, who was my partner during the first saturation dive in the *Hydro-Lab*, invited me to join his diving expedition, roughly 600 miles north of the Arctic circle. Designated Arctic IV, it was sponsored by the James Allister MacInnis Foundation, and its target was Resolute Bay on the southern end of Cornwallis Island at about 75°F north latitude in the Northwest Territory of Canada. I had been living in the Bahamas for four years and wondered if I had now been so acclimated to the tropics that I lost the ability to withstand the rigors of coldwater diving.

Before moving to the Bahamas, most of my diving experience had been off the coast of New Jersey, and much of this in frigid winter waters with only an old-fashioned wet suit for protection. This really became thought provoking when Joe said that I would be one of the first people on earth to actually live under the ice for a prolonged period. I was so excited by the prospect and honored to be chosen for the task that the frigid waters of the Arctic became a non-issue, at least for the time being.

In April 1975, I flew to Toronto to meet a Canadian Forces military C-130 transport planc that would carry us to the Arctic site. The flight was a routine supply route to service outlying military bases, which were part of the early warning system for possible Soviet missiles and aircraft coming from the north during the Cold War. We left Toronto and headed north in the big lumbering plane—first stop Thule, Greenland. Onboard, aside from the Canadian Forces crew, were a handful of military and civilian personnel headed to the Alert Early Warning radar station on the shores of the Arctic Ocean. Two physiologists from the U.S. Navy and Tom Bain, (the son of Lynden O. Pindling, Prime Minister of the Bahamas), were also on their way to Resolute.

Although the plane offered little in the way of comfort, we each had access to a small window, which gave us a limited view of the incredible ice- and snow-covered mountain ranges of northern Canada. After a quick stop at Thule, we proceeded to Alert, the northernmost military station in the world, where we spent the night.

I was fascinated by the indoor curling rink at the station. Even with outdoor temperatures averaging about 10 degrees below zero, the rink was equipped with refrigeration coils under the ice floor. Apparently curling requires an absolutely smooth ice surface to play the game properly; freezing by natural means would make the ice too rough to use. I wondered how it was done in the old days.

After a relatively smooth landing, the pilots maneuvered the huge C-130 along the icy runway to a small building where we were picked up by a Bombardier tracked vehicle. Resolute was all ice and snow; everywhere I looked was white. Even in spring the temperature hovered around two to five degrees below zero. The bay was frozen solid. When we got out of the plane, winds whipped fine snow in the air, whiting out the horizon. It was impossible to see contrast or detect distance. I'd been in this situation many times diving in murky waters, but this was different. We were standing on land, and I was totally disoriented. The Bombardier driver, keeping us on track by following a series of dark stakes that marked the side of the road, finally brought us to a camp on the shores of the bay.

The camp contained several simple but comfortable barracks, a mess hall, small store, and even a movie theater, which was open once a week. It was used as

Scientist donning a dry suit for a dive under the Arctic ice.

a kickoff point for Arctic oil exploration and would be our base for the month-long expedition. Nearby was an Eskimo settlement.

My partner for this pioneering venture, Jim English, was a Canadian diver working at the time for Memorial University in Newfoundland. Following dinner, MacInnis and his team briefed us on our goals, and we began to prepare for our dives. Between the scientists and the support crew there were about a dozen men involved in the project. The dive site was in fairly shallow water, about 60 feet, covered by 7 feet of solid ice. The Canadians had already cut two holes to the ocean below. One was small and covered by a large heated tent; the larger uncovered hole was for placing and recovering equipment and instrumentation. MacInnis reminded us that the relatively small holes were our only way in and out of the water and screwing up while under the ice could have dire consequences.

My role in the expedition had two objectives. First, I would conduct various scientific experiments, including measuring dissolved oxygen from the bottom of the ice to the ocean floor, and I would collect Arctic marine fauna. The second objective was to demonstrate that people could live under the ice for prolonged periods, in this case for 24 hours. The Canadian team would monitor crude oil as it migrated up through the seven feet of ice following a small intentional spill by scientists at the underside of the ice shelf. (The oil-spill experiment produced some intriguing results. The oil reached the surface in just a few days, showing that a major Arctic underwater oil spill could be catastrophic, locking the oil in the ice for who knows how long.)

The most important pre-dive advice we received was how to avoid getting eaten by a polar bear. MacInnis had invited one of the region's game wardens to give us his advice, which boiled down to this: "If you meet a bear on the ice flow, do not run. Stand still. If it becomes aggressive, play dead, and hope it's not very hungry." With the image of a 1,000-pound, hungry polar bear burned into my brain, I was happy to be spending most of my time underwater. (I didn't know at the time that polar bears are pretty good divers and, if I were close to the surface, I could still be lunch.)

The next day we began forays under the ice to get acquainted with Arctic diving and to survey the area we would be studying. Jim English, two safety divers, and I donned the cumbersome dry, variable-volume Unisuits and prepared for our first dive. The temperature of the water under the ice was just above 28°F. Although freshwater freezes at 32°F, the salt content in seawater keeps it liquid for a few degrees colder. An exposed diver would last only minutes in this water and would probably go into shock almost immediately.

The heated tent gave us a place to get our gear ready. I was wearing long underwear, thermal pants, two pair of wool socks, and a wool sweater under my dive suit, so I was sure the frigid water would not be a problem. Finally, we put on oversized swim fins, masks, and two separate air tanks equipped with a special octopus regulator that stored a small amount of alcohol to prevent it from freezing. We forgot to bring the alcohol, but "Screech," a Newfoundland rum that was favored at the camp, and in plentiful supply, was an adequate replacement.

Screech was originally from Jamaica and was used to barter salt cod from Newfoundland. It was a rough, high-octane, nameless rum that, as I heard it, got its label during World War II when an unsuspecting American soldier passing through tried to emulate the Newfoundlanders' practice of throwing down a hefty drink in one gulp. Doing so, the soldier screamed out in pain. When someone asked what the noise was, a man replied, "The screech? 'Tis the rum, me son." So the name stuck.

The last pieces of equipment were important life-saving features: two five-pound lead ankle weights and forty pounds of weight around our waists supported by a shoulder strap. The Unisuit had an attachment that let divers flow a layer of air into the suit from the breathing tanks. This provided some insulation from the cold water and also acted as a buoyancy compensator.

But such buoyancy could be extremely dangerous. If a diver's legs rose above his head, air could rush there from the suit, turn the diver upside down and start an uncontrolled, rapidly accelerating ascent to the surface. Some years before, it happened to a NOAA diver in 50 feet of water off New York, resulting in a fatal embolism. Ankle weights solved the problem, but made swimming difficult. Still, having your legs over your head isn't always fatal if you're under the ice and near the surface. The Canadians taught me the trick of turning upside down under the ice, purposefully letting the air rush to my legs so I could walk on the bottom of the ice pack, upside down. This had no practical purpose, but it was fun.

The hole in the ice created a seven-foot long, water-filled shaft to the ocean below. As I descended, the surrounding ice diffused the light, creating a surrealistic, mystical entrance to the underwater world of the Arctic. The light from above became a mix of different shades of greens and blues down to the bottom of the hole where we could see just blackness. It was exquisite, like passing though a dreamlike portal into a parallel world.

Atop the ice pack, the Canadian team had plowed a 50-foot-wide path to the hole, allowing even more light to penetrate below. Swimming out from the bottom of the shaft, I found myself in a muted, shadowy place of crystal clear water. The clarity was beyond anything I'd ever seen—beyond the pristine waters of the Caribbean. I could easily see to the bottom 60 feet below and visibility must have been more than 200 feet. Apparently, with no wind-driven surface currents, no waves, and little or no convection, the water was almost still, allowing most suspended material to settle out of the water column.

It was an alien environment teeming with life. Kelp seaweed covered much of the ocean floor's fine muddy sediment. Jellyfish with flowing tentacles two-to three-feet long moved slowly through the water. Because the motionless sea had no influence on them, their tentacles were spread out in all directions in a pattern I'd never seen. Arctic pout three to four inches long swam slowly by me. The kelp and exposed rock harbored worms, brittle starfish, and other invertebrates. The bottom not covered by kelp housed large mussels, other bivalves, and small gastropods.

Most striking of all, it was a world in slow motion. In the 28°F water, Arctic organisms were doing everything to conserve energy. The pumping action of the mollusks was almost undetectable. When the brittle starfish were disturbed, they moved rapidly across the ocean floor only for a second or two, then stopped. I had brought nets to capture fish, but found that small specimens such as the Arctic pout were so placid I could catch them with my hands, even though I was wearing heavy waterproof mittens.

The dive was so exhilarating that I didn't notice the cold slowly creeping around and into my body. Later, I began to feel it on my exposed face and especially on my lips. It was an insidious cold, different from being exposed to frigid air. The temperature of the seawater was the same over every inch of my body and it came on slowly. By the end of the dive, some 60 minutes later, the chill had burrowed through the Unisuit, through the sweater, through the long underwear and wool socks, and deep into my bones.

After the first dive, we were confident we could explore this hostile world. Undressing in the tent, frozen to the bone, however, I wondered how we would fare in the planned 24-hour saturation dive. No one had done it before. Was it possible we were setting our sights too high?

We were confounded. We swam from one depression to the next, but the scene was always the same—death and decomposition.

During our second dive, we were able to make longer excursions from the entrance hole in the ice. The 50-foot strip of plowed snow overhead gave us plenty of light to study the communities of bottom organisms. Under the snow-covered areas, we needed hand-held lights to see anything in detail, even though we were only 60 feet down. I was halfway into the second dive when I discovered the dead zones. There were depressions in the bottom sediment, some only several feet in diameter and others as large as 17 feet. The larger depressions were about three feet deep. When I approached them, I could see a dome of light gray haze over each one, about as high as the depressions were deep. I shined a light into the domes and saw a carpet of dead and dying fish, snails, mollusks, and brittle stars along the outer edges and inside the depressions.

We were confounded. We swam from one depression to the next, but the scene was always the same—death and decomposition. Suddenly, the focus of my project shifted from collecting live specimens to studying these depressions of the dead. We suspected that the dome of hazy gray water above the depressions was low in oxygen and, by a stroke of luck, our limited inventory of instrumentation included a meter that measured dissolved oxygen. The meter was not waterproof, but it had a 150-foot cable and probe. With this long cable, a diver could swim the probe to the nearest depressions while oxygen levels were monitored from the surface.

After probing several depressions, we were amazed to find that the readings weren't just low, they hit absolute zero. There was no oxygen from the bottom of the depressions to the top of the domes. Anything swimming or crawling into those waters would die quickly from oxygen deprivation.

The bigger question became: What caused these Arctic dead zones? Answers started coming during the 24-hour saturation dive and several weeks afterward when sediment and water samples taken inside the depressions were analyzed by the University of Miami. Eventually we came up with a theory. The depressions were ground out by icebergs in this relatively shallow water during each summer's thaw. Once dug, the anaerobic conditions of the sub-sediment and other factors set up a chain reaction of decaying matter. With no water movement present to flush through the depressions, a condition of continuous oxygen depletion was possible. Animals became trapped in the oxygen-starved water, died, and subsequently decayed, taking even more oxygen from the water.

To compound the problem, the University of Miami reported that the samples we took showed traces of 2,4-D, a common herbicide used on North American farmland and as part of the jungle defoliant, known as "Agent Orange" during the Vietnam war. Additionally, the Miami chemists found traces of oil in the sediment at the bottom of the depressions.

The presence of oil was not surprising since ships came into Resolute Bay during the summer months, but the herbicide residue was a mystery. Since then, of course, pesticides and herbicides have been found over much of the globe. Recently, scientists have even found traces of PCBs, DDT, and other toxins in the blubber of whales.

When reports of our dead-zone find hit the Canadian newspapers, several oil companies attacked our sampling techniques. It was true that it was unsophisticated. We used only the containers we had on hand to collect sediment and water from the depressions. It was so unsophisticated, in fact, that it prevented us from publishing our findings in a scientific journal. Even so, the evidence was strong; the samples were contaminated.

The evening before the saturation dive we took in the movie at the tiny theater. The long daylight at this latitude meant that we went into the theater in the light and came out in the light. As we approached the theater, we saw several snowmobiles with young local Eskimo couples all decked out in fur parkas and mukluks. They were there for the movie as well. These were not the ice-flow-dwelling, igloo-living, set-grandma-out-on-the-ice-for-the-polar-bears kind of Eskimos of my imagination. Modern civilization had arrived. Inside were numerous Eskimo couples. The theater was chilly so we all kept our gear on throughout the movie—the original *Lolita*. It was hard to concentrate on the film as the Eskimo couples snuggled together. Here we were in the middle of the Arctic surrounded by Eskimos on their "date night." No rubbing noses. A few kisses maybe, but no traditional nose action. It was too interesting not to be a voyeur. Tomorrow I was about to set out on a great exploration, and the movie house experience set the stage.

Armed with a new scientific goal, we began preparing for our 24-hour dive. My partner, Jim English, an accomplished Canadian diving engineer, managed an underwater laboratory at Memorial University named *LORA-1* built by the University's Ocean Engineering group with a team of students during the previous year. The lab, about the same size as the *Hydro-Lab*, was sitting in 30 feet of water in Conception Bay, Newfoundland. The expedition's chief, Joe MacInnis, was also a hyperbaric physician and would serve as the medical backup for the project. It was a huge comfort to have Joe close by when we were doing any kind of experimental diving.

A physiologist from a U.S. Navy experimental lab in California had arranged to monitor our core body temperature for the duration of the dive. Even with the dry diving suits, there was little known at that time about the effects of prolonged exposure to below-freezing water temperature on the human body. The major thrust of this exercise, aside from our scientific goals, was to demonstrate that humans can

Author inside the SPID *during the 24-hour dive under the Arctic ice.*

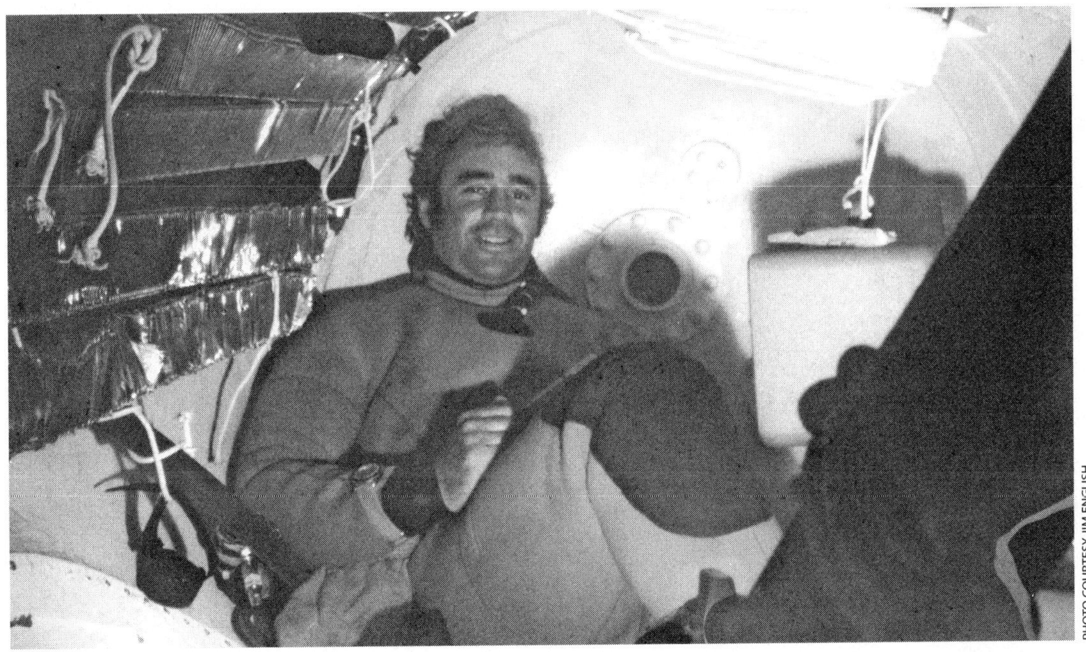

PHOTO COURTESY JIM ENGLISH

live and work effectively underwater, even under the harsh conditions presented by the Arctic. This became commonplace in Arctic oil exploration only a few years later.

Several days before the saturation dive was to begin, the Canadian team lowered our underwater habitat through the large hole in the ice near the divers' entrance. The habitat was designated *SPID*, for Submersible Portable Inflatable Dwelling. It was one of the many brain-children of Ed Link who, along with MacInnis, orchestrated another pioneering *SPID* dive in 1964. For two days off the coast of Great Stirrup Cay in the Bahamas, Jon Lindbergh and Robert Stenuit stayed in *SPID* at 432 feet for two days. At the time, it was the deepest saturation dive ever. As I watched them lower *SPID* into the ice hole, I thought about the warm water of the Bahamas.

SPID was tiny; the living quarters were barely five feet long and four feet in diameter. It was made of an iron frame, lead ballast, and a heavy duty sausage-shaped rubber balloon. When they launched it beneath the ice, they filled the balloon with air until it looked like a small blimp floating above the frame. Air pumped from the surface maintained the pressure inside *SPID*, allowing the submersible to have an open hatch on the bottom and serving as our living quarters. A small oil-fired heating system on the surface, normally used to heat hot-water suits during oil field dives, would warm *SPID* somewhat by flowing water through hoses to simple

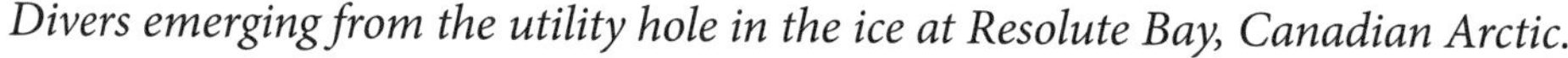

Divers emerging from the utility hole in the ice at Resolute Bay, Canadian Arctic.

radiators mounted inside. Communications consisted of a simple two-way wired walkie-talkie and a satellite telephone system—an astonishingly high-tech piece of equipment in those days. And, as a final touch, *SPID* would hold a few thermos bottles filled with hot coffee and soup. This, and the open water beneath the ice, was to be our home for a full day.

The morning of our dive, MacInnis and his support team gave us a briefing on such possibilities as a lost diver, hypothermia, and injury. It was then that the physiologist announced that we had to swallow a small transmitter in the shape of a pill that would send a signal from our bodies through the water by way of a subsurface probe to a surface receiver, which he would monitor. The changes in sound frequency were calibrated to the temperature surrounding the transmitter, thus measuring our body core temperature. This served two purposes—to collect scientific data on the human body under extreme conditions and to make sure we weren't freezing to death.

It took about an hour to get ready. We donned heavy underclothes and the Unisuit, filled the regulators with Screech, swallowed the transmitters, and put on the heavy lead weights and double air tanks. Just about the time I was completely bundled, one of the support crew asked me, "How ya gonna take a piss?" Oh man, I thought, I'm going to be wrapped-up like a mummy for twenty-four hours. "How come no one mentioned this very obvious problem before?" I asked him. "Don't sweat it," he said with a knowing grin, "you'll figure it out." And I did. It meant that in the very cramped quarters of the *SPID* we would have to unravel part of the Unisuit as well as layers of clothing and pee out of the hatch. It was an arduous task that prompted a lot of waiting until we could absolutely not hold it any longer. To add to the problem, the cold causes your penis to shrivel up and almost recede into your body. Finding it was a job in itself.

The *SPID* was set just under the ice with the hatch at only about 15 feet deep. As soon as we entered the water the 24-hour clock was started. Man's first stay under Arctic ice had begun. First, English and I practiced getting in and out of the habitat with the cumbersome suit and equipment. It was tough. My biggest worry was that Jim, a sturdy Canadian diver, would thrive in this frigid situation while I, who had been living in the tropics for four years, would shrivel up from the cold.

When we left *SPID* for the first excursion, we spent an hour exploring the study sites already visited on previous dives. We found several more "black holes," which is what the expedition had begun to call the dead zones. All had about the same configuration, a grey haze over a shallow lifeless depression. When the cold forced us to take a break, English and I squeezed into *SPID*'s cramped quarters after placing the double tanks on the ballast frame. We could only sit upright, still in our dry suits, with our legs stretched past each other. The radiators' warmth helped our hands and faces; the hot coffee was definitely appreciated.

It didn't take long before we settled into a routine—about an hour of diving and then a period of warming up inside *SPID*. The dry suit worked fairly well in the water, but not so well inside the habitat. Its insulating qualities maintained some of the cold around our bodies so we never really warmed and, in fact, over time we got progressively chillier. While inside we conducted a number of motor skill tests to make sure our condition was stable.

But the cold didn't really matter. I felt lucky, very lucky, to be there. The sea once again displayed its magnificence. The clear, still water capped by seven feet of ice, was home to many animals. Some had clearly evolved to fit the environment. One unidentified invertebrate we discovered had saw-like ridges on its back that it used to dig a nest in the ice. Mussels were commonplace. They make their living pumping water through their bodies to extract food. In the cold Arctic waters, the pumping was very slow. In the lower latitudes around New England and New Jersey, it was easy to see their rapid pumping action, especially in the summer months.

The Arctic pout that we observed has evolved a circulatory system with an anti-freeze chemical that prevents the blood from freezing in the most severe circumstances.

Under the ice, I tried to observe a mussel's pumping action, but couldn't see it. It was as if the animal were dead. Because there's a direct correlation between temperatures and pumping rates—the higher the temperature the quicker the pumping action—it follows that more food would then be available to the faster-pumping animal. Even so, many of the bottom invertebrates I saw in the Arctic were quite large, meaning that they were old, probably very old.

Fish in the Arctic region experience extremely cold water most of the year. Only during the short summer season do temperatures rise enough to break up and melt the ice in Resolute Bay. The Arctic pout that we observed has evolved a circulatory system with an anti-freeze chemical that prevents the blood from freezing in the most severe circumstances.

Not all of the wonders involved living things. The pressure caused by the thick ice cover created a number of curious icicles, which we called "ice-a-tites" (icicle stalactites). Freshwater pushed down from the surface by ice movement at the shoreline froze at the bottom of the ice cover and grew very fragile icicles underneath, some over seven feet long and five to six inches in diameter. The ice-a-tites were about three-quarters hollow and open at the end. Close-up, we could see the fresh water flowing through narrow channels inside their walls.

On our last excursion before dinner, English and I collected dead specimens and sediment samples from some black holes. After about 50 minutes we were headed back toward the *SPID* loaded with plastic bags and jars when the second-stage regulator suddenly fell out of my mouth. When I picked it up, I saw that the mouthpiece had come off. But when I tried to jam the emergency octopus regulator in my mouth, it would not go. After several attempts, I realized that the original rubber mouthpiece was still inside my mouth. My exposed face was so completely numb from the water that I couldn't feel the mouthpiece. I couldn't get the mouthpiece out with the cumbersome mittens and my face muscles were so frozen I couldn't spit it out. I had no choice but to remove my left mitten to clear my mouth. After several tries it was cleared and once again I was breathing. The whole episode took only about 30–40 seconds, but it seemed minutes longer. Back inside the *SPID*, the warm air inside started the blood in my hand flowing again, causing excruciating pain for a while. I always wondered why I didn't get the same pain in my face, which was much more exposed to the cold sea.

Once during a rest period in the *SPID*, Joe MacInnis arranged for two calls from us via the satellite phone. The first was to Ed Link, whose habitat we were occupying. Ed was in New York at the time and was keen to hear of our great adventure. The second call was to Dick Clarke, who arranged to be in the *Hydro-Lab* sitting 50 feet deep off the coast of Freeport, Bahamas. It's the first call I know of from one underwater lab to another—certainly the first between such opposite environments. The water temperature outside the *SPID* was about 28.5°F and outside the *Hydro-Lab* it was over 80°F.

Jim and I had mixed emotions when the 24th hour arrived. We hadn't slept for more than 30 hours; we were bone cold, cramped, and uncomfortable. But when the end came, it was somehow sad. The Arctic dive was unique; it may never be done again. Since the *SPID* was in relatively shallow water, it was not necessary to do a full-blown decompression, so we breathed pure oxygen off and on for several hours to purge the excess nitrogen accumulated in our bodies.

All in all, the expedition was a success. During the 24-hour dive we made nine excursions from the *SPID* averaging 44 minutes each, totaling 6.6 hours. The following evening, after some sleep and hot food, the Navy physiologist briefed us on our core temperature regime during the dive and said that although we were chilled from the cold water, our core temperatures never dropped to a dangerous level. Then he handed us each a pair of latex gloves and said that the transmitters we swallowed were expensive and he wanted them back. The things we do for science.

Later that night at a party, Tom Bain and I were inducted into the "Arctic Streaking Society." Initiation involved running around outside the camp building in the buff. I don't remember much of that night, but later someone described the strange sight of three Screech-soaked guys, two from the Bahamas, one black, the other tanned to almost black, and a white-skinned Canadian, all running buck naked through the Arctic snow in two-below-zero temperatures.

Love those Canadians—love that Screech.

24

THREE DAYS UNDER THE NEWFOUNDLAND ICE

A SHORT TIME AFTER the success of our 24-hour dive under the Arctic ice, Jim English proposed a saturation dive under the ice in Conception Bay off the coast of St. John's, Newfoundland. Jim helped build an underwater laboratory about the same size and configuration as the *Hydro-Lab*. The difference was that it was only a few hundred yards from shore at 26-foot depth. The life-support umbilical that provided air flow, power, communications, and heat came from an onshore station. The lab, designated *LORA-1*, was built by engineering students of Memorial University to support engineering and biological research projects and to train students.

Dick Clarke, Morgan Wells, and I were invited by Jim to conduct a 3½-day scientific dive in February 1975. The purpose was to observe winter behavior and conduct some temperature studies on fish. I was interested in the possible effects that warm-water effluent from a power plant could have on hibernating fish during the winter months.

When we arrived in Newfoundland the weather was threatening a snowstorm. It was cold and Conception Bay was frozen solid. Unlike the Arctic, the bay had frozen over several times and ice was moved about by currents. Instead of a smooth, uniform surface, the bay was covered with ridges and protruding chunks of ice. The *LORA* team cut a small hole just above the habitat and hoped that currents would not move the ice while the dive was on. The night before we were scheduled to enter the *LORA*, one of the worst snowstorms in recent history began, and continued through the next morning. Although it was going to be difficult to get to the lab site, we made the decision to go ahead.

Everything else was ready. The lab's life-support system was tested and food, blankets, water, and other amenities were stocked in the lab. We gathered in the project's shore station and dressed in heavy clothing, covered by the dry diving Unisuit. The three of us, Jim, and several technicians pulling sleds slogged out to the hole. It was tough going through several feet of snow and the irregular ice. The techs pulling the sleds had a particularly rough time of it.

We were very mindful of the danger of soft spots in the ice. After about 20 minutes, we reached the hole in the ice that would allow us to dive down to the *LORA*. There was no other marker to tell that the lab was below, just the rough cut hole. Bubbles flowed up from the lab from the heated air pumped by a compressor located at the shore station.

The lab was surprisingly comfortable, considering the water temperature was 28.6°F. The walls were covered with a foam insulation that prevented the rapid conduction of heat into the frigid sea. One problem though—the heated air flowing into the lab immediately moved to the top, which was only about 6½ feet high. With little mixing, the result was a severe layering of temperature, measuring about 85°F on the top and somewhere in the 40s on the deck. Over a 40° change in only 6½ feet. We were forced to wear heavy footwear during our entire stay in the lab, while the rest of our body was fairly comfortable.

Once we got ourselves situated, we donned diving gear and entered the open water. Like the Arctic dive, we were restricted by the cold seeping through our heavy protective suit, long underwear, sweaters, socks, and all. An hour or less at a time was all we could do in the cold water. The ice and snow on the surface prevented much of the sunlight from getting through, so we always carried lights to see in the shadowy areas. As expected, the fish life was dormant. Species either migrated to warmer offshore grounds or were hibernating among the rock outcroppings. Kelp and other marine macroalgae covered some of the bottom. We could see large numbers of active, small periwinkle snails everywhere. Other invertebrates, such as starfish, moved slowly along the predominantly sand and gravel bottom sediment. Lobster were active at night and stayed close to the rocks during the day.

On the second dive of the first day, we discovered large numbers of cunner, a fish I had studied off the coast of New Jersey, hibernating in and under the rocky reef not far from the lab. These fish, unlike those in the Arctic, did not have a natural antifreeze component to their blood. In this temperature they were in a state of being super-cooled. We could easily pull a fish from its hiding place without any resistance. They were totally at the mercy of their harsh environment.

I had known at the time that a cold-blooded species in a super-cooled state could freeze with even a slight change in temperature or by being subject to a vibration, including that from sound. It did not seem logical to me, so on the second day we swam out to the rocks and pulled about a 10-inch cunner from its hiding place. I had previously broken off a piece of ice from the underside of the surface cover. With the fish in hand, I touched the tip of the ice to the side of the cunner. Almost instantly, ice crystals started to form at the point of touch, spreading out in all directions along the fish's body. Within a minute or so the entire cunner turned into a solid chunk of ice.

Dick, Morgan, and I kneeled on the bottom, forgetting about the cold that was now creeping into our suits, totally mesmerized by this event. We could see the ice crystals slowly, but steadily, travel from the point of origin. It seemed impossible, and though I felt sorry for the unfortunate fish, it was an amazing thing to witness.

Our next experiment involved capturing several hibernating fish and subjecting them to warmer water in tanks set up inside the lab. Our hypothesis was that if a power plant dumped warm water into the ocean during the winter, it could possibly be harmful or even fatal to hibernating fish. We took four hibernating and dormant cunner and set them in two tanks inside the lab. One tank was subjected to a rapid increase in temperature and the other to a slower rate of change. In both cases, the fish responded and eventually became quite active. Okay. The simple

Dick Clarke in the LORA *lab under the ice in Conception Bay, Newfoundland.*

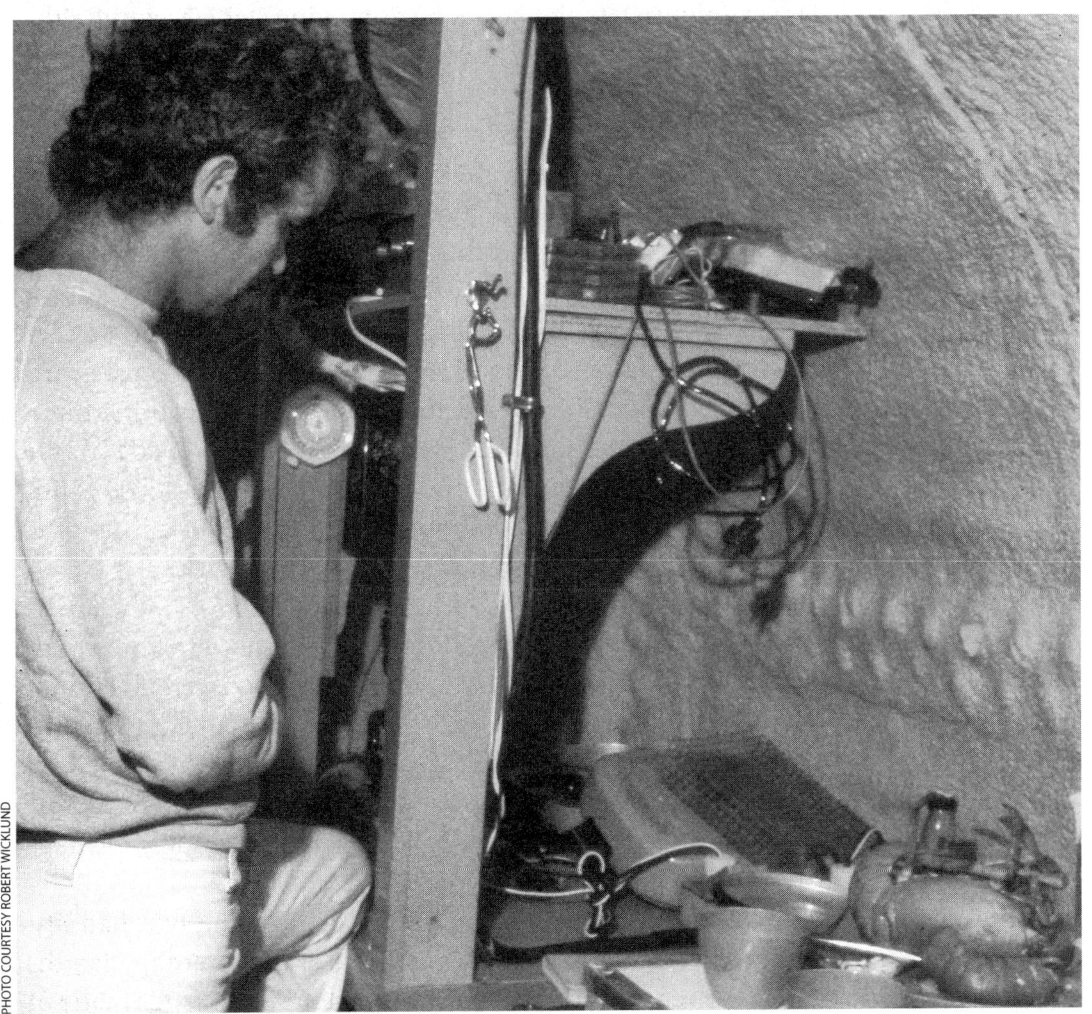

PHOTO COURTESY ROBERT WICKLUND

experiment seemed to indicate that the fish might respond similarly if flushed with a sudden mass of warm-water effluent from a power plant or other source, but what would happen if the water suddenly changed back to its original cold temperature?

We then introduced the cold water back to the tanks, one rapidly and the other allowing a slow acclimation to the change. The rapid change resulted in a shock to the fish that eventually was fatal. The others survived and went back to a hibernating state. Although not exactly a controlled scientific experiment, it hinted at an important consideration for placing such things as cooling towers for nuclear power plants in cold regions of the world where marine animals are hibernating, especially if the warm-water effluent has an inconsistent flow.

During our 3½-day stay in the *LORA*, we constantly looked out through a transparent acrylic dome on the top of the lab to view the hole in the ice just above us. We were concerned that currents or a storm might start the surface ice moving, which could either close the hole or take it away altogether. The dome was a two-edged sword—it gave us comfort to be able to see the hole, but at the same time we worried that one of the surface crew might mistakenly drop a heavy object into the hole, which would land on top of the dome. If the dome broke, it would flood the entire lab. Even though we were in relatively shallow water, it would be difficult, at best, to enter the extremely frigid water and make a free ascent to the surface without any protection.

I thought about the possibility that a couple of Mounties would be waiting for us at the surface to take us away to jail. What a way to finish an incredible dive.

One evening we decided to have a bang-up meal right from the sea. We collected snails, which were plentiful, and grabbed a couple of lobsters from a nearby rock reef. These were all boiled up inside the lab and, along with a few other bits of food stuffs, we ate like kings that evening. Following the meal, we made a radio check with Jim English and crowed about our good luck finding the lobster. Jim's line went silent. Every time we mentioned the lobster, Jim broke in with another subject and in a roundabout way told us to shut up.

The next day Jim came down for a visit and told us the bad news—the lobster season was closed. Oh man, we didn't even consider that. Here we were, three of the most environmentally conscious people you could find, and we screwed up—totally insensitive to local wildlife laws. I guess being in that alien world made us forget that we were still connected to civilization. I thought about the possibility that a couple of Mounties would be waiting for us at the surface to take us away to jail. What a way to finish an incredible dive. Jim must have worked his magic though; we never heard another word about the incident.

On our last night after a full day of dives, I drew the top bunk that had little space due to the curve of the wall. It was exceptionally hot at the top of the lab that night, maybe close to 90°F. The combination of the heat and the close space made me feel a little claustrophobic. Although the lab's deck was just the opposite, something around 40°F , I pulled down the mattress and blankets and sacked out right next to the open hatch. The hatch had a lip that kept the water level several inches below the inside deck. On the other end of the lab, a small pipe, about four inches above the hatch level, vented air out at a constant rate. The vent was above the hatch to prevent the air from belching out of the hatch in loud burps. The gentle flow of heated air coming into the lab was the only sound we heard, and it was balanced to keep the level of water stable.

During the night, with the lab in total darkness, a loud explosion woke us with a start. Moments later, icy cold water started to rise in the hatchway, covering my arm. I jumped up, scrambled around in the dark, and yelled, "We're flooding!"

A few moments later someone got to a light switch, and we saw that several inches of water had risen in the hatch and a little was now on the deck where I was lying. What had happened? Confused, we started to get our dive suits together for a possible emergency ditch. We called the shore station and told them the situation and that we were preparing to get out. After a few minutes, we realized that the water level inside the lab was not rising any further.

With a little more time, we started to explore the lab's hull to see if its integrity had failed. When we found some ice on the deck, just opposite of where the air flows into the lab, the mystery was solved and we knew we were safe. Water was condensing out of the air flowing to the lab through the pipe running the long distance from the shore station, and it was freezing near the opening.

At some point the opening became totally blocked by ice, stopping the flow of air into the lab. With no air coming in and the outside pipe continuing to vent, the water moved up the hatchway. With pressure building up in the air pipe, it finally blew the ice into the lab with a loud bang. This incident proved to be another situation in which things are not always what they seem at first blush.

The dive ended the next morning with some breathing of pure oxygen and an ascent to the surface hole. It was a great experience with few problems, and quite remarkable considering the harsh environment in which we were diving. It was Jim English and his crew that made it happen, and safely.

25

PROJECT SCORE

BY THE END of the fourth year of operation, NOAA was considering other projects to support that would jeopardize the continuation of the *Hydro-Lab* Undersea Research Program. Although it was not certain that our program would end soon, we hatched an idea for an innovative project that would allow scientists the opportunity to work at depths and for lengths of time never before achieved. It would be a joint venture between NOAA, the Harbor Branch Foundation, the Perry Foundation, Duke University, the MacInnis Foundation, and Seneca College in Canada, represented by Bob Landry. It would involve such diving support systems as the *Hydro-Lab* undersea laboratory, the *Johnson Sea-Link* lockout submersible, the *Sub-Igloo* habitat, and various other innovations, including remote talking stations and rebreather systems.

The objectives were to study the ecology and geology of the deep reefs on the vertical wall to 250 feet and to demonstrate the usefulness of a submersible-habitat complex in achieving scientific goals. It was, after some debate, named the Scientific Cooperative Operational Research Expedition (SCORE).

The plan included moving the *Hydro-Lab* to a 65-foot depth, where 16 scientists and technicians would saturate for five days each and make daily excursions to either 200 feet deep on a rebreathing system or to 250 feet in the lockout chamber of the *Johnson Sea-Link* submersible.

The tables for the excursions were tested in Phase I of the project in the hyperbaric facility at the Duke University Medical Center. These studies actually tested divers to 300 feet, but problems were found with oxygen toxicity when one subject experienced convulsions in the test chamber. The limits of excursion diving from the *Hydro-Lab* base depth of 65 feet was then restricted to 60 minutes at 200 feet and 45 minutes at 250 feet.

Following the Phase I tests, the ocean dives began on April 1st and ended on April 27th, 1975. The first dive on rebreathing systems began with a near-fatal accident within minutes of entering the water.

The remainder of the first dive and subsequent missions of Project SCORE demonstrated the usefulness of extending the diver-scientist's ability to work at deeper depths and for extended periods of time. We had to shift our thinking and remove

PHOTO COURTESY DICK CLARKE

R/V Johnson *launching the lockout research submersible* Johnson Sea-Link *during Project SCORE.*

the rebreathing systems from our plans because of the accident. We were uncertain of the cause and felt it too dangerous to continue with the systems.

The rebreathers were replaced with double scuba tanks with a surface-support boat and divers bringing extra tanks of air to the edge of the drop-off. During the 27-day period, 34 excursions were made to 200 feet and 13 to 250 feet. The 200-foot excursions were made by the scientists simply by swimming out to the deep reef and drop-off and returning at a predetermined rate as dictated by the new decompression tables.

The excursions to 250 feet were made in the lockout chamber of the *Johnson Sea-Link* submersible. Two scientists, saturated in the *Hydro-Lab,* transferred into the lockout chamber of the submersible parked nearby. Once the divers were in the chamber, the sub proceeded to the drop-off and attached to an ingenious system developed by Ed Link to allow it to hang in midwater at 250 feet. The system was a heavy chain attached to an anchor placed far up on the slope. The chain hung over the drop-off to 250 feet.

The pilot of the *Johnson Sea-Link* maneuvered the sub close to the chain at the right depth and grabbed it with the hydraulic manipulator arm. Once secured to the chain, the sub took on ballast water to make it slightly negatively buoyant. The sub hung in open water near the almost vertical slope. Directly under the sub, the bottom was over 500 feet down. At this point the sub's aft dive chamber and its two occupants were still at the equivalent pressure of 65 feet. Once the clock started for the excursion dive, the chamber was quickly pressurized to 250 feet, the hatch was opened, and one person at a time swam out and over the slope to begin the studies.

The diver wore a helmet with a tether that provided breathing gas and communications back to the sub. The voice communications were taped in the sub to allow the scientists to record their observations, hands free. The success of the excursion dives using this first-ever technology was exciting indeed. Scientists had the experience of studying a portion of the earth that had not been previously touched. Only a little over a mile offshore of land and civilization, they might just as well have been on the moon.

With the exception of the first dive on the rebreathers, all of the remaining dives were conducted safely. We did experience some minor difficulties, including a scientist becoming sick right after decompression. We put him through a brief second decompression schedule for several hours in the onshore chamber, after which he showed no further symptoms.

Dr. Sylvia Earle, a dear friend and world-renowned spokesperson for the protection of the oceans, was one of the main scientists and the only female participant in the project. I met Sylvia some years back at a diving symposium and we immediately became friends. She was one of five all-female aquanauts who

Johnson Sea-Link *approaching the* Hydro-Lab *to pick up saturated scientists for a one-hour excursion to 250-foot depth during Project SCORE.*

PHOTO COURTESY DICK CLARKE

saturated in the *Tektite* habitat operating in Lameshur Bay, St. John, in the U.S. Virgin Islands. Having vast diving experiences all over the world, Sylvia later became chief scientist of NOAA and Explorer-in-Residence for the National Geographic Society.

Sylvia is a small bundle of sheer, unbelievable energy. Even though we are good friends and she is about half my size, she has no problem putting me in my place when she thinks it is needed. Of course, if I don't buy into the notion that she is right, it often leads to an occasional friendly disagreement.

It was against this backdrop that Sylvia and I clashed during one of her excursion dives out of the *Johnson Sea-Link*. Following the sub securing its place on the chain at 250 feet, the aft chamber was pressurized to ambient depth and Sylvia got out. She headed for the drop-off hoping to find new algae or to map the extreme depths of species normally found at shallower locations.

About 10 minutes into the dive, Sylvia started to feel a little nausea due to exertion from the heavy weight of the umbilical and other collecting equipment. Because the scientists were saturated, lifting gear or buoyancy compensators were not used, as they were deemed too dangerous. An uncontrolled ascent due to a faulty compensator or from over-inflation by the diver's hand would be fatal. She reported to the pilot of the sub, who relayed the information back to us on shore. Dave Youngblood, the project physician, immediately ordered Sylvia to abort her dive and return to the *Hydro-Lab*. Once Sylvia was back in the lab, Dave dove down to examine her and could not find any problems.

He did, however, tell her that she could not make any more excursion dives to 250 feet until he could figure out what happened. Well, the shit hit the fan. Sylvia was not taking that lying down. I heard her voice over the radio, "Bob, I didn't come here to sit around for five days in the *Hydro-Lab*. I want your okay, as project manager, to continue the dives," she said.

Now, from past experience I knew what was coming and that I was in for some tough negotiations. "Can't do it. I have to follow the advice of our physician," I said.

"Well, wait a minute, I feel fine, so tell Dave that you're going to rescind his advice. After all, it's only advice." Now fully in the grasp of Sylvia's discontent and in a strange way her charm, I was at least thankful that she was sitting on the bottom of the ocean and I was on shore.

The conversation went on for some time. It was not that Sylvia was insensitive to my plight or that she didn't care about safety; it was her passion for the ocean and desire to experience every possible moment of its beauty and mystery. Clearly, she didn't want to miss this opportunity, and I felt and understood her pain. If the roles were reversed, I would be saying the same thing. Needless to say, I had to hold fast to my decision, and Sylvia could not continue the dives. Even today, some 30 years later, Sylvia occasionally still renders some friendly ragging about the incident, and I still laugh about the promised punch in the nose.

Typical of Sylvia though, she didn't walk away from the project empty-handed. She found and sampled a species of algae entirely new to science and named it after the *Johnson Sea-Link* submersible.

The project drew national attention. Jordan Klein, owner of Mako dive compressors and underwater cinematographer, worked with us to produce a one-hour documentary on SCORE. To highlight the extreme diving and science that was expected from the project, Jordan was convinced that, as exciting as the project was, a well-known celebrity was needed to attract the attention of a television audience. So he went ahead and offered Lloyd Bridges a contract to appear in a segment and to be the narrator of the documentary. In one sequence, I was to team with Bridges and take him for a ride in a wet submersible named the *Shark Hunter*. Lloyd sat behind me as I piloted the small sub in shallow water and around the *Hydro-Lab* and coral reefs, all the time being followed by an underwater cameraman.

After the dive we went aboard the *R/V Johnson*, where we were given a script of dialogue describing the amazing things we saw on the bottom of the ocean. Well, with several cameras rolling this is how it went:

Lloyd Bridges in his well-trained, booming voice, "Bob, that was incredible; the ocean is a beautiful place" (or something like that).

Illustration depicting layout of Project SCORE off Freeport, Bahamas. Hydro-Lab *was at 65 feet;* Sub-Igloo *was at the edge of the wall at 90 feet. The* Johnson Sea-Link *served as a taxi for scientists from the* Hydro-Lab *to 250 feet over the wall.*

"Yes, Lloyd it is," I read, answering in a stiff, choked, squeaking voice.

"Cut," said the Director. "Try it again."

"Yes, Lloyd," now sounded even worse.

It was "cut" over and over, but I still could not get it right. I felt like a hand was reaching out from the camera, grabbing me around the throat, and cutting off air and blood to my brain. I had to admit to myself that I was terrified of the camera and working with such a polished actor. Sharks—no problem; deep diving—no problem. But this was my Waterloo. This part of the project was a total disaster for me, and I mentally removed acting from any possible future career path.

The rest of the production went smoothly, except for filming the actual dives from the sub at 250 feet. On several dives a camera was inside the acrylic forward dome of the *Johnson Sea-Link* recording the scientist leaving the sub and the exchange between diver and pilot. It was dramatic footage with a lot of discussion about safety and being careful.

One of the cameramen, "Big John" McLaughlin, a rough-and-tumble commercial diver, twice came into the camera scene from below the sub, wearing just a bathing suit and single tank, and carrying a huge underwater camera. He was below the sub! Poor Jordan was trying to dramatize the events of the scientific dive, while "Big John" was tooling around in front of the camera at about 265 feet deep, as if the whole thing were taking place in 10 feet of water.

The project was completed and the film was in the can, but I understand Jordan could not sell it to anyone, so I guess it remains sitting on a dusty shelf somewhere.

The remainder of the SCORE project went well, although we were initially concerned about pumping straight air to the lab at the 65-foot depth, which raised the partial pressure of oxygen to just about double the 21 percent at the surface. This rate differential over time can be harmful to divers. As a technological project, SCORE was a huge success and demonstrated how the combination of the right equipment can support science, even under difficult conditions.

26

DIVER DOWN!

DURING THE KICK-OFF dives of Project SCORE, one of the participating scientists came close to death. It was a beautiful summer morning in 1975 when disaster struck 140 feet deep along the almost vertical slope that makes up the margin of Grand Bahama Island.

After months of planning, training, and preparation, the first excursion dives of Project SCORE were finally about to begin. The normal excursion profile set up for the project was to saturate four scientist-aquanauts in the *Hydro-Lab* at 65 feet deep, and for two of them to swim about 800 feet once a day to the drop-off and descend to 200 feet deep for one hour. The return was a slow swim back to the habitat with no decompression stops.

We demonstrated this on straight air dives from a previous 50-foot saturation dive in *Hydro-Lab* involving Dick Clarke, Gerri Wenz, and me. Dick and I made the dives using three sets of double tanks on a 1,200-foot excursion out to the drop-off with an 18-minute swim back, which replicated a continuous decompression from 200 feet to the 50-foot depth of the *Hydro-Lab*. We did this once every day for a week, without incident.

The excursion dives that were about to begin would be different. Harbor Branch had obtained two closed-circuit rebreathing systems that theoretically would allow a diver to remain at depth for up to six hours, breathing a helium-oxygen mix. The rebreathing system included two small tanks, one containing oxygen and the other helium. An integrated computer was pre-programmed to allow the two gases to flow at the right mix for the 200-foot dives.

The gases were recirculated through a scrubber filled with lithium hydroxide that removed the accumulation of carbon dioxide from the diver's exhalations. At the same time, the system added the right amount of oxygen that was consumed by the diver. The gases were then used over and over with just a small amount of loss. Three redundant meters on the diver's wrist allowed for frequent checks on the accuracy of the mixed gases.

The rebreathing system brought a number of advantages to the project, including the elimination of nitrogen narcosis at the deeper depths. This would afford the scientists not only a measure of safety but also the ability to think clearly while conducting their experiments. The rebreathers also eliminated the need to change tanks three times over the one-hour dive period.

All in all, the decision to incorporate the rebreathers into the SCORE project seemed to be a good one. But, as rebreathers went in those days, they were very unpredictable. If everything was going well they were wonderful. As a complex machine, they were also prone to complications, and several people had died in the past because of rebreather breakdowns, or inadequate training in their operations.

No one expects to face a life-threatening incident when leaving sunny skies, balmy tropical breezes, and calm seas to enter blue, warm waters clear enough to see the bottom some 75–100 feet below.

We decided that the first excursion dive would be the actual beginning of the mission. The two scientists were Dr. Bob Jones, then Director of Harbor Branch, and Grant Gilmore, a fisheries scientist for the same institution. They would don their diving gear onboard the *R/V Johnson* and go straight down the slope to the 200-foot site for one hour, instead of starting from the *Hydro-Lab*. This would give us an easier first check of the rebreathing systems. I would accompany the two divers down the slope for about 10 minutes to act as safety diver and to generally observe how the scientists got along with the new equipment, but I would wear a simple set of double air tanks and an octopus regulator instead of a rebreather.

A short briefing that morning included Roger Cook, Harbor Branch's diving chief, dive physician Dave Youngblood, dive engineer Denny Breese, several rebreather technicians, and me. By mid-morning the briefing was over, all equipment checked, and the three of us jumped off the stern deck of the *R/V Johnson* to start the dive and project.

No one expects to face a life-threatening incident when leaving sunny skies, balmy tropical breezes, and calm seas to enter blue, warm waters clear enough to see the bottom some 75–100 feet below. Since the *Johnson* was anchored offshore of the *Hydro-Lab*, this dive was just about straight down to a 90-foot depth where the *Sub-Igloo* was placed. From there the scientists continued down the slope to their 200-foot destination, following a final equipment check. The visibility was about 100 feet and water temperature was over 78°F with very little current flow. It couldn't have been better for this dive.

As the two scientists descended with me close behind, I started to get an uneasy feeling about Grant. He was constantly checking his wrist gauges, often stopping, coming back upslope a few feet, and then starting back down again. Several times I swam to Grant and checked his gauges. Everything looked fine. His flow rates were in order and the oxygen levels were right on. Grant motioned that he wanted to continue the dive, and we proceeded down.

Bob Jones slowed his swimming to stay within reasonable distance of his partner. At this point my air supply was getting short, and I was now in a decompression mode, but I was still uneasy about Grant's diving behavior and continued to follow the two. At 140 feet, along an almost vertical slope, Grant stopped again and appeared distressed.

Once again I swam to him and motioned "Are you okay?" Grant didn't respond and stared straight ahead. His eyes were wide open but motionless. After some time, he pointed up meaning that he wanted to go back to the surface. We had by now reached a serious decompression requirement, and Grant was looking bad, perhaps ready to panic and swim rapidly to the surface. This is always one of the most dangerous situations in diving. A fatal embolism, drowning, or the bends is always possible under these circumstances. I motioned to Grant and pointed upslope to where the *Sub-Igloo* was stationed at a 90-foot depth and about 200 feet away. I felt it would be safest to get to the habitat and regroup. We could even go inside and talk about Grant's problems.

Shocked by this rapid turn of events, my heart sank as I thought I was witnessing the convulsions of a dying man.

The events that occurred over the next few minutes are somewhat fuzzy. Everything happened so quickly that I suppose much of my reaction was pure instinct based on a lot of experience with divers in trouble. After I motioned to him to swim to the *Sub-Igloo*, Grant spit out his mouthpiece and stared with unblinking eyes. I immediately grabbed my spare second-stage regulator and tried to force it into Grant's mouth, but his teeth were clenched tightly. After several unsuccessful attempts to give Grant the regulator, he reached up and pulled off his mask. His eyes rolled up under his lids as he turned over on his back, convulsing violently. Shocked by this rapid turn of events, my heart sank as I thought I was witnessing the convulsions of a dying man.

What could have happened? I needed a moment to think what to do next, but there was no time. Bob Jones was downslope somewhat and appeared alright. We were at 140 feet, and Grant was convulsing more violently now. I looked at my air gauge and there was less than 500 psi in the double tanks. Probably less than 20 seconds had passed since Grant pulled off his mask.

Grabbing Grant by the collar of his wet suit, I headed up toward the *Sub-Igloo,* the only logical and closest sanctuary. I swam as hard as possible, towing Grant behind. My breathing became excessive from the exertion and apprehension over Grant's condition. It sounded like a puffing steam engine in my head, exaggerated by the profusion of bubbles streaming from the second-stage exhaust of my regulator.

This was bad. With little air left in the tanks and my heavy breathing, I was afraid we may not make it to the *Sub-Igloo*. I had to slow down, but couldn't. Grant had not been breathing for some time now and, if there were any chance to save him, I had to keep going as fast as possible.

Turning my head back for a moment, I could see that his jerking motions were slower. Grant was probably already gone, I reasoned, but I didn't know for sure and had to keep going. Bob was heading toward us, but he was too far away to help at this point. It's a helpless feeling to have a person's life in your hands and you are doing everything possible, but somehow it doesn't seem to be enough. What would happen if I ran out of air and had to abandon him? It was unlikely that I could have even saved myself under those circumstances.

After a minute or so, with my air supply down to nothing, I could see the *Sub-Igloo* only a short distance away on top of the slope like a glistening phoenix waiting to help us out of our dilemma. As we approached the structure, I started to take off my tanks and remove the cumbersome rebreathing system from Grant. Bob Jones reached us by then and helped lift Grant through the hatch and into the airspace. We had made it, but Grant's condition looked grim. A bloody froth was coming from his mouth, and he was not breathing.

With every function on him apparently shutting down, I feared that he could have embolized coming from 140 feet to 90 feet. Standing in the opening of the hatch with Grant in my arms, I attempted mouth-to-mouth resuscitation. About 30 seconds later Grant started to breathe, I believe spontaneously, for my CPR efforts under these conditions were clumsy at best.

Bob removed his diving gear, and we were able to lift Grant up onto a seat within the *Sub-Igloo*. His breathing was shallow, and he was conscious by this time. Within moments however, Grant started to rave and scream and go into dramatic convulsions again. We were afraid he might fall or even jump out of the *Sub-Igloo* in his state, so Bob and I grabbed him by the feet and shoulders and hung on for dear life.

Grant's motions were so violent that we were all thrown about within the tiny habitat. The chamber filled with fog from our heavy breathing. Finally a support diver from the surface came down to check on me because I was long overdue from my dive. He came to the *Sub-Igloo*, and we yelled to him as best we could about our situation. We needed assistance quickly. We needed increased airflow into the *Sub-Igloo* and the lockout sub *Johnson Sea-Link* launched to transport Grant to the surface chamber onboard the *R/V Johnson*.

On the surface the sub and ship crew scrambled to get the sub in the water, and Dave Youngblood established communication with the *Sub-Igloo*. While Bob and I continued to wrestle with what seemed like super-human strength coming from Grant, we tried to communicate his condition to the doctor.

Ten minutes later, Grant was still screaming incoherently and convulsing. We were exhausted and the CO_2 buildup made breathing more difficult. By this time the airflow increased, which made things a little better. Fifteen minutes from the start, Grant came out of his convulsive state and calmed down. A couple of minutes later we were talking to him.

He said that he had no recollection of the past events. When the *Johnson Sea-Link* appeared on the bottom, its lockout chamber was pressurized and Grant and I were escorted to the sub one at a time. We kept Grant's swim fins off him in case he went into convulsions again, so we would have better control over his actions. After reaching the surface and transferring to the ship's decompression chamber, we settled into a six-hour decompression schedule with no further problems.

> The events following the accident are still troubling to me. Grant was not yet out of the woods and needed to be airlifted to a stateside hospital.

We had no idea what led to Grant's incident. He was a fairly seasoned diver and had completed extensive training on the rebreather. The fact that he was continuously checking his oxygen meters suggested breathing problems. He also appeared to be frequently hitting an override button on the rebreather that manually gives extra oxygen to the diver. When he went into the second set of convulsions in the *Sub-Igloo,* we figured it was oxygen poisoning due to adding too much to his system through the manual override button.

Sometimes divers who are not used to rebreathers feel they are not getting enough breathing gas. Convulsions are symptomatic of oxygen poisoning, but the length of time that Grant was convulsing was far too long for oxygen poisoning and was more symptomatic of carbon dioxide poisoning. That would mean that the CO_2 scrubber was not functioning properly or that the scrubbing chemical was bad or even missing. The system was checked and declared in good shape by the Harbor Branch techs. We will never know what caused Grant's difficulties.

The events following the accident are still troubling to me. Grant was not yet out of the woods and needed to be airlifted to a stateside hospital. Dave Youngblood, as Harbor Branch's hyperbaric physician, knew that the aircraft owned by Seward Johnson, co-founder of the institute, was sitting on the Freeport runway and ordered it to fly Grant and him over to a Florida hospital. Apparently, a higher authority within the organization rescinded Dave's order and declared the plane off limits.

It appeared that they didn't want Seward involved in any way. Perhaps they thought that this problem, on the heels of the incident in which two people died in the *Johnson Sea-Link* just a year before, might cause him to have second thoughts about continuing his heavy funding of the institute. Dave went ballistic. An employee's health and possibly life were at stake and he was prevented from taking the best measures to treat him. Dave lost, and they had to wait extra time for another plane.

Dave resigned soon after the project ended. It was dirty politics at its best, and tainted the reputation of the Harbor Branch Institution, at least in my eyes. Thankfully, Grant fully recovered and stayed on with Harbor Branch for many years as a productive scientist.

I never heard a word from anyone at the institute about the incident, not even an acknowledgment that we went to extraordinary lengths to save his life.

Considering how desperate they were to sweep the whole thing under the rug, I never expected any further contact. Hearing about Grant's scientific achievements from time to time over the years was rewarding enough for me.

27

SWEET REVENGE AFTER TWENTY YEARS

I NEVER REALLY CONSIDERED revenge particularly rewarding. Having said that, I must admit that there was one incident in my life when revenge was handed to me on a silver platter, and I still find it gratifying to recall.

This story begins way back in 1952, when I was about to graduate from eighth grade at a New Jersey elementary school. It was late spring and I needed a suit to attend the graduation ceremony. I had never owned a real suit before; this was to be my first.

So, one morning about a week before the event, my father said, "Let's go get you a suit," and off we went in his car to the home of Wise Clothes. Wise Clothes was certainly no Brooks Brothers, but it was well-advertised in the local papers. Frankly, my father was no more of a clotheshorse than I was and he didn't know of many haberdasheries anywhere else.

This was pretty much big time for me—I was about to enter the world of grown-up suit owners. "Maybe when I wear my new suit I won't be afraid of girls and will actually be able to talk to them," I thought. Back then I had a stuttering problem, and when confronted by a young lady I would be just about catatonic. I knew in my heart that I was not cool. As we used to say, I was a "square." But I just knew the suit was going to change all that.

Approaching the building, I saw the bold letters above the door that read "Wise Clothes," and I was thrilled. I knew that when I passed under that sign, my ticket to manhood would be secured.

Once inside, the first person to greet us was the proprietor himself, Mr. Fred Wise. Now, Fred Wise was a man of enormous proportions; portly would be an understatement. As he lumbered toward us he introduced himself and asked, "What can I do fer ya?"

I thought to myself that it was strange he didn't have a suit on, but maybe there were no suits big enough. After establishing why we were there, Fred said mister so-and-so would take care of us, and I was immediately dragged over to a mirror by two salesmen, obviously keen to make this a quick sale.

After some rapid measurements, which involved a set of knuckles slamming into my balls, one of the salesmen draped a large jacket on my frame. The jacket loosely fit my chest, but the arm length was far too long. He pulled the excess of the jacket from the back saying, "This suit is you, kid."

The legs of the matching pants were so long that they could have fashioned a matching vest from the excess material. The fact that I was slightly bent over from the assault on my private parts didn't help matters.

"Don't worry, kid, we'll put a conservative peg on the pants, take in the jacket a little, and shorten the arm length. You're gonna be looking like a hotshot from downtown in this suit," said the salesman.

I looked at my father, and he just smiled and shrugged his shoulders. So, it became official; a suit was being altered just for me. I wondered if I should walk differently in my new suit, maybe strut a little.

One week later, I had my suit. Graduation was the next day and I was excited. Opening the box, my anticipation was huge. I started with the pants, slipping my foot into one leg. The peg around the pant leg was so tight I could hardly get my foot into the opening, and the rest of the pant leg was baggy to say the least. When I finally donned the whole suit and checked it out in the mirror, the jacket was wide at the shoulders and the pants were way wide and closed down to a tight fit at the ankles. It resembled a 1940s zoot suit, the same one I saw in *Lil' Abner* cartoons drawn by Al Capp and read about in Damon Runyon novels. I thought I was staring in the mirror at a comic book character. Well, needless to say, I was mortified. I hated that suit, and I hated big Fred Wise more. No strutting in this thing, that's for sure. I graduated anyway and had to suffer with the suit for a few more years. I became more pissed off every time I wore it. I remained pissed off for another 20 years.

Well, needless to say, I was mortified. I hated that suit, and I hated big Fred Wise more. No strutting in this thing, that's for sure.

Flash forward to 1972. I was now the Director of the *Hydro-Lab* Undersea Research Program in Freeport, Bahamas. One day I received a call from an agent of the Parkway Company that manufactured diving wet suits. Parkway was interested in marketing the Unisuit, a cold-water dry suit for which they just bought the rights.

They asked if we would be interested in providing the *Hydro-Lab* as a backdrop for a promotional photo shoot, and if I would be personally interested in modeling the suit underwater. They also wanted me to model it for a brochure that showed the purchaser how to properly get into the suit. They would pay some amount to the project, and I remember that they would pay me $100 for my part, which I considered a lot of money at the time. I said sure, and several weeks later the Parkway team came to Freeport.

Just before they arrived, I found out that Parkway was now owned by none other than Wise Clothes.

"Give me a break," I said out loud. "Am I dreaming?"

The thought hit me like a ton of bricks. Even more bizarre was the day they arrived. I was on the dock preparing the boat to bring everyone to the *Hydro-Lab* site, and down the companionway comes good old portly Fred Wise. He was still alive and looked pretty much the same.

"It's Fred Wise," I thought, "probably bringing me a baggy Uni-zoot suit to wear for the whole diving world to see what a putz I really am. Fred isn't finished with me!"

The Bahamas was a world away from New Jersey and here I was, once again, with Fred Wise. I walked up to him and said, "Mr. Wise, do you remember me?"

"No, kid," he replied. "Whatta ya want?"

"My name is Bob Wicklund; I'm the director of this program and your Unisuit model."

"Okay, good, but why would I remember you?" he asked.

"When I was a kid you sold me a piece of shit for my graduation suit and I'm still pissed off. If you want to continue this operation, the price is now $200," I blurted out loud without really thinking.

Fred probably thought I was crazy, and decided it wasn't worth wrangling over $100 with a madman. Well, I did the job and got my money, a reckoning that took twenty years to accomplish. Do I sleep any better now? Not really, but it's been fun to think about.

That's not quite the end of the Unisuit story, but it no longer involves Fred Wise. Two years later I was invited to participate in the Arctic dives, and I had not even seen, much less worn, a Unisuit since the photo shoots in Freeport. Now I was going to actually use one in the frigid Arctic waters.

While preparing for the first dive under the ice at the Resolute Bay campsite, I was in a small room with several Canadian divers. All of them practically lived in Unisuits and were able to put them on and take them off with ease. I, on the other hand, had forgotten how to do it, but I did not dare ask the Canadians for help because they would surely rag me to death. I was supposed to be a hotshot saturation diver, and I couldn't even put on a simple diving suit. They were about to have my head.

After a few moments of silent panic, I happened to, by some miracle, look across the room and there, among a jumble of equipment, was a stained and crumpled Unisuit brochure with me in over 25 photos illustrating the steps necessary to don the suit.

I moved over into a dark corner of the room, opened the brochure so no one could see, and I slowly put on the Unisuit following my own instructions. I had to bear my own face, panel after panel, leering at me and seeming to enjoy my predicament.

I was successful and no one was the wiser. I had dodged a bullet—a close call for my reputation. If the Canadians had caught me, especially with the brochure, there would have been no mercy.

28

MEETING LOWELL WEICKER

SEVERAL WEEKS INTO the project in 1975, we had a major visit by members of Congress, including several from the House of Representatives and one member of the Senate. Secretary of Commerce Pete Peterson and his wife, NOAA personnel, and media groups also arrived.

It was a big deal which I did not fully grasp at the time. I was pretty much wet behind the ears when it came to politics and the high levels of Washington, DC. I did know, however, that this group, in one way or another had their hands on our funding, and it was important to the program that we put on our best face and showcase our very visible use of divers, an underwater lab, and lockout submersibles in deepwater research.

Once the group arrived, including Representatives Bill Alexander of Arkansas and John Murphy of New York, who was also the Chair of the now defunct House Merchant Marine and Fisheries Committee, we arranged for some of the guests to dive on the *Hydro-Lab* site and a few others without diving experience to take a quick course with the UNEXSO instructors. One of the people taking a first-time diving course was Lowell Weicker, U.S. Senator from Connecticut.

Following several hours of instruction, the Senator told one of my young assistants that he was ready to see the offshore operation, and he wanted to dive on the *Hydro-Lab* site. The young man said something to the effect that he needed more training before he could dive. Lowell, I was to find out in no uncertain terms, was an impatient man and used to getting what he wanted. He was immediately finished with the assistant and told him to get the person in charge to talk with him, which, of course, was me.

The assistant came and told me that there was some big guy who insisted on going on the next boat out to dive on the *Hydro-Lab* site.

"Tell him he can't go. With a couple more training sessions and a test, maybe he'll be ready," I said.

"You better tell him yourself. I tried and he wants to talk with you," he answered.

I was very busy, so I thought that I would just tell this guy, whoever he was, that he couldn't go on the boat, and that would be that. I climbed the stairway to the top of the 18-foot-deep training tank, where I saw this man sitting on the edge of the tank with his feet in the water.

"Hello sir, I understand you want to go on the afternoon dive boat. You can go on the boat, but you can't dive," I said with an attempted firm voice.

The man hadn't said anything, and yet I felt I was being mentally picked apart piece by piece.

I realized immediately that I was almost looking him straight in the eyes, and I was standing and he was sitting. I mentally attempted to stretch my pathetic five-eight frame without much satisfaction. The Senator sat for a moment without saying anything. He was looking at and through me.

Life for me was fairly simple up to this point—deep diving, sharks, storms, close calls underwater, but now I sensed that I was confronting something entirely different. The man hadn't said anything, and yet I felt I was being mentally picked apart piece by piece. "Look, I traveled all the way from Washington, and as a member of the Senate Committee that oversees the oceans, I need to see what is happening offshore and I don't intend to sit on the beach, sipping tropical drinks and staring out to sea. I want to see what is going on firsthand, so let's go," he said still looking at me as if I were being analyzed and catalogued. Maybe I was being filed in the asshole or dimwit section, or perhaps I was in the okay category. I already knew that this was not going to be as easy as I thought.

"For reasons of safety, we can't allow you to dive down to the *Hydro-Lab* with the others who have experience," I murmured. "You just took the initial training and it is not enough to qualify you for a dive to 65 feet, but maybe we can try something else."

I suggested that later on the two of us go out to the *Hydro-Lab* site and dive only to 15 feet. The water was clear enough for him to see all the action on the bottom without compromising safety.

"Okay, what time," he quickly asked. So it began, and little did I know that we were about to embark on a new phase of undersea adventures—my simple life, bare feet and all, was about to change.

That afternoon the Senator and I sailed out to the *Hydro-Lab* site in the 23-foot *Bahama Hunter* to make our shallow dive. While donning our dive gear, I sized him up. He was a big man and looked strong. I contemplated the worst-case scenarios should something go wrong with the dive. If I lost him, would I get the electric chair or maybe just life on bread and water? The Bahamas still hung people. Ugh! *No one was going to lose anyone.*

Once in the water, I could see that he was comfortable on the surface and he was obviously a competent swimmer. We were right over the *Hydro-Lab* and luckily the *Johnson Sea-Link* submersible was just transferring scientists to its lockout chamber.

Once we poked our heads underwater and submerged to 15 feet, the drama on the bottom of the sea was laid out before us. Two divers were making the short swim between the *Hydro-Lab* and sub. Two others were serving as support divers.

The aluminum hull and acrylic dome of the sub glistened in the sunlight that penetrated the clear sea. The yellow *Hydro-Lab* sat motionless on the sandy bottom. There were bubbles everywhere, streaming up and around our bodies as we swam slowly around in a circle. The Senator made no sounds or motioned to me in any way.

For about 20 minutes we watched the transfer of divers and the sub moving slowly off toward deep water and disappearing into the blue gloom of the sea. I wondered if the Senator were okay, and if he were enjoying his dive and the scene below. Maybe he found it boring compared to life in the fast lane of Washington, DC. When we finally finished the dive and came to the surface, he spit out his mouthpiece and literally screamed. My heart jumped.

"Son of a bitch that was the most exciting thing I've ever seen!" he quickly exclaimed, followed by a few expletives and more excitement.

I thought, *This guy is alright.* I wished some of the marine scientists I knew could get as excited about things that went on in the ocean. The Senator was pumped. When we returned to the boat, he insisted that over the next few days he finish the dive training so he could really experience the ocean from every vantage point.

Within a very short time, Senator Lowell Weicker, Representative Bill Alexander, Deputy Administrator of NOAA Howard Pollock, and I spent a three-day saturation dive in the *Hydro-Lab*, the first time in history that members of the U.S. Senate and of the House actually lived on the bottom of the ocean.

By this time, I was well-educated on the importance of the people with which I was dealing, and it was an opportunity to demonstrate how diving science could help us understand and protect the oceans. Howard Pollock, a former Congressman from Alaska, was quite a character. He had lost one of his lower arms to a hand grenade accident in World War II, which seemed to have little effect on his diving capabilities.

During another mission, I took Howard on a tour around the *Hydro-Lab* in the wet submersible *Shark Hunter*. While we were passing by the lab, one of its occupants accidentally dumped some food out of the hatch. Once it hit the water the stuff disintegrated into a dark plume that flowed out into the mild current. Howard, sitting behind me, started yelling through his regulator and hitting me on the shoulder. I couldn't understand why he was so excited and brought the sub up to the surface where we could talk. Once we broke into air, I turned to Howard and asked why the fuss.

"Didn't you see the smoke coming out of the lab? There must be a fire inside," he yelled. After explaining to him what had actually happened and that smoke could not flow underwater, he felt a little foolish, but I commented that we all have a tendency to bring our earth-bound experiences under the sea where they don't always apply.

By the end of the year, the MUST office of NOAA decided that they wanted to support the multi-national project *Helgoland*, planned for a two-month mission in New England, and informed me that funding was going to end for the *Hydro-Lab* program. I desperately fired off a letter to Senator Weicker asking him to use his influence to save our program. He called me several days later to tell me that he was going to concentrate on ocean issues in the Senate and, instead of pushing on NOAA to keep the *Hydro-Lab* in place, he wanted me to come work for him and be his main staffer on the oceans.

Who me? Would I have to wear shoes?

I was still naive about politics and didn't fully understand what the offer meant. After a lot of gut-wrenching thinking, I decided that I would take a crack at it for a year. Little did I know that I was about to embark on a journey that would serve me for the rest of my professional life.

The departure from Freeport and the *Hydro-Lab* was very sad indeed, but Dick, Gerri, and I took great pride in the record we set. The program had accomplished more than a hundred missions with 343 individuals saturated over a 4½-year period. The *Hydro-Lab* still stands as the most successful scientific habitat program in the world. No one died, and with the exception of the near-tragedy during the SCORE project, accidents were minor.

The *Hydro-Lab* itself was soon bought from Perry by NOAA, refurbished and placed off the coast of St. Croix in the Virgin Islands. After about a five-year stint there, it was replaced by the *Aquarius* undersea laboratory and the *Hydro-Lab* was shipped to Washington, DC, where it was placed on display at the Smithsonian Institution for several years.

29

CAPITOL HILL DAYS

My first day on the job in Washington was like being on another planet. Almost everyone in Weicker's office was younger than me and wore ties. They were lawyers, political scientists, and economists. Many of the younger staff appeared to have been scrubbed clean and polished by some machine and sent off to work bright-eyed and bushy-tailed. A few older, scruffier staffers looked like they had been thoroughly beaten over and over by the political process that ran Congress—lifers for sure.

My friend and diving buddy, the Senator, took on a totally different personality in this setting. It was disconcerting to realize how much larger he loomed here and the power that exuded from the office.

Even after the first month or so, I was not sure that I would ever fit in. I had to learn a whole new language and how things worked related to legislation, appropriations, committees, subcommittees, the floor, hearings, bill conferences, and much more. Not knowing exactly what to do with me, the Senator placed me on the Government Affairs Committee, which had little to do with the work that I was supposed to be handling. I was pretty much a place holder.

The first year was all learning. Tim Keeney, who became a good friend, was a lawyer and an ex-Navy Seal hired by the Senator to handle a number of issues. Tim walked me through a lot of the early maze that was Congress and allowed me to manage a few minor shots for the oceans and other environmental issues.

Claudia Ingram, Senate staff director for the Appropriations Subcommittee on Commerce, Justice, State, and the Judiciary, later becoming Lowell's wife and First Lady of Connecticut, was also a guiding force for me. Many other staff became my mentors. Al Stayman was a young marine scientist, who came to work with me under the Sea Grant Program. Al later came back to take my job and went on to various Committees.

To my delight, the Senator wanted to continue diving and seeing the ocean firsthand. On one early trip to the Virgin Islands, I was his support diver to a depth of 120 feet, the deepest dive he had ever made. It was intended to be just a bounce dive, meaning when we reached the depth, we would start back to the surface after just a minute or two.

As soon as we started the descent, Lowell's big body frame and inexperience caused his air consumption to be extraordinarily high. I constantly watched his pressure gauge that showed his air going fast. Once we reached 120 feet, I signaled to immediately start back. Lowell wanted to stay longer, but his air was down to 1,000 psi. I insisted on leaving with exaggerated hand motions and Lowell started up. He knew he had to heed my diving advice even though he was the Senator. We reached the surface safely, but with little air left in Lowell's tank.

That's not the end of the story. A week later I walked into the office and the other staff started booing and throwing pencils and other things at me. They showed me a newspaper article written about our trip describing the air problem with the Senator and my role as Dive Master in charge of Lowell's safety.

"You had your chance," they joked. It was all in fun, and I made a few points that day.

After some experience dealing with Congress, it quickly became clear to me that it is an imperfect system and, like the rest of the federal government, it is clearly inefficient. Over the two-year life of a Congress, for instance, some 20,000 bills and resolutions are written and recorded. Of those, only about 600 ever see the light of day.

This is a good thing, otherwise we would be so deeply buried under laws that we could not function as a nation. Many of the bills and resolutions written are to satisfy or impress a senator's or representative's constituents back home or to appease a major campaign contributor.

Throughout the seven-plus years I spent on Capitol Hill I learned, to my dismay, that nothing happens in Congress on merit alone. Even though an effort is clearly for the national good, it takes much negotiation and compromising to reach a goal. Congress consists of 535 individuals with their own agendas. Some of these are in positions of power, such as a majority leader or chair of a powerful committee, who has to be reckoned with regardless of the circumstances or worth of an idea.

Early in the game, I was handed the responsibility of a bill that would, among other things, place some environmental safeguards on mining polymetallic nodules from the deep waters of the Pacific seafloor. The valuable nodules, most the size of potatoes, were widely scattered over a vast region of the Pacific abyssal plain, and their discovery raised a lot of excitement among a number of nations interested in mining the metals contained in them. The nodules were created over millions of years by manganese, nickel, copper, and other metals precipitating out of the seawater solution and forming around small objects. Mining companies were mainly interested in the nickel, copper, and cobalt.

Author with Senator Lowell Weicker, NOAA's Barbara Moore and unknown diver preparing to dive off St. Croix, VI.

Since the region targeted was in international waters, the bill became contentious over the move to make deep seabed mining the "common heritage of mankind," meaning that we share the wealth with the international community. In fact, deep seabed mining was a major player in the formulation of the United Nations Convention on the Law of the Sea.

This, of course, did not sit well with U.S. corporate interests. It appeared that powerful corporate lobbyists convinced Congress and others that being an

If mining went on without any restrictions, how would we know of its impacts? The proposed method of ships dragging large suction hoses along the seafloor would likely do extensive damage to the fragile deep-ocean ecology.

international player and sharing the seas would be bad for the U.S., and to this day our country remains a non-party to the Law of the Sea Convention. The same holds true of the Kyoto Accord, where U.S. companies oppose any cutback in the production of greenhouse gases. The U.S. is now one of only a few nations that will not sign the Accord. The arrogance of our corporate interests and the caving of our government on these issues are appalling and continue to this day.

Eventually the Deep Seabed Mining bill was passed, but not until we were successful at including a very contentious section that would protect a portion of the ocean bottom from any mining.

Over lunch one day, my friend Sylvia Earle threw out the idea that it would serve well to have at least a section of the ocean seafloor protected from mining, which could be used as a baseline for comparison to evaluate the ecological impact of mining operations. I immediately saw the value in her logic. If mining went on without any restrictions, how would we know of its impacts?

The proposed method of ships dragging large suction hoses along the seafloor would likely do extensive damage to the fragile deep-ocean ecology. With Sylvia's help we drafted a section of the bill that would set aside a percentage of the ocean seafloor we named "Stable Reference Areas" and submitted it to the Republican side of the Commerce Committee, which was handling it for the Senate. Lowell was a senior member of the Committee and was a supporter. Of course the Republican staff of the committee were appalled that we would offer such an anti-business amendment to the bill, but they had to consider it anyway.

Several months later, some of the Committee staff came to tell me that the bill was ready to be marked up in Committee and asked that we withdraw the section. I firmly refused on behalf of my boss. They said, in that case, they were going to take it out anyway and we could deal with it when it went to the Senate floor.

Lowell was out of touch that day, and I had to think of something. If the Stable Reference Areas were not part of the Committee bill it would be a lot more difficult to add on later. I turned to the staff and said that if our language is taken out of the bill, Senator Weicker would order a hold which could kill it all together. I was lying through my teeth.

I wasn't completely sure if the Senator would go that far, but all I had to lose was my job. They laughed nervously and basically said that they didn't believe me. I invited them to call my boss, which I was pretty sure they were not going to do. They would have to get the chairman of the Committee involved, which would look bad for them.

With a lot of teeth gnashing and a little modification in the language of the bill, they caved. It was my first of a number of high-stakes bluffing incidents necessary to accomplish something in Congress. I felt a little dirty, a little Machiavellian, but not too much since I believed in what we were doing.

Between Capitol Hill duties, I arranged a couple of three-day saturation dives for the Senator in the *Hydro-Lab*, now placed in Salt River Canyon off the shores of St. Croix, Virgin Islands. The first included Lowell, Stan Waterman, a renowned underwater cinematographer, and me. The dive did not accomplish much scientifically, but it allowed Stan to spend a lot of time filming reef fish behavior and it helped to solidify Lowell's commitment to ocean issues in Congress.

On our second dive, Lowell and I were joined by our new friend, author Clive Cussler. Like Stan Waterman, Clive was a delightful fellow, and we hoped that this experience of living on the bottom of the ocean would give him new insight into the importance of the marine environment. Although known for his adventurous tales of intrigue, often revolving around the ocean, and his exploration of sunken Civil War ships, I found Clive himself to be quiet and somewhat reserved.

Clive relished the three days in the *Hydro-Lab*, taking in the whole experience of not only having unlimited diving time but also living in the ocean like some pioneering settler. Following the dive and a 17-hour decompression, we were back to the terrestrial world. The following night, after Lowell went to bed (which was always around 9:00 p.m.), I convinced Clive to join me on a trip to Christensted for a beer or two. We stayed through the wee hours listening to steel drum and reggae music, and hit the rum hard. We had a good time, and it was obvious that this was not a regular thing for Clive.

As Weicker continued his interest in underwater research, we worked with NOAA to establish the National Undersea Research Program (NURP) and decided that there should be another, more advanced laboratory to complement or replace the *Hydro-Lab.*

When NOAA was created in 1970, a division was added to address undersea technology support for marine science. Named the Manned Undersea Science and Technology, or MUST, the program operated for 10 years, after which we concluded that a new, more research-oriented program was needed, including regional partners around the country.

As Weicker was the ranking member of the Senate Appropriations Committee with jurisdiction over NOAA, we set out to add funds to design and build a new state-of-the-art undersea system. NOAA determined where the lab would be placed and the institution that would be responsible for its operation.

In the early years of the *Hydro-Lab* program, a team from the University of Southern California conducted several saturation dives with an eye on setting up a program in waters around Catalina Island, 26 miles off the Los Angeles coast. This was the catalyst leading to USC being selected for the new undersea program.

PHOTO COURTESY BERNIE CAMPOLI

Aquarius *undersea laboratory located off the coast of Key Largo, Florida. Owned by NOAA and operated by the University of North Carolina Wilmington.*

Over a several-year period, Lowell's position on the Appropriations Committee allowed us to design and build the lab. Although it was supposed to be a mobile system, USC designed it to be more or less stationed only at Catalina and fixed to an underwater railway to be hauled in and out of the water.

NOAA was not happy with the results, and when a decision was made to replace the old *Hydro-Lab* in St. Croix, the now-constructed 43-foot long undersea laboratory, later named *Aquarius,* with far more capability than the *Hydro-Lab*, was moved to the Caribbean island to be operated by the West Indies Laboratory.

After Hurricane Hugo left St. Croix in ruins, the *Aquarius* was moved to Key Largo and partnered with the University of North Carolina Wilmington. There still was interest in a mobile system and a large towed catamaran barge was constructed to lift and launch the lab and also serve as the surface-support system. Over time the barge became cumbersome and impractical and was eventually replaced by a large life-support buoy.

Twenty years later the *Aquarius* is still operating in the Florida Keys.

30
JAMES WATT

When Ronald Reagan won the 1980 presidential election and the Republicans took over the majority in the Senate, Lowell became the chairman of the Commerce, Justice, State, and Judiciary Subcommittee on Appropriations. It was a powerful position as far as the oceans were concerned. The subcommittee had jurisdiction over NOAA, Marine Mammal Commission, and other agencies with interests in marine affairs. Although I had been planning to leave Congress around this time, this new turn of events put us in a position to really makes things happen.

During the preceding years, however, with Senator Hollings as Chair and Lowell as the ranking minority member of the CJSJ subcommittee, we could do just about anything we wanted anyway. Hollings' main staffer, Deb Stirling, for whom I have tremendous respect, and I worked together on ocean issues and I could not imagine things changing that much with this shift in power. Over the next two years and before I finally left in 1982, we beefed up NOAA's program significantly, kept the Marine Mammal Commission viable, and saved the Sea Grant program from going belly-up.

During that time, I helped engineer a bill to increase research on the environmental effects of oil drilling on Georges Bank, a prolific New England fishing ground. The Department of Interior was considering opening the bank, as well as other sites on the east coast continental shelf, to oil exploration. The bill was mislabeled the "Georges Bank Protection Act" even though it was primarily a research bill and not necessarily for protection. Of course, the oil industry went ballistic and lobbied hard against the bill. The oil lobbyists came in droves. Following a number of assaults on my office, I did what I could to avoid them.

My office was on the first floor across the street from the Russell Building and more than once, when the main office called to tell me that oil lobbyists were on their way over to see me, I would open the window and jump out for an early lunch or just a break.

I would usually return to jeers from my co-workers, something along the lines of me being a "pussy." I was no match for three or four guys in 1,000-dollar suits with handkerchiefs in their pockets. They were cookie-cutter lobbyists and spouted the same rhetoric I had heard many times. I was a lone staffer in a J.C. Penney jacket with a rumpled tie in the pocket. These guys wore me out with mind-numbing droning about their issues. So I considered an escape out the back window as a viable option.

One morning in 1982, the Senator called me to say that James Watt, Secretary of Interior, was coming to see him regarding the Georges Bank legislation. I had spoken to Watt on the phone the day before and it was obvious he was angry with the Senator's stand on the issue. Lowell wanted me to attend the meeting and he asked me to bring any information I had. The meeting was behind closed doors with just the three of us. Before the Secretary could get started, the Senator told him that I was the expert on the bill and he should direct his questions to me. Watt immediately went into a tirade about the deviousness of the bill and how it would impede the nation's ability to remain energy-strong. I tried to explain that it was only to increase research on the ecology of the Bank, considering its importance as a fishing ground, and I didn't see how that would impede anything.

He called me dishonest, stupid, and other names I can't remember. I looked over at the Senator and could see he was enjoying the whole thing. He was not going to stop me from defending myself.

Watt went directly for my throat, accusing me of an agenda to scuttle offshore drilling everywhere. He called me dishonest, stupid, and other names I can't remember. I looked over at the Senator and could see he was enjoying the whole thing. He was not going to stop me from defending myself. I came back at Watt, saying I didn't work for him, so he should stop the nonsense. He could call me anything he wanted, but that didn't change the fact that he didn't know what he was talking about, and unless the Senator told me differently, we were not going to change or drop the bill. It was a contentious meeting, and I was grateful to Lowell that he gave me the latitude to deal with this bully.

True to form, Watt later addressed a group of drilling contractors and stated, "The deviousness of that (Weicker amendment) approach was wicked. But I hold Weicker innocent. I don't think he knew what his staff was up to. That amendment would have scuttled the OCS plan for 26–30 months. It was a vicious attempt to kill our program, using a Senator who didn't fully understand the implications."

So, in a public speech and later quoted in the *Capitol Energy Letter*, he claimed that I deviously manipulated my boss and clearly tried to get me fired by embarrassing Weicker. When Lowell heard this he just laughed. He had little respect for Watt as well and was not going to waste his time with this petty man. We eventually had to pull the legislation anyway. It would have been an amendment to a larger Outer Continental Shelf drilling bill that, in the end, went nowhere.

My days on Capitol Hill were rewarding and frustrating at the same time—rewarding in the knowledge that I played a small part in helping to create needed ocean and environmental programs, and frustrating in the way things were done and the backdoor approaches on issues, which I believed, idealistically, should have needed no game playing to become law or to provide funding. It is the nature of the beast, after all, that will never change. You either play the game or stand on the sidelines.

But, underlying it all, I came away from Washington secure in the knowledge that our Constitution is working much as the framers intended.

31
U-352

BEFORE I LEFT Capitol Hill, Denny Breese offered to take Lowell and me diving on the *Unterseeboot 352,* or *U-352*, a German submarine sunk May 9, 1942, in 115 feet of water off Morehead City, North Carolina. The sub was discovered and attacked by the Coast Guard Cutter *Icarus* with depth charges. Mortally wounded, the sub surfaced for several minutes and then sank. Thirty-three of the original crew of forty-nine survived and became POWs in the U.S. for the remainder of WWII.

On our dive to the wreck, which was lying on the sandy bottom at a 45 degree angle and mainly intact, we were able to sit on the conning tower and view most of the vessel. History was all around us.

That would be pretty much the end of the story, however the Senator learned that the remains of the sailors, who went down with the *U-352*, were still in its hull, not to mention unexploded torpedoes and other ordinance. Stories came back that bones from the German crew were put on public display and some divers were using "bang sticks," short-barrel underwater firearms, to hunt fish around the wreck. Knowing that explosives become unstable over time and that the torpedoes had been inside the *U-352* for over 30 years and were dangerous, Lowell decided to contact the Navy and direct that the sub hull be sealed. He also cited international law in that sunken warships are considered memorials and remains of their fallen sailors should be left alone.

Well, soon after the media got wind of his intention, the shit hit the fan in the diving community. Divers sent letters by the dozens stating that the Senator was interfering with diving the *U-352* without good cause and that this was only the beginning of government regulating sportdiving. After several weeks of media coverage and communications from angry divers, a large diving club in Maryland invited Lowell to address one of their meetings. Of course, I got the job.

A few days later I entered a huge hall packed with about 300 people. This should be relatively easy, I thought. After all these are my colleagues, further deluding myself. As I walked up the aisle my bubble burst when I heard muffled voices uttering "Kill the Bastard," followed by a chorus of "Kill, Kill, Kill!"

Once I got on stage and started my presentation, the chorus ended, but I was bombarded with angry questions. I tried to explain that it was primarily a safety issue and there was no intent to stop diving on the *U-352*.

A few minutes into the talk a guy got up and started to move toward me yelling "I'll get him!" He was a small man with forearms like Popeye and noticeably drunk. As he approached, I looked at my microphone which had a metal ball on the mouthpiece. My strategy was, if all else failed, to conk him with the mic.

I was about to cold-conk Popeye in front of hundreds of his angry friends, and the amplifier would transmit the 'thunk' for blocks around the building. I could envision the next day's headlines: Senate staffer mauled by angry mob, nothing left to identify. Just before the man reached me, a couple of others in the front row tackled him and dragged him out. The rest of the event was still raucous, but uneventful, and with no real resolution.

The next day I reported to Weicker. "Jeez, Senator, it was awful. Hundreds of my diving buddies wanted to kill me. I'm lucky to be here." Lowell's response was "Hey, stop whining, what do you think you get paid for?" That put it all in perspective.

Several months later, the Navy used the sealing of the *U-352* hull as a training exercise and that was the end of it.

32

DIVING ON THE *HELGOLAND*

In late summer of 1975 and early in my Senate days, NOAA sponsored a two-month undersea project off the coast of Massachusetts to study the spawning of the commercially important herring. Little was known of the herrings' reproductive behavior, and it was thought that an underwater laboratory could help scientists unravel their mysteries. It was a joint undertaking between the U.S., Germany, Poland, Canada, and the USSR.

The primary facility to support the project was the *Helgoland* undersea laboratory built and operated in Germany. The *Helgoland* was a large, relatively sophisticated habitat built to withstand the rigors of the often stormy and always cold North Sea. Once it arrived in U.S. waters on a Polish ship, it was placed at a 103-foot depth, over eight miles off the coast of Massachusetts on Jeffreys Ledge in the Gulf of Maine.

The project was beset with problems from the beginning. Cold water, ranging from 45–53°F and depth kept the average open-water time to one hour and twenty minutes per day. Stormy seas and other problems allowed only two out of a planned five missions to be completed. Following decompression on one of the missions, during heavy seas with large waves passing overhead, a German scientist swam to the secondary stop just below the surface and held on to the umbilical connecting the life-support buoy to the *Helgoland*.

When the scientist came to the surface, he suffered a massive embolism and died. It is speculated that, as the diver tried to keep his depth by holding on to the umbilical, he may have held his breath for a moment just as the trough of a wave passed overhead. If his lungs were full when the peak of the wave passed by and he didn't exhale during the trough, it could be enough of a pressure change to cause an embolism. On a later mission, an American diving technician also experienced a possible embolism, but he was moved to a chamber quickly enough to save him. To make things worse, the herring did not cooperate and the spawning never happened where it was predicted.

I was invited by NOAA to dive to the *Helgoland* and be an observer for a couple of days. When I arrived, an old friend, Dick Cooper from the University of Connecticut, greeted me and gave me an update on the project. Dick spent many years studying lobsters and he was one of the best diver-scientists in the country.

Divers had observed the spawning on Jeffreys Ledge during this time of year in the past, so the lab was placed close to the observed spawning grounds to allow the scientists a lot of study time. When we assembled in the morning to discuss the day's activities, I was told that, since I was NOAA-certified diver, I would be responsible for the safety of two photographers that were going to film the work of a Polish scientist. The photographers were not certified and I figured I was going to have to babysit two guys who probably could barely swim. *Here we go again.*

When I went into the next room, there was my old friend "Big John" McLaughlin and another guy, Courtney Brown, who turned out to be a well-known movie stuntman with vast diving credentials.

"Hi Bob, looks like we're going to be diving buddies," said John.

I was immediately relieved; these were two of the best divers in the world and it was going to be a piece of cake, I thought. Well, that turned out not to be exactly true, as I later discovered.

That afternoon John, Courtney, and I joined another team and headed offshore on one the of the dive boats servicing the project. It took about 45 minutes to reach the *Helgoland* site, some 8½ miles from the Rockport base station. Our dive and the filming were scheduled to be no more than 30 minutes with a short decompression stop. John and Courtney each carried one 16-mm camera in a large underwater housing equipped with lights.

When we reached the bottom, the scientists were already out of the lab and at work. The visibility was about 50 feet and the ocean bottom was dark sand with intermittent patches of kelp. John and Courtney went about their business of filming while I stayed within sight of them, enjoying the freedom to observe the local fish population.

About 20 minutes into the dive, I heard muffled yelling from one of the two photographers. I assumed they were calling me to assist in a setup for a particular shot, or something of the sort. When I approached, Courtney held up his pressure gauge showing he was out of air. I looked at my gauge and saw that I still had a fair amount of air, so I handed Courtney my octopus (reserve second-stage) regulator. We were a little over 100 feet deep and my air supply would now deplete very quickly with the two of us sucking on the same tank. I motioned to Courtney to swim to the surface, but he signaled that he had one more scene to film and only needed a minute more.

We moved back to the scientists as I constantly monitored my pressure gauge. Seconds passed and the needle on the gauge was visibly moving, but Courtney kept filming. Finally, when my air supply was getting dangerously low, I grabbed Courtney's tank strap and started hauling to the surface. Courtney just hung with his camera pointed at the scientists and continued filming.

By this time I was pumping hard, knowing that time was quickly running out. During our ascent, Courtney kept filming until the bottom was out of sight. We ran out of air at about 40 feet and both of us had to make a free ascent, which under stress can be risky, not to mention that we were supposed to stop for a short decompression.

On the surface, I said, "Shit, man, I hope that film was worth it."

"Hey, thanks a lot, that really worked out great," he answered.

Usually this kind of thing happened to me because the diver I was with was inexperienced. In this case, it was Courtney's casual approach to diving and his zeal to bring home the bacon that put me on the spot.

I thought that eventually this would probably be the way I would die, since it didn't seem possible for me to avoid these predicaments.

33

MISSION TO CUBA

LOWELL WEICKER OFTEN pulled the chain of his Republican party, not just for the fun of it, but by being his own man. Few people that I met over my career were as true to themselves and their philosophies as Lowell. There was never any doubt where he stood on any political, social, constitutional, or any other issue. This did not always sit well with the conservative faction of the party, especially when their ideologies clashed.

One day in 1979 the Senator called a few of his staff together to announce that he would seek State Department permission to launch a diplomatic trip to communist Cuba to meet with Fidel Castro. I knew the shit was going to hit the fan when some of Lowell's Republican buddies found out. Even the Carter White House would throw a fit.

Almost since Castro's takeover of Cuba from the Batista regime and following the Bay of Pigs fiasco, U.S. policy toward the country has been one of almost total isolation. An embargo was put in place, which persists today, almost 50 years later. Cuba was considered a threat to the entire Caribbean and U.S. region, with its perceived ambition of exporting communism wherever possible. Fueled by a small group of Cuban expatriates based in Miami, opposition to any contact with the Castro regime was fierce.

The Miami Cubans made substantial contributions to the Republican Party and in return they expected to call the shots on U.S. Cuban policy, even holding the Democrats at bay on this issue. Even though the Soviet presence on the island is now longtime gone, and U.S. policy toward most other communist countries has become more relaxed, our government's disdain for and lack of diplomacy with Cuba continues.

Lowell's purpose for this visit was simple: Cuba was a large part of the Caribbean and ignoring the role that the country played in terms of the tropical marine environment was ludicrous. The Caribbean and West Indies consist of many small island nations connected by a common ocean. What happens in one country's waters could affect many others. Currents carry the eggs and larvae of many species of marine organisms from one place to another, so if a spawning population is affected by bad management practices in Cuba, for instance, it could affect the recruitment of stocks in other countries, including the U.S. The intent, therefore, was to find some common ground to conduct marine research that would be helpful not only to the two countries, but to the entire Caribbean basin.

Following a bucketful of teeth-gnashing, the State Department finally capitulated with the understanding that this diplomatic mission would involve scientific issues only, and Lowell agreed. As soon as the Miami Cuban faction found out, our Washington office was inundated with calls and letters condemning the trip, calling us traitors, communists, and much more. This was more or less shrugged off as radical ranting by a group with nothing but self-interests.

So, on a sunny day in October 1979, the mission left Miami in a private plane owned by Shaw Mudge, a successful and somewhat eccentric Connecticut businessman and close friend of the Senator. The mission consisted of Lowell, Shaw, several staff including me, Lowell's cousin, Florence, who was fluent in Spanish and would act as interpreter, and two pilots. It was well-known that Castro spoke English, having had some education in the U.S., but he would only speak in his native tongue, thus Florence was to be an important part of our team. My role was to provide marine expertise in our talks with Castro.

We arrived at the Havana airport in late afternoon and were met by a group of Cuban government officials, including a young woman interpreter, who greeted us on the tarmac and whisked us through immigration and customs very quickly. They were courteous and efficient, but not overly friendly.

Soon after, we were barreling down the road to Havana proper in a convoy made up of vintage 1950s cars, some in absolutely mint condition. In fact, there were 50s and some 40s automobiles everywhere, mostly American-built. Following the revolution that ended in 1959, no new cars were exported to Cuba from the States, so the streets of Havana were almost frozen in time with pre-1960 automobiles.

We found out later that, out of necessity, the Cubans made many of their own parts to keep the cars running and looking good. It was an amazing feat. Along the highway into Havana there were numerous billboards celebrating the Soviet cosmonauts, Che Guevara, and communism in general. Although I didn't understand Spanish, the messages were clear. It was interesting that we saw little sign of the Soviet presence in the form of soldiers or war weapons. I guess we expected that they would be everywhere on the island. Was their scarcity for our benefit or was this the way it really was all the time?

We arrived at a large, former American hotel, which was virtually empty, and were escorted to our rooms by the government agents. It was clear that we were not at liberty to roam around without an escort—something about our safety, the interpreter said. We were given a few small gifts and our hosts told us that they would be back in a little while. Within a half hour there was a loud knock on the door. Two of the agents appeared and pretty much ordered me to come with them immediately. I wondered what was up.

There was no hint of our next destination. I met Lowell and the others in the hotel lobby and we were directed to get into a number of cars. Within minutes we pulled up the long driveway to the huge presidential palace. It dawned on me right then that we were about to meet with Fidel Castro himself. We had been in Cuba for a little over an hour and already had been granted an audience with the president. There was a bit of nervousness on my part. Here I was, a lowly Senate staffer about to meet the president of Cuba, an international icon, a communist leader who was declared an enemy by my own government. What a rush, and I knew that I was about to enter a new phase in my professional career. I also have to admit that the Senator's coattail under these circumstances was somewhat comforting.

Entering a huge room, we could see Castro standing on the other side with a handful of aides by his side. He was tall, bearded, and looked exactly like the many photos I had seen of him. His high level of confidence was immediately evident. He was unmistakable, dressed in his classic military camo uniform. This was a historic moment as the two leaders from opposite sides of the political spectrum approached each other, stood eye-to-eye, and obviously sized each other up. Certainly Castro was well-briefed on our mission to address marine issues, but considering the longtime, negative stance of the U.S. Government toward him, did he believe that Lowell was genuine in his intent? The two men then smiled and shook hands. This was going to be interesting, I thought.

Following introductions and handshakes with Castro and his entourage for the rest of us, and a photo shoot, we sat down to casual chitchat. The discussions began with such things as baseball, which has always been a passion of the Cubans, and Castro's upcoming speech to representatives of the unaligned nations. Castro's female interpreter and Florence were busy relaying each sentence to us and to the Cubans and soon we got around to marine issues. Castro was particularly interested in the plight of the Caribbean population of sea turtles. He talked about the declining stocks of green sea turtles in Cuban waters and the general declining catches of fish on the world stage.

It was fascinating to hear, but I wondered why this all-powerful dictator, who could make any policy he wanted without going through anyone or any organization, didn't put fish and other marine species that are in trouble under lock and key in Cuba.

We found out later that turtle meat was on most restaurant menus in Havana. He certainly had demonstrated his knowledge and concern to us that night, but as in

PHOTO COURTESY ROBERT WICKLUND

Fidel Castro describing the Cuban Revolution to Senator Lowell Weicker.

other countries, including the U.S., issues of economics and special interest groups require a certain amount of political posturing and finessing—even in a communist country, even under a dictatorship.

The evening meeting lasted an hour and went smoothly, and I had the opportunity to speak to Castro directly about a few problems involving coral reef ecosystems and fisheries in the Caribbean. He turned to Lowell on a few occasions and asked what "El Scientifico" thought on some issue, referring to me. That was my official handle for the rest of the trip, and Lowell delighted in ragging me about my new name as much as possible.

An hour later we said our goodbyes and left the palace with our escorts. The hour went quickly, and at no time did the conversation stray toward politics unless it concerned the protection of the marine environment. We were hopeful that this would lead to direct action by the two countries to protect the Caribbean seas, even if in a small way.

Our next stop was a restaurant that was one of the favorite haunts of Ernest Hemingway. It was old and quaint, pretty much the same as when the famous author spent a lot of his time there years ago. In the middle of dinner, one of our escorts went into the kitchen and brought out a small aging man holding some black and white photographs. It turned out that the man was the owner of the restaurant before the Cuban government took possession; he was holding photos of Hemingway and himself taken in the very room in which we were dining. It was exciting to see the pictures, but sad as well. This poor man, probably the dishwasher now, proudly showed us his mementos of a happier time, now long gone.

At the end of the meal we were served coffee and a pack of Cuban cigarettes. The Cuban officials lit up immediately, but none of us were smokers. Interestingly, a pack of cigarettes was served with all our evening meals.

During the next several days, we were transported over a large part of the island to witness a well-choreographed display of nationalized programs providing services to the Cuban people. We first toured a representative dairy farm. It was explained to us that the government, having limited funds, had to choose between several agricultural programs, one designed to provide a steady supply of fresh milk to the children of Cuba. The milk program won out and small farms with central milking stations were built all over the country. Each had, if my memory serves, about 100 head of milk cows. The cows were a cross between Holstein and Brahma breeds, which assured high yields of milk in the harsh, hot tropical climate of Cuba. Government trucks came by several times a day to pick up the raw milk. The operation was efficient, clean, and impressive. I had expected to see old rundown farms with a few cows each.

We visited the harbor to view the national fishing fleet. Although a small country, Cuba sailed a very large distant-water fleet of trawlers and factory ships. These were familiar to me. Before the U.S. declared a 200-mile economic and fishing zone, some of these ships fished off our coasts, and I probably had seen some off New Jersey years before. The Cuban spokesman for the day explained that the catches brought in by these ships were for local consumption only. Species such as spiny lobster, grouper, and snapper were valuable and too costly for general consumption. They were exported and, most likely, went to high-end restaurants.

A large part of the fleet was in port this day and was unloading box after box of frozen horse mackerel caught in the Pacific Ocean. We told our guides about our concerns over the damage that these large distant-water fleets were inflicting on the global fish stocks, but received no response. Here was a tiny developing country with a major fishing fleet, capable of working anywhere in the world's oceans. We believed that if a few more of these were put into production, the fish stocks would be gone. It was another wake-up call to the fragile nature of ocean resources.

Our last stop included a lecture on the Cuban health system, which demonstrated the improvements the country had made over the years. The large reduction in infant mortality and gains in tropical disease prevention were very impressive. But, throughout the presentation, which included their work on certain cancers, it was obvious that the presenter skirted the issue of lung cancer. After observing roomfuls of Cubans lighting up their cigarettes in restaurants filled with smoke, we wondered what the incidence of lung cancer was in the country. We never found out from this briefing, but in later years Castro himself quit smoking cigars and initiated a national effort to curb smoking.

In the afternoon of our third day in Cuba, after having met many of the top officials along the way, we boarded an old twin-engine plane with several dignitaries and flew to the Isle of Pines, now named the Isle of Youth. The make and model of the plane was unknown to me, but I sat next to the aft door, which did not close properly, and wind whistled though the cabin for the whole trip. The Cubans with us were undaunted, but I expected the door to tear off at any moment.

The flight path was not a straight line to our destination; we frequently changed directions. We were also directed not to take pictures along the way. It was apparent that we were avoiding sensitive military regions, but when we flew directly over the Bay of Pigs, which should not have been in our flight path, the plane circled and our hosts made sure that we knew what we were seeing.

At the Isle of Youth we learned the meaning of its name change. The Cuban government built a number of school complexes there, providing education, housing, and agricultural work programs for both Cuban and foreign students. Each complex housed 600 students, who spent part of the day studying and part working the adjoining fields and fruit groves. The setup was not unlike the dairy complexes we toured two days earlier. The foreign students were from third-world countries in Africa and elsewhere. Each school complex was fairly isolated and several, I believe, housed only Cuban students while the others were just for the foreign students. Our hosts drove us through lush fields with large numbers of kids tending their various crops and fruit trees.

About an hour later we arrived at a school for students from Namibia in South Africa. The school children gave us a rousing one-hour presentation of dance and song. The little I could understand had some political bent praising the virtues of communism. I also noticed that there were posters on walls depicting the American Eagle about to pounce on a prey that represented Puerto Rico.

During the performance, I overheard Shaw Mudge in the back of the room talking to a Cuban who understood English. Shaw was describing his business, manufacturing flavors and fragrances, and how it worked. I looked at the Cuban and only saw a vacant stare. He was completely in the dark and had no idea what Shaw was saying. The capitalist was clearly getting nowhere with the communist and it made me laugh.

34

DIVING WITH FIDEL CASTRO

FOLLOWING THE TOUR of the school system, we spent the night in a local hotel and left early the next morning on an old but well-kept fishing vessel, which brought us to the local coral reefs for a day of diving. The boat was equipped with tanks, compressor, and other diving gear. It had a large deck space and a long canvas canopy to keep us out of the tropical sun. Within an hour we arrived on a pristine coral reef and dropped anchor.

As Lowell and the rest of our visiting team prepared to enter the water, checking tank pressure and testing the regulators, the Cuban captain pointed toward the horizon where we could just see a high-speed vessel heading our way. Within 10 minutes, the boat, about 50 feet long and creating a large wake, passed by and circled several times. On the bow was a Cuban soldier dressed in fatigues and holding on to a fixed, large-caliber deck gun.

We were startled and thought we were about to be boarded. Our boat's crew were unconcerned; they seemed to know what was going on, so we relaxed. Soon another larger vessel came into view. As it approached, we could see that it was equipped with several fixed guns. We learned that it was Castro's private yacht and the president had sailed all night to reach us, following his speech to representatives of the unaligned nations gathered in Havana. We were completely surprised and wondered if the Cuban president were going to dive with us.

The yacht anchored some distance from our boat and a smaller boat ferried Castro, some other Cuban dignitaries, and a team of tough-looking bodyguards carrying automatic weapons over to us. He was dressed in a shorty wet suit and it was obvious he intended to do some diving.

With permission from our hosts, I unpacked my camera and started to snap photos. Lowell and the president continued discussions where they had left off four days earlier in Havana. They talked about the beauty of the clear water and reef that was easily seen from the deck of the boat.

In the middle of the conversation, Castro told us that he and his men were going to get some lobster for lunch and ordered his bodyguards into a rubber

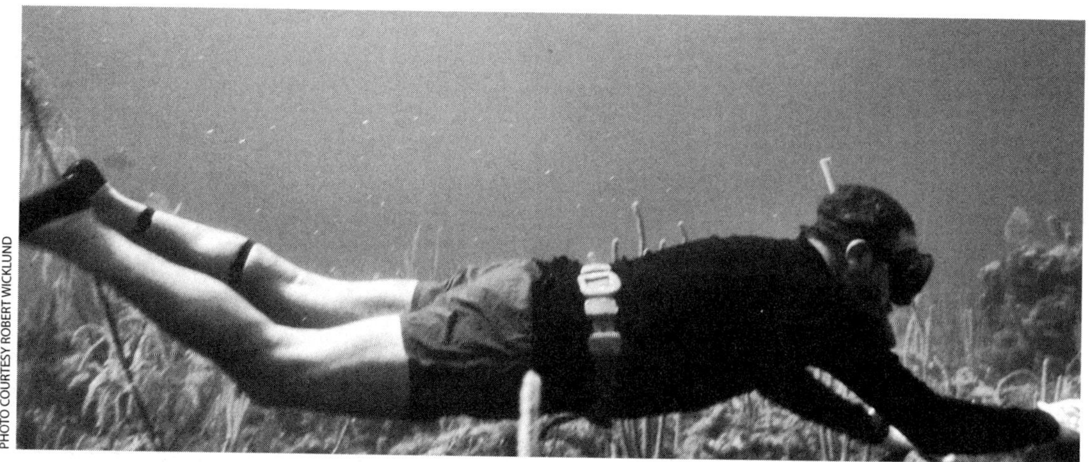

PHOTO COURTESY ROBERT WICKLUND

Fidel Castro breath-hold diving to a depth of 40 feet off the coast of the Isle of Youth, Cuba.

dinghy, weapons and all. When they left, heading toward shore and a shallow reef, Lowell turned to us and jokingly exclaimed that we were about to dine on the first lobster blasted with a machine gun. About a half hour later, the dinghy returned with Castro triumphantly holding up a good-sized spiny lobster for us to see—sans bullet holes.

Onboard and just before lunch, Castro summoned an older man, who we learned was his personal physician, and asked him to bring his scalpel. The doctor proceeded to take the thick meat from the lobster tail and deftly slice it into very thin strips. We were all offered the slices as a delicious, not to mention exotic, sashimi appetizer.

After lunch, we proceeded to dive the reef. Lowell and I toured the beautiful coral gardens, which appeared to be in excellent shape. The corals were healthy and the fish population was impressive. It was obvious that these reefs saw little diving activity and not much commercial fishing, if any. At the end of the dive, Lowell went to the surface and I stayed down a little longer to photograph the reef.

A few minutes later, something caught my eye to the left. It was Castro breath-hold diving to a depth of 40 feet and moving right by me. I instinctively raised my camera and snapped a picture. It was unbelievable. I was probably one of only a handful of people who had ever been alone with Fidel Castro and on the bottom of the ocean, no less. He moved effortlessly among the coral heads without the assistance of scuba. At this point in my diving career I had encountered a lot of strange things, but this was something else altogether. I was surprised that he was diving without a bodyguard. (I had this same experience with Lynden O. Pindling, Prime Minister of the Bahamas.) Perhaps none of Castro's team could keep up with him.

A few moments later, Castro swam back to the surface, leaving me with a photo in my camera that later appeared as a two-page spread in *People* magazine. Following another dive, we were invited to the yacht and Castro gave us a personal account of the Cuban revolution complete with maps and photos. Regardless of our differences in politics or philosophies, it was fascinating to listen to this firsthand, blow-by-blow description of his battle, and eventual victory, against the Batista government.

The trip was over in four days, but before we left the president, he and Lowell agreed to work on an exchange of marine scientists between the two countries. We extended an invitation to Cuban scientists to participate in a saturation dive in the *Hydro-Lab* now in St. Croix, Virgin Islands, owned by NOAA and operated by the West Indies Laboratory of Fairleigh Dickinson University.

I met, talked, and briefly dived with one of the most controversial figures of the twentieth century. He is a warrior, a hard-line communist, and by virtue of my citizenship—my enemy. There was little that I could relate to in Castro's ideology, but I found him to be charming and bright. The fact that we kept our meetings focused on marine science made it possible for the Senator and Castro to come to terms.

35

THE CUBANS COME TO THE U.S. VIRGIN ISLANDS

BACK IN WASHINGTON, we proceeded to work on the scientific exchange between the United States and Cuba. The concept wasn't totally out of the question, for U.S. scientists had been traveling to Cuba for years, but the sticky part was bringing the Cubans to our soil. It seemed that the *Hydro-Lab* project in St. Croix would be the best solution. It was far from the mainland and relatively small, so security would be easier, and it was the site of an ongoing coral reef research program to which the Cuban scientists could relate.

We invited the Cubans to send a team of three diving scientists to make a saturation dive in the *Hydro-Lab* for a week, conducting research of their choosing. First though, Lowell had to work some magic to get the White House and the State Department to agree. As we expected, the proposal to bring Cuban scientists and accompanying government officials to U.S soil was not well-received.

The radical faction of the Miami-based Cuban-American population quickly found out about the proposal and raised hell. It was a balancing act that took a lot of finesse and just plain luck. We had to deal not only with the U.S. Government, but also with the Cuban Interests Section. There was no official diplomatic exchange between the two countries, but Interests Sections of 20 people each were set up to maintain some communication. The Cuban Interests Section was located at the Czechoslovakian Embassy in Washington and the American counterpart was in Havana.

Following much haranguing and some blistering public condemnations by the Cuban-Americans, we received permission to proceed. Meanwhile, a radio station in Miami was broadcasting that we were intentionally bringing communist spies to St. Croix, who would have access to military submarine operations conducted off the island.

One day, while in my office just across from the Senate Russell building, I received a call that there was a reporter from some conservative magazine who wanted to interview me about the St. Croix project. I thought it would be a short visit, so I agreed.

Five minutes later the door to my office slammed open, nearly torn off its hinges, and I heard a gruff, somewhat female voice say, "Where's this guy Wicklund?"

Right then I knew I was in for it, but it was too late. More than once I had escaped out the back window of the building to avoid an onslaught of oil company lobbyists, but this woman caught me flat-footed. I am a public servant, so I must be pleasant and cooperative, I told myself.

When she came through the second doorway to my office, I saw this short, heavyset person with dirty-looking, stringy hair, and a puffy face with a scowl that revealed she already hated my guts.

"Okay, let's hear it. What does Weicker think he's doing?" she blurted out.

Blah, blah, blah, etc., I answered.

"You must be pretty stupid to think that this fiasco your boss is advocating is helpful," she went on, adding a number of other caustic remarks.

Her appearance was about as unkempt and dumpy as I had ever seen with a demeanor to match.

"Stupid? Listen, I don't have to take your abuse. If you want to continue this conversation, keep it civil," I again answered.

"You have no choice, I'm here to ask questions and you're here to answer," she literally spit onto my face.

"Wrong, lady, this interview is over, and I don't give a rat's ass even if it means my job, so get lost."

She left yelling, again almost ripping the door off its hinges.

I figured it was going to be a rough road ahead. I had to admit however, I was intrigued by this woman. She was, in a bizarre way, perfection. Her appearance was about as unkempt and dumpy as I had ever seen with a demeanor to match. She had scraggly, oily-looking hair, an awful dress and a mouth straight from the streets. She came after me like a Sherman tank. I think if I weren't already so cranky from dealing with the issue, she would have chewed me up and spit me out onto the floor. She had to be the magazine's (the name of which I have forgotten) secret weapon.

When the project was finally underway, Elliott Finkle, Director of the National Undersea Research Program which funded the *Hydro-Lab*, was thrown into the fray. Elliott was a tough Jewish guy from New Jersey, who didn't suffer fools gladly. His job was to coordinate the project from NOAA's and the federal government's standpoints. Elliott and I became close over the years and, as the Senator's ocean staff, I helped look after the undersea program, relying on Elliott's guidance in terms of funding needs and such.

Following several months of planning, we were finally able to arrange an initial visit to St. Croix by Cuban scientists and some government officials, including one we had met in Havana whom I'll call José. This was not the actual research project, but more of a planning mission to survey the reef system and discuss details of the project.

Our group included Senator Weicker, me, some NOAA officials, and Elliott. The Cubans brought four scientists with diving experience and three government people. We were hosted by the West Indies Lab, then directed by the late Dr. Robert Dill, marine geologist, educator, old friend, and wild man.

The first couple of days were dedicated to briefing the Cubans on the *Hydro-Lab* program, followed by dives in and around the lab. The lab was sitting in 50 feet of water in a natural canyon just outside the mouth of Salt River Bay. The Cuban scientists were interested in the unique marine geology of the site, as well as the fish life on the canyon banks. Everything appeared to go smoothly except for the constant bombardment by the Miami Cuban-American group. They even went as far as to name some of our visitors as known spies. We didn't hear any of this from the U.S. State Department or the FBI, so Lowell pushed on with the project.

We all stayed in the modest dormitories of the West Indies Lab, along with about 30 students. We ate our meals in a combination dining and recreational building in the center of the campus. One evening following dinner, we were sitting and chatting with the Cubans and students when I saw someone in the darkness just outside the screened walls of the recreation area motioning to me to come outside. It was José.

When I stepped out, he pulled me aside to profess his fascination with an oriental student in our discussion group. He asked me to set up an introduction and to basically give her a good impression of him. I looked at José— he was a short fellow with a hairdo and clothes that reminded me of the fifties. His approach to the situation was also from the fifties. I had to suppress a laugh, so as not to insult our guest, but he was funny. Apparently the revolution froze more in time than just the cars.

I went back to the group to continue our discussion and about a half hour later, I heard a hissing sound coming from outside. It was José again motioning to me to come out. He had a jacket on and was holding one arm close to his chest. He opened his jacket slightly to show me a bottle of booze.

"I got the whisky, so how are you doing," he blurted excitedly.

It was too much and I let out a laugh that I'm sure everyone inside heard.

"Get rid of the bottle and come inside in about 10 minutes," I told him.

I approached the girl, whom I didn't know, and told her that there was someone dying to meet her, and I would like to make an introduction. She said okay. When José came back, I made the introductions and left them alone to talk. Five minutes later the girl stood up abruptly and left, leaving poor, broken-hearted José alone. I didn't know what he said to her, but I could imagine. José was definitely not cool, but he was a funny guy nevertheless.

The following evening, after we had all gone to our dorm rooms and prepared for bed, I heard very loud shouting coming from the men's bathroom at the center of the building. The Cubans shared a couple of rooms on the opposite side of the building. I came out into the hallway, just down from the men's room to see what the commotion was about.

"Kill the commie bastards," was the first thing I heard followed by a string of obscenities and more reference to the Cuban commies. It was a group of student boys in the men's room who were obviously drunk. I was the only member of the U.S. team in that particular dorm; I had to do something very quickly to quell a potentially ugly incident. I knew that if I could hear their ranting, the Cubans could hear it as well.

Not knowing what else to do, I barged into the men's room, approached the biggest of three kids and pushed him against the wall. I knew from previous experience that having gray hair was a definite advantage and a deterrent to getting my face pushed in; I was counting on it, and the element of surprise, working against these three young strapping boys.

"You better shut your damn mouths," I yelled. "You can wind up in jail for starting an international incident," I lied to them.

As drunk as they were, it worked, and they immediately quieted down. My ruse was successful, and I saw them off to bed with a sigh of relief. There were no other incidents that night.

This visit was followed, some months later, by a Cuban team of scientists, who went though training and successfully completed a one-week scientific saturation dive. Soon after, Ronald Reagan became president and the Republicans gained control of the Senate, which basically doomed any further scientific exchange with the Cubans for the time being. It was a good run and we learned a lot about an important part of the Caribbean that previously had been a mystery to us.

In retrospect, the continued isolation of Cuba by the U.S. has kept the flame of hostility lit. If left to the devices of world events, Cuba would probably now be less of an issue, as many other former and existing communist countries are no longer a problem to us today.

36

TREASURED DAYS

Soon after leaving the Senate, the strong urge to return to the sea brought me to Southport, North Carolina. My old friend, Denny Breese, set up a project to salvage unlimited (so we thought) riches aboard sunken ships in a region known as the "Graveyard of the Atlantic." The remains of hundreds of ships lay on the continental shelf off North Carolina. Some were put there by sudden and vicious storms, common around Cape Hatteras, others by German U-boat attacks during World War II.

On previous diving expeditions around the Cape, we had surveyed a wrecked freighter in about 100 feet of water. Its sides had split wide open spilling tons of manganese ore onto the sandy bottom and exposing much more within its holds. This ship, lying peacefully on the bottom of the ocean, had met a violent end when a German torpedo slammed into its side some 30 years before our discovery. The manganese, we thought, could be recovered and sold on the open market. Other shipwrecks, yet to be discovered, might yield oil or durable goods.

During our survey of the manganese freighter, a school of large amberjack flashed by me in an obvious escape from an unseen danger, and they kept coming. While I was ascending from the wreck at about 50 feet in depth, the fish, each about 20–30 pounds, burst on the scene from one direction, some passing so close I could feel their rush in swirling vortices of current. These fish were in a hurry. I stopped and waited for the inevitable arrival of a predator large enough to send these fish into such a panic. It was probably a pelagic shark such as a mako. My eyes strained to look beyond the murk and, just as quickly as the school started, the last fish passed by and they were gone. No predator came, but without conscious thought I had taken my breathing tank off my back and held it in front, anticipating that a shark coming after the jack just might mistake me for something worth eating. I was going to offer up the tank, as foolish as that seems now.

In hindsight, this reminded me of my first physical before entering the Coast Guard in 1959. I was among several hundred young men who were ordered to take off our clothes in the locker room of a New Jersey armory gymnasium and proceed to the open gym for a medical examination, with only our wallets in hand. Once inside and realizing that the room was full of female, as well as male, nurses and doctors, we all, to a man, desperately attempted to hide behind our wallets—a sight to see. As one can guess, it was a miserable failure, as hiding behind the scuba tank would have been to avoid a shark. In my mind, and in both cases, I was attenuating—getting smaller, slimmer, and easily hidden behind the wallet and behind the tank.

Some lessons are never learned. This was the third time I observed a school of fish reacting to unseen danger without actually being in the immediate presence of an adversary. The evidence is strong that regardless of visibility, whether in clear tropical waters or in murky rivers, marine organisms are capable of detecting each other over long distances.

Other dives were made to inventory shipwrecks and their cargos without much luck. Several months later we attempted to find the *Central America*, an old clipper sailing ship that was converted to steam power, which sank in 1857. It sailed from Panama with 578 passengers and crew and a commercial shipment of gold from the California gold rush. On September 4th the ship weighed anchor bound for New York, but never made it. A storm of hurricane proportions hammered the ship relentlessly until it sank September 12, 1857; only 153 of the 578 people onboard survived. The sinking of the *Central America* was considered the greatest maritime disaster of its time.

To add insult to the tragedy, the nation was in a recession and New York bankers were relying on the *Central America's* shipment to help ease the financial crisis and to pay depositors' demands in gold. Word of this loss set off a panic.

Early reports of the sinking hinted that it might not be too far from shore. An eyewitness reported that he saw a light off the North Carolina coast only several miles from shore just about the time the ship sank, and a body believed to be from the *Central America* was buried on shore not far from the sighting.

With little resources at hand, and even less credible information, we barreled ahead convinced that the gold-laden ship was ours to find. After several weeks of preparation and a little voodoo calculation based on reports from fishermen that a large object had been found sticking out of the shallow, sandy bottom near the eastern end of Cape Lookout Shoals, we headed for the site anticipating that this was the *Central America*. The object by description could be the large one-cylinder steam engine that records indicated was placed in the *Central America*'s hull.

The trip from Beaufort, North Carolina, to the shoals was rough. Over seven-foot seas tossed our small 42-foot boat for three hours before we reached the spot, which our best estimate indicated was the location of the wreck. In addition to the heavy seas, the currents were horrendous for diving, clipping along at just under two knots. We anchored the boat and I used the attached rope to pull myself down to the bottom, which was only 40–50 feet deep. Currents on the bottom are normally somewhat less than those on the surface, but here any diminishment of current was undetectable. The rush of water whipped me from side to side as I held onto the anchor line, and sand swirled over large ripples built up on the bottom by the relentless currents. It was like an undersea hurricane, and I could do nothing more than hold on and peer around in the 20-foot-or-so visibility.

After quickly aborting this dive, we decided to weigh anchor and I swam freely, dragging a line with a float attached. Denny followed the float, so the boat would be close by when I returned to the surface. About 10 minutes into the second dive, I spotted a number of fish normally found around a reef. Surmising that they may be near an object, I followed the school, which fortunately was moving with the current, and a moment later a large shadow loomed high out of the sandy bottom. It was unmistakably an engine, and a very old one at that. Wooden wreckage surrounded the area, which I was able to grab onto and pull myself around to the lee side of the motor. Few times in my life compare with the excitement I felt at that moment. As it turned out, it was not the *Central America*, which was found some years later in 8,500 feet of water. Our wreck, still not identified, was miles and many fathoms from the actual site. Still, the one-cylinder engine that I held onto was from the same era and much like the one that powered the *Central America*, and the thrill was real.

I've had many exciting moments during my thousands of dives, but those associated with a belief that treasure was found were in a class all their own.

It has been my experience that the value of treasure diving is in the frequent gut-wrenching moments of anticipation and pure excitement surrounding even the most trivial of finds. Most treasure diving would otherwise be nothing more than a string of failures—no riches, most probably significant financial loss, and sometimes loss of life. I've had many exciting moments during my thousands of dives, but those associated with a belief that treasure was found were in a class all their own.

The experience of following the fish that led me to the wreck supports other personal observations and research by others showing that fish can navigate from relatively long distances to find a reef. The fish were at least 200–300 yards from the wreck when I first saw them, in visibility of approximately 20–30 feet. The fish went for the wreck in a relatively straight line, and previous experience urged me to follow them, successfully so, to the site. Wrecks, like natural reefs, offer food and protection and are gathering places for many fish and invertebrates. Even small, schooling fish will gather around a wreck, presumably for protection. Predators such as the bluefin tuna seek out these artificial reefs to feed on the smaller fish.

I have heard, but not confirmed, that tuna will leave one wreck and head straight for another as far as 60 miles away. Is it memory? Do these fish know the location of these wrecks and navigate directly to them? I doubt it. Although much research needs to be done, I believe that the acoustical powers of marine organisms are great, and tuna and other species can actually hear or detect low-frequency sounds over long distances in the dense medium of water. Perhaps the tuna can actually hear the sounds that a school makes even many miles away. Blue whales apparently use extremely low-frequency sounds to communicate with their own species over thousands of miles.

It was during the 50-foot saturation dive in the *Hydro-Lab* off the coast of West Palm Beach, Florida, with Joe MacInnis that I first encountered the ability of fish to detect others out of visible range. On one of the two mornings, I sat on the sandy bottom photographing the feeding behavior of a school of scad. We were right on the edge of the Gulf Stream and the small five- to eight-inch fish were distributed from the bottom of the ocean to its surface, numbering in the thousands and peacefully feeding on the plankton that flowed by on the currents. I spent several hours watching and taking photos in about 60 feet of visibility, interrupted only when changing to fresh breathing tanks. Early on I noticed that many of the scad had injuries, some rather severe. Most of these continued to feed regardless of their injuries. After about 20 minutes, the scad suddenly started to move downward in unison, continuing until they were massed near the bottom. I was completely surrounded by a wall of fish.

Considering the size and speed of the albacore, I would have been in trouble if one hit me during the attacks. Quite frankly, I was more than a little nervous each time I saw the fish start their attack from the surface.

Within minutes a school of about 20 false albacore, members of the tuna family, came into view near the surface. Like football-shaped fighter planes, the albacore streaked by and disappeared. Moments after the albacore left, the scad went back to their routine of feeding, assuming the same distribution from bottom to surface as before. After another few minutes the tuna circled back in pretty much the same pattern, but this time, when they were right over me, they pointed down and attacked the scad that had hovered, once again, near the bottom. The two-foot-long, twenty- to thirty-pound fish came streaking toward the prey and me. It was absolute bedlam as the large predators dive-bombed all around me, turning just before hitting the bottom. It was at this point I could hear loud snapping sounds as the predators bit at the scad.

I was able to photograph the albacore on their surface approach and just as they turned down, but the attack was too fast to capture up close. Clouds of sandy sediment kicked up by the fish also obscured much of the scene. Over the next hour, at least six or seven attacks took place right around me, all in the same pattern. Although I could feel the rush as many of the big fish came within inches of my body, at times in almost zero visibility, none touched me. Considering the size and speed of the albacore, I would have been in trouble if one had hit me during the attacks. Quite frankly, I was more than a little nervous each time I saw the fish start their attack from the surface.

These observations convinced me that the scad were fully aware of the approach of the false albacore, identifying them as a danger long before they arrived on scene or were visible. At the same time, the albacore knew of the scad's presence and identified them as a source of food before the prey were actually seen.

Although there is not a lot of scientific evidence, I theorize, based on many observations that all marine species, or at least most, give off sounds that can identify them individually or in groups.

Living habitats, such as coral and artificial reefs, inhabited by marine organisms may give off distinctive sounds, which can be identified by approaching animals. It may be the collective sounds of a variety of organisms through movements, grunts, and snapping that distinguish one reef from another. For instance, many fish, when startled, emit a very audible cracking sound from a swift movement of their caudal (tail) fin. These sounds are most likely produced by cavitation—"the formation of partial vacuums in a liquid created by a swiftly moving solid body." The bubbles created by a moving boat propeller are an example of cavitation, and snapping shrimp opening and closing their claws very fast cause cavitation which produces a sound. Low-frequency sounds might be emitted by animals simply swimming in the dense medium of water.

Late in the summer of 1983, we attempted to find a barrel of gold coins about one mile off Ft. Fisher, Kure Beach, North Carolina.

During the Civil War, a Confederate blockade runner attempted to sneak past a fleet of Union warships standing off the North Carolina coast to prevent any enemy vessels from leaving. This particular ship was reported to have onboard a small wooden barrel with gold coins sealed inside. The intent was to smuggle the coins through the blockade and into Charleston to help buy weapons for the Confederate war effort. The ship sailed out through an inlet and down the coast one dark night and was spotted by a Union ship somewhere near Ft. Fisher. Just before the Union ship dispatched a boarding party, the captain reported seeing someone kick an object overboard in the dim light. Later inquiries confirmed that the object was, indeed, a barrel filled with gold coins. The Union captain dutifully recorded the incident and took land bearings, which were less than two miles away.

For two months off and on, Denny, my son Bob, and I searched for the barrel or its contents, towing a magnetometer every square inch of several square miles of ocean bottom. When we got a hit on the recorder, one of us would dive to the bottom, which was only about 30 feet deep, and use a handheld version of the larger towed magnetometer to scribe the size and shape of the object buried under the sand sediment. On one afternoon I prepared to dive from a small rubber boat to check out a possible site. With a set of double tanks on my back, I stood up and jumped from the boat. At that very moment a rather large shark—larger than the boat, species unknown, but big—swam right underneath me.

There are events, I can now confirm, that happen in slow motion. I know it all took place in a split second, but I recall being in mid-air, like some cartoon character, watching my progress toward the shark, and hitting the water. Even though the shark's back was practically out of the water, I swear I did not touch it. It was apparently as surprised as I was and was gone in an instant. Convinced that the shark was more frightened than I was, I decided to continue the dive rather than hassle with removing my gear and climbing back onto the boat—no shark sightings for the rest of the day, but also no treasure.

Our only interesting find followed a hit on the magnetometer and confirmation by the handheld system of a three-foot field of metal under the sand. Of course we started mentally spending our newfound wealth, until 10 minutes of digging with a homemade underwater vacuum revealed a three-foot-long steel stay, part of the rigging from an old sailing ship. When I left the surface minutes before, the crew was so excited that I did not have the heart to come up with the bad news right away; I sat on the bottom for an extra half hour. Why not? By this time I knew that treasure diving was about excitement and fun, not riches. That extra half hour of excitement was worth the trip for some of us.

Considering that notes were taken during the capture of the ship, the barrel was seen being kicked overboard, and the water depth was only 30 feet, it would have been fairly easy for some of the sailors to have returned after the war and used diving technology of the time, or even free dived to recover the barrel. Its value would have made the effort worthwhile, especially if it were soon enough after the war that the barrel had not yet been buried under the sand bottom. It's been reported that the 16th- and 17th-century Spanish used natives to free dive into the holds of galleons wrecked in coastal storms, successfully recovering much of the riches carried by these ships. Free diving was not out of the question.

37

THE DARKEST MOMENT

Seldom do any of us face an absolute test of self and faith. I don't mean in a religious sense, but a test of all that is conscious life—mind, body, instinct, and emotion. All that has been your life is put on the line, in no uncertain terms, and a feeling of casual caution abruptly changes into pure and unrelenting terror. That moment was handed me one October 1983 night 210 feet under the cold, dark waters of the Atlantic Ocean.

The culmination of our great undersea treasure experiment came in the fall of 1983, and it was then that I faced the ultimate test of survival, still as vivid in my memory as the day it happened. In early September, I joined a team of explorers and divers, including my son Bob and friend John Duggar, to survey and extract a bounty of treasure from a shipwreck 80 miles east-northeast of Virginia Beach, Virginia. The Ward Line 6,200-ton passenger-freighter steamship *Merida* was on its way to New York in 1911, returning from Vera Cruz, Mexico, and Havana, Cuba. Onboard was a group of people escaping the Mexican revolution. Some were reported to be from the Mexican aristocracy who had their vast wealth onboard with them.

It was also reported that the ship was carrying 15 tons of silver bars in its strong room and the Maximilian jewels in the purser's safe. On May 12th the *Merida* was rammed by the *Admiral Farragut* in heavy fog. Both ships were severely damaged and the *Merida* quickly sank, but not before all onboard were safely rescued. Most of the riches onboard, however, went down with the ship.

In 1982, while I was still working for the U.S. Senate, Denny Breese, a few others, and I traveled to the reported site of the sinking in Denny's 42-foot dive boat, *Tern,* to attempt to verify that the wreck was indeed the *Merida*. After only a five-hour trip, we found a large wreck in 210 feet of water with the dive vessel's depth finding system. There was time for one dive and I was tapped to do it. The purpose of this expedition was to find some artifact on the wreck that would confirm it as the *Merida*.

Without much financing, the effort was pretty much a hit-and-miss operation. Diving equipment consisted of 210-cubic-foot air tanks, a helmet with surface

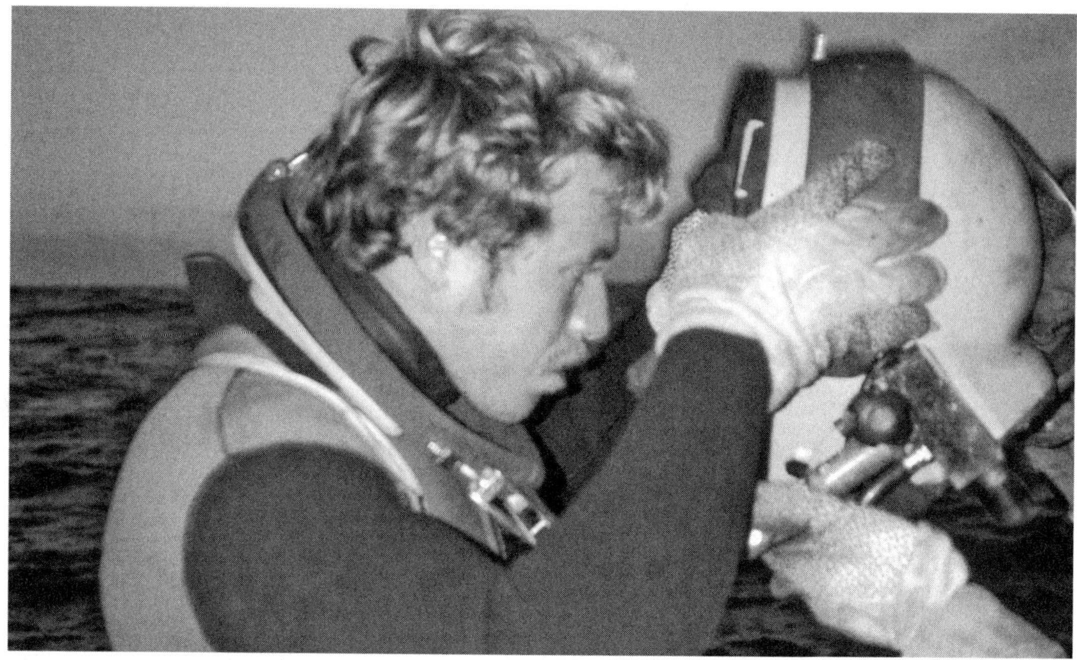

Author's son Bob preparing to dive on the Merida *shipwreck.*

communications, full wet suit, dive lights, swim fins, and not much else. The dive profile was set at 210 feet for 30 minutes with a 1½-hour, in-water decompression. No decompression chamber was onboard. Diving at this depth on straight air meant that my concentration would be somewhat impaired by nitrogen narcosis, compromising not only my ability to find some identifying artifact, but my safety as well. I had made many dives beyond 200 feet on straight air in the past, so I was confident that I would be okay.

Nitrogen narcosis, or so-called "rapture of the deep," is a real threat to divers. The deeper a diver goes, the more intoxicating nitrogen becomes, which can severely compromise his or her ability to reason. Narcosis has different levels of effect depending on the individual and the day, very much like drinking alcohol; however, unlike alcohol, as soon as the diver comes back to shallow water the effect is gone almost instantly—no hangover.

Three minutes into the dive, the huge wreck came into view. The 50-foot-plus visibility revealed the stern section. It appeared to be sitting on its port side with much of its bottom and keel exposed. The majesty of the sight, along with a touch of narcosis, made for some rather excited, high-volume blather over the communications system to the surface crew. I was quickly reminded that there were only about 25 minutes left in the dive, which shut me up and sent me on my way toward the bow of the wreck.

It was hard keeping my attention on the business at hand as schools of bait fish, amberjack, and hake swam all over the wreck. Northern lobster adorned many holes and crevices. Used to diving with scuba tanks, which gave me swimming freedom, I found the umbilical, consisting of an air hose, rope, and communication wire, very restricting and I was often in a pulling match with the surface hose tenders. They tried to anticipate my moves so as not to give too much slack in the umbilical, which could tangle in the wreck.

Eighteen minutes into the dive, I spotted a large brass porthole ring, about three feet in diameter, lying between some jagged steel beams and unattached to the ship's hull. It weighed about 25 pounds. Putting it aside, I continued the search for another seven minutes without finding anything that could identify the wreck, and then swam back to the ring. Denny asked me if there were any writing or stamps on the ring; I saw something but could not make it out. Time was getting short, so I put the ring over my shoulder and started my ascent. The extra weight made it impossible to swim and I had to pull myself up the umbilical. When I was within 100 feet of the surface, Bob swam down with a line, tied it on the ring, and it was hauled to the boat. After a long decompression and dinner, a fresh breeze turned into a storm that whipped up heavy seas and ended the expedition.

The porthole ring was proof the wreck was indeed the *Merida*. It was stamped with the name of the shipbuilder. This find eventually led to an extended expedition funded by a man named Harry John, heir to the Miller Brewing Company of Milwaukee, Wisconsin. The project was completely supported by Mr. John, including a fully equipped, 180-foot offshore supply ship with a four-point mooring system, redundant surface-supplied dive systems, two decompression chambers, and a large crane.

The diving complement consisted of a team from Subsea International, two professional salvage experts from England, John Duggar as project manager, and my son Bob. Denny Breese provided onshore logistics, and I joined the dive team to explore and map the wreck.

From September through November 1983, the salvage ship was set in a four-point mooring system directly over the wreck of the *Merida*, 80 miles off the coast of Virginia and the mouth of the Chesapeake Bay. The dive team from Subsea was set up for one-person excursions on a 24-hour schedule every day the weather permitted. Each dive to 210 feet was for 100 minutes of bottom time with a 1½-hour, in-water decompression, followed by a quick move to the surface, removal of dive gear, and a 4-hour stay in the deck decompression chamber. With the required long surface interval, only one dive per day was possible for each person. The dives were surface-supplied air to 90 feet, switching to a helium-oxygen mix for the remainder of the excursion until once again back at 90 feet.

Standard dive equipment included a SuperLite helmet with demand or free-flow breathing system, surface communications, weights, knife, and a couple tiny Q-lights. Water temperature at the beginning of the project was in the low 70s on the surface, but it was only in the high 40s to mid-50s on the bottom, requiring a special suit that distributed heated water pumped from the surface around the diver's body. A diver's descent, return to the surface, and in-water decompression were on a platform, or stage, controlled from the surface.

I cycled into the dive schedule and most of my 25 or so excursions took place at night. During the first several dives, we could easily see the results of explosives placed on the wreck by past salvage efforts. Our information at the time indicated that a salvage crew had attempted to recover the wreck's treasures in the summers of 1932 and 1933. Because of no record of any treasure having been found and a belief that diving and salvage technology were inadequate back then, most of us thought that the silver bars and other riches were still probably on the wreck.

The more we saw, the more we realized that this wreck had been seriously worked over. Twisted steel was everywhere and proved to be a hazard to the divers. On one late evening, a Subsea diver cut his breathing gas hose on sharp steel and had a rough time getting back onboard the ship safely. A quick-thinking surface supervisor advised the diver to shove the open end of the separate pneumo hose, which took accurate depth readings by flowing air to the diver and measuring the back pressure, into his helmet. The surface crew then pumped a small stream of air down to the diver through this hose, enough to get him back to the stage and on deck. On another night dive I got my umbilical hopelessly tangled in the wreck and wasted the whole dive freeing myself from the mess.

So, throughout September, October, and into November, we searched, used C-4 explosives in strategic locations to gain entry into the wreck, and brought numerous artifacts to the surface—dinnerware, Mexican brooms, sisal and large mahogany logs, all perfectly preserved in the cold water and mud, but no silver, gold, or other booty. The explosions, of course, had a devastating effect on the fish around the wreck. The lobster and other invertebrates, without the gas-filled swim bladders that most fish possess, did not seem to be affected. I didn't like this part of the operation, but it was out of my hands. During the in-water decompressions at 40–60 feet, however, I was thrilled to see small schools of filefish, bluefish, and dolphin fish, obviously on their fall migration runs, unaffected by our activities.

Sometime in October, Subsea decided to place a 50-foot length of fire hose filled with liquid explosives on the partially upturned bottom of the wreck. This would presumably give us easier access to the cargo hold where the treasure was believed to be stored. The ship was positioned directly over the working area and the hose was lowered by a deck crane and put in place by the divers. After fitting an explosive primer cord and cap, the charge was set off with a tremendous blast.

The problem was that the crew forgot to inform the captain that they were ready and, when the charge went off, the ship was still over the explosive-laden hose. Even though the explosion was at least 200 feet under us, it literally lifted the stern end of the ship and rattled its deck plates from stem to stern. The captain, who was napping at the time, ran up the companionway with eyes as wide as dinner plates. Fortunately, for some of the crew, keelhauling had been outlawed a long time ago.

Author preparing to dive on the Merida *shipwreck.*

By mid-October, the seas prevented diving operations almost two out of three days. The down days were miserable, setting on the four-point mooring and just hanging on. Some of us with delicate stomachs had long quit eating the cook's greasy Cajun-chicken-fried everything. Plain rice became the staple diet. The two movies onboard were played at least a hundred times. The only saving grace was that the crew's slimy tobacco spit was washed away occasionally by the heavy seas. Just about everyone onboard adopted the habit and at times it was hazardous, as well as disgusting, to walk on the deck.

Sometime in October, at about 3:00 a.m., I prepared for a long dive into the ship's hold to dig in the mud with a powerful water jet system. Aside from the life-support umbilical and hose to the hot-water suit, I had to drag another rather large water hose through which high-pressure seawater was pumped from the surface. After the water hose was lowered to the bottom, I prepared to jump into the sea and enter the stage. I knew it was going to be a difficult task, but little did I anticipate that a very defining moment in my life was close at hand. I reached the bottom within several minutes and found the water hose right away in the gloomy, dark sea.

At 90 feet during the descent, I was switched from straight air to a helium-oxygen mix. The inert helium gas eliminates the narcotic effect experienced by divers under the influence of the high pressure associated with deep water. At 210 feet some divers, breathing straight air, can become completely disoriented and dangerously disabled. The downside of breathing a helium mix is that it carries heat away from your body at about four times the rate of air.

Although the ocean waters in this region normally become unstable and turn over in the fall, mixing the cold bottom water with the warmer surface, the water temperature was still in the mid-50s, making the hot-water suit an absolute necessity for such long dives. After dragging the water hose and life-support umbilical to the entrance of the ship's hold, it took over 20 minutes to negotiate the openings into the wreck. Rusted, jagged steel from previous explosions was everywhere and frequently grabbed one hose or another. I was on a demand regulator fitted on the SuperLite helmet. This saved the costly breathing gas, allowing flow only when a breath was taken. The free-flow valve was shut off, only to be used in an emergency.

The inside of the ship's hold was pitch-black. The small Q-light on my belt afforded only a very narrow beam to guide my way. Previous mapping dives paid off as I finally reached the site. Once in, I called the surface crew to start the water jet pump. At the end of the hose was a "T" nozzle that diverted the water 90 degrees downward and also 90 degrees upward. The opposing force of the water flow kept a diver from being pushed upward, allowing him to stay relatively stable on the bottom. The water came with a rush, immediately blowing mud and contents of the hold everywhere. After several minutes of this, the visibility was completely

The author breathing oxygen in a decompression chamber after a 100-minute dive to 210 feet on the Merida *shipwreck.*

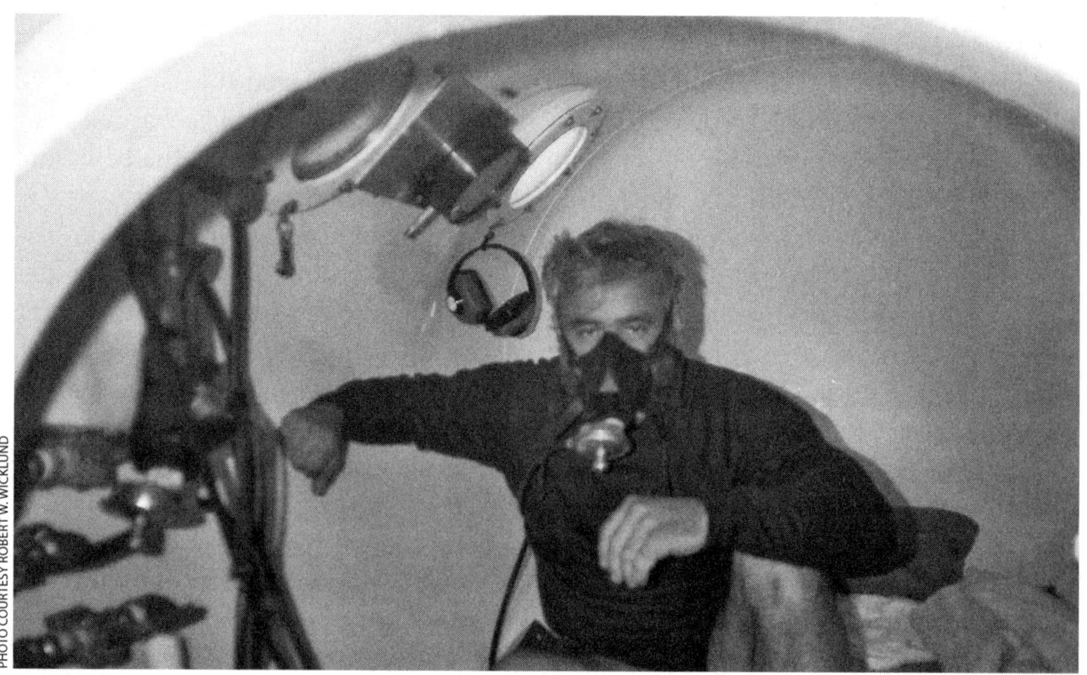

PHOTO COURTESY ROBERT W. WICKLUND

gone. The only way I could see my light was to place it smack on my helmet's glass faceplate. It was a strange sensation—ultimate darkness.

The sound of my breathing seemed amplified and the dull roar of the water jet heightened. I became more aware of other things such as the hot water flowing through my suit, burning my knees where the water first entered, and the creepy feeling of sisal flowing around my body from the jet's action. Sisal, used to make rope and other products, was everywhere, apparently a major part of the ship's cargo. After about 30 minutes, I could only imagine what the room looked like. I could have been standing on top of the silver bars and never know it.

Then it happened. I mistakenly pulled the end of the water jet across my chest and the upward-flowing nozzle shot water under my helmet, almost blowing it off my head. In an instant it was completely filled. Unfortunately, I took a breath at the same moment the mouthpiece from the demand regulator was blown partially out of my mouth from the force of the jet. For what seemed like forever, I stood motionless, by myself, in this darkest of places with my helmet flooded, some water in my lungs, and no chance of immediate rescue.

Although there are not many instances in life like this, it seemed at the time—at that moment—as a path to life or death was set out before me, that giving in to panic would be almost a luxury. To act defensively, to make the mind think and to react, would be painful.

I was over 20 minutes away from the entrance to the wreck and that would be the same for a rescue diver. The darkness, muffled sounds, and cold water around my head contrasted with the warm water flowing around my body was a surreal sensation. It felt as if I were physically and mentally removed from the scene, reading about it in a dime-store novel. Although there are not many instances in life like this, it seemed at the time—at that moment—as a path to life or death was set out before me, that giving in to panic would be almost a luxury. To act defensively, to make the mind think and to react, would be painful. Panic was, however, my immediate enemy. I had to steel myself against its overwhelming grip. Drowning and suffocation were in my helmet with me, challenging my resolve to stay around a little longer.

In the end it was my call. Nothing else in the world could save me. I was isolated, trapped inside a 75-year-old wreck on the bottom of the ocean. Like Jonah, I was in the belly of the beast. The absolute darkness, cold, thoughts of my family, and the will to live mixed cruelly in my thoughts.

Seconds went by before my mind took it all in and thoughts of survival started to emerge. Almost automatically, I reached up and grabbed the free-flow valve on the top of the helmet and turned it full on. Several seconds later all of the water was gone and I could hear myself coughing and choking. I let the helium-oxygen mix continue to flow as it gave me comfort against the feeling of drowning. The tiny airspace inside my helmet felt more like an oasis in the black ocean than ever before, and I desperately clung to that thought. Less than a minute went by and I started to relax a little when the topside dive supervisor, who didn't yet know what happened, yelled over the communication system, "Turn that damn free-flow off. Don't you know how much helium costs?"

Choking back the little water left in my lungs, I simply replied, "Go screw yourself," which as much as anything brought me back to the real world. The exchange was something that made sense to me in this alien situation. It stirred my ire somewhat and that was good. Maybe my fellow diver really did know and tried to push my buttons on purpose. In any case, it helped a lot.

The dive was terminated, but I was not out of the woods. I had to get back to the stage on my own. I was only able to feel my way back, following the umbilical hose to the outside of the wreck where the hand light could do some good. My umbilical was constantly getting hung up on the jagged wreckage of the ship, which made the trip more difficult. My thoughts went to my son Bob, who was on deck. He was an excellent diver and would have come to my rescue in an instant. I also thought, if I didn't make it, how horrible it would be for him. Two hours later, following an uneventful in-water decompression, I was safely on deck and in the decompression chamber.

Contemplating the events later, I wondered why we evolved with panic as an response to danger. Was it a cue to flee for primitive man, like prey when confronted by predators? It doesn't help in most dangerous situations, such as my experience inside the broken hull of this ship, where panic would have been a killer.

All subsequent dives were relatively easy and, as usual, we came up empty-handed. Persistent late fall storms and heavy seas finally drove us back to shore. That was about it for my treasure diving career. Close calls, empty hands, and a hell of a lot of fun!

38

BACK TO THE BAHAMAS

JOHN PERRY OWNED a magnificent island in the Exuma chain of the Bahamas. For a mere $70,000, he and a few of his colleagues bought the island in the mid-fifties as a tropical retreat. At that time the Bahamas was still part of the British Commonwealth, and Perry's deed was supposedly a Queen's Grant, which theoretically gave him a lot of latitude in the disposition of the island. John eventually bought out his partners and often joked that because of the grant he could declare independence and run the island as a sovereign nation. He even seriously thought of creating his own currency, which he called "Hydro Marks."

Lee Stocking Island is about 600 acres in size with high cliffs, rolling hills, eleven beautiful beaches. It's just six miles from Barraterre, a tiny village on the northern point of Great Exuma Island with a population of about 100—Lee Stocking's closest neighbors.

Lee Stocking is one of many small and medium-size islands extending about 110 miles from Nassau to Great Exuma Island. A population of about 500 is spread throughout the Exuma islands. To the east of Lee Stocking is Exuma Sound, an over 4,000-foot deep narrow cut in the Great Bahama Bank. On its west side a sand-covered bank, averaging only 10 to 15 feet deep, extends to the Tongue of the Ocean, some 40 miles away. Miami is 300 miles to the northwest, as the crow flies, from the island. The nearest hospital, in Nassau, is over 100 miles by plane or boat. Lee Stocking Island, in every respect, is a remote region of the world.

During my tenure on the Hill, I kept in touch with John and made a few visits to the island, often consulting with him on potential research possibilities. John talked constantly about his dream of making the island a research facility and energy self-sufficient. Early on, he built three prototype windmills, which generated A/C power for small portions of the island when the wind was strong enough. When John learned that I had left Washington, he asked Gerri and me to come back to the Bahamas and get something going on the island. At this point he had built a 3,000-foot runway, a road, some buildings, docks, and a power station with diesel generators. So, having checked treasure diving off my list, Gerri and I accepted

John's offer, applied for the appropriate work and other permits from the Bahamian government, and in 1984 we moved to Lee Stocking Island.

For the first week or so we familiarized ourselves with the operation of the generators, and the rather primitive electrical system installed by local electricians. Wires were running everywhere, switches were upside down, and many places had no power at all even with an electrical wiring system in place. Often the ground wire wasn't attached to anything. Several buildings had "ghost" currents that would come and go for no apparent reason. One day we would measure 15–20 volts of current right from the side of a washing machine; the next day it would be gone. It was the same with a house that John built for his private use. When taking a shower, guests would often experience a sharp, tingling sensation. The tub faucet would also occasionally provide an additional shot of electricity.

I remembered the very funny book *Don't Stop the Carnival* by Herman Wouk in which the new owners of a Caribbean hotel constantly dealt with the island-way of doing things. It seemed that we had been transported into that world. Luckily, there was a young Bahamian technician, Danny, already living on the island, who was familiar with some of its idiosyncrasies. Danny worked for Perry Oceanographics and his primary responsibility was to keep the windmills operational. There were also several workers from Great Exuma Island, a few somewhat skilled in masonry and carpentry, who came each weekday morning by boat. Kerlean cooked wonderful

Gerri Wenz coming through the hatch of a portable habitat off Lee Stocking Island.

Bahamian dishes and was in charge of the kitchen and housekeeping, and Doyle was the island groundskeeper.

Gerri and I spent some time exploring the island and the waters around its shores. The eleven beaches were covered with deep calcareous sand and were separated by hard rock shoreline eroded by wave action into treacherously jagged edges that we called "iron shore." Even a minor fall on these rocks would almost certainly result in severe cuts and abrasions. On the island's south end, cliffs rose out of the water unlike most of the Bahama islands, which have low, fairly flat profiles. Coconut Beach, on the lee side of the island, had a grove of coconut trees lining the shore, planted there years ago. Small black and red mangrove forests were found here and there. Most of the island was covered by low brush with some Lignum Vitae trees and a few invasive Australian pines. The crystal clear waters surrounding the island reflected light from the shallow bottom in hues of deep and turquoise blue, depending on depth, with green and yellow interjected by shadows of coral heads and grass beds. The setting was indeed worthy to be called paradise.

In and among the brushy overgrowth were remnants of an old settlement with rock walls and stone foundations. This region, particularly Great Exuma Island, was settled by Loyalists to the British Crown emigrating from the Carolinas and other U.S. colonies during the 18th century. They moved their families, slaves, and sometimes their homes, brick by brick. They soon discovered that these islands had little soil

Deep Rover *and* Shark Hunter *meet in shallow water off Lee Stocking Island.*

to farm and the settlers eventually abandoned their new homes and farmsteads. We speculated that the Lee Stocking Island ruins had been built by slaves who had been left behind, but we will probably never know for sure.

The first few months we had this whole island paradise practically to ourselves. Aside from planning the island's future, we spent hours diving and snorkeling on the shallow reefs. Lobster, conch, and fish were abundant and made up many of our meals.

Just north of Lee Stocking Island, we discovered a small area in 25 feet of water covered by large and small coral heads and surrounded by thick stands of sea fans and soft gorgonian corals. Reef fish thrived there and it was home to the largest population within miles of the island. Thousands of grey, lane, and schoolmaster snapper roamed the area in tight schools and many more thousands of French, striped, white, and other grunts swam among the soft corals swaying in the current. Large barracuda hung almost motionless within the schools waiting for an opportunity to take lunch or dinner.

During our hosting of the "Sea Space Symposium" on Lee Stocking Island, my friend, Andy Rechnitzer, an official in the office of the Oceanographer of the Navy, and Elmer Wheaton, an entrepreneur and member of the President's Commission on the Oceans, were so enthralled by the beauty of the site they named it "Rainbow Gardens," which became its official name. Other members of the Symposium, including Sylvia Earle and astronaut Buzz Aldrin, were also regular visitors to the magic of the Gardens. It was interesting that the abundance of life at Rainbow Gardens was matched by only a few other sites we visited along the Exuma Island chain. Even some sites that were similar in appearance had just a small percentage of fish life. Was it the way that currents brought in nutrients, or was it a recruitment-rich place where eggs and larvae were frequently carried? Now, after many years of general decline, I wonder if it still is "Rainbow Gardens."

Once we gained an understanding of the marine system surrounding Lee Stocking Island and the logistical problems of maintaining a research program on this very isolated island, we started to formulate a plan for the next few years. Food, repair parts, equipment, and general supplies were available by a weekly flight of Perry's twin-engine plane or by the *Undersea Hunter*, one of our research vessels, which came to the island every few months. Most of our food came every few weeks on the mailboat, a 70-foot, wooden-hulled vessel which loaded at Nassau and traveled down the Exuma chain, stopping wherever mail and supplies had to be delivered. Passengers could travel anywhere the boat went for a few dollars—meager accommodations, but cheap.

When the boat arrived at Lee Stocking, close to the end of its route, we all turned out on the dock to help unload the food and take it to our commissary, a small building with shelving, refrigerators, and freezers. Inevitably, by the time

PHOTO COURTESY ROBERT W. WICKLUND

Research submersible Gamma *being launched from Lee Stocking Island.*

the mailboat arrived days after leaving Nassau, some of the frozen goods unloaded were almost completely thawed out. Regardless, the mailboat system was surprisingly efficient most of the time. Our biggest problem was the primitive telephone system that constantly broke down, leaving us with a ship-to-shore radio to get food orders into the Nassau merchants, as well as for any other communication with the mainland.

We soon decided that the island should be the site of a major marine and coral reef research facility with diving to be used for much of the research. John Perry agreed to dedicate the island to this cause and donated the full use of several vessels, including the 85-foot *Undersea Hunter* and a 32-foot aluminum catamaran, *Exuma Hunter*, with a hydraulic platform designed to launch and retrieve a two-passenger wet submarine from the ocean surface. The Perry plane was also available to us when needed. On the Exuma Sound side of the island we had a small ambient-pressure habitat in 26 feet of water. It was twelve feet long by eight feet wide, and six-feet high at the peak of its sloped roof. It had a large window on one end and an open hatch at the other end. With all this in place, we started a modest reef study program close to the island while continuing to explore the varied habitats—grass beds, fore and mid-reefs, and the deep slope down to 200 feet.

Being a businessman, John Perry had been particularly interested in using the island as a commercial marine farm focusing on the cultivation of the spiny lobster, which was the most highly prized species in the West Indies. Before we came to the island, John, unfortunately, decided to create a lobster pond on the island and dammed a magnificent, two-acre mangrove wetland. The mangroves were cut, burned, and pulled to create the pond. By the time we arrived the entire stand of mangroves was dead.

The idea was to stock the pond with adult lobster and hope they would reproduce on their own. The project was doomed to failure before it even started. The people involved had little or no understanding of the life history of the spiny lobster—their mating, critical larval stages, metamorphosis, feeding requirements, cannibalism—everything they needed to know and of which little was known at the time. So, when we inherited that project, I advised John that if aquaculture were to be an important part of our research program, we had to concentrate on a much less complicated species.

We created the "Caribbean Marine Research Center" as the research arm of the Perry Foundation and the Bahamas Undersea Research Foundation (Perry's Bahamian non-profit entity), and started building research facilities. (Later on, Sylvia Earle agreed to chair the Board of Directors of the foundation.)

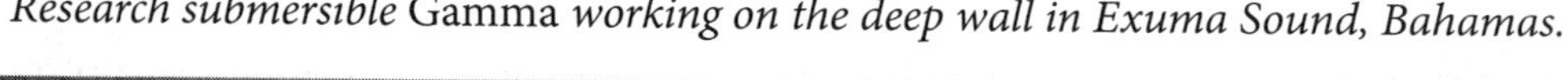

Research submersible Gamma *working on the deep wall in Exuma Sound, Bahamas.*

Most of the existing buildings had to be renovated and others had to be constructed to accommodate future employees and to support research projects. The power plant required bigger generators with backup. A reverse osmosis system to produce freshwater from the sea was put in place. Aquaculture ponds were built. We rewired almost the entire island. Later a dormitory was built to accommodate scientists and students. Most importantly, the diving system was upgraded to accommodate at least a dozen scientists and technicians at any one time. By the second year, Lee Stocking Island had 28 buildings and 11 boats ranging from 14 feet to 85 feet long. We received modest funding from the undersea program at NOAA and finally, after negotiations with its director, Elliott Finkle, we became an official Center of the National Undersea Research Program (NURP).

The Bahamian people of the outer islands, including the Exumas, were gentle, warm, and totally delightful. The locals we employed were, for the most part, hardworking and contributed much to our success. We had a little problem with their time-honored tradition of "totin' rights," meaning that if a tool or anything else is left lying around for a while, it's fair game and a person has a right to "tote" it away. This led to a steady stream of tools, lumber, tiles, nails, you name it, walking off the island. We noticed early on that Lee Stocking Island tote'n rights had helped build some of Barraterre. The ceiling in a local bar had L.S.I., the original freight identifying mark, still visible, as did posts under a house porch. No attempt was made to hide it. It made us laugh, and we decided it was a small cost of doing business in the islands.

We were given another lesson in island protocol when one of the workers, who was paid on an hourly basis, started coming to work late one month. At the end of the pay period we simply added up his time and gave him a check minus about 10 hours. He immediately came to me and said that he should get his full pay. I knew this was going to be interesting and asked him why we should pay him for a full day. He replied, "Those days I come in late, I works extra hard." I almost fell out of my chair. I knew by now that there would be no debate. We just let it ride and got it back with some extra time from him later on.

It was also interesting trying to convince the workers that vacation meant they had time off with full pay. Several came to me one day saying they were about to go on vacation and wanted their vacation pay. I told them they already had their full paycheck, but that didn't set well. "We want our vacation pay so we can have fun on our time off." They wanted "vacation" money on top of their regular pay. It took some time to get through to them.

Doyle came to my office one afternoon soaking wet with bleeding scratches on his head. "We has a problem, mon," he said, insisting he was okay and asking me to come with him. I followed him to a rock seawall on which he had been leveling sand with a Bobcat. The Bobcat was laying on its side in about 10 feet of clear water. Doyle had gone over the wall with the machine and was able to swim out of its protective cage. Assured that he was not badly hurt, we pulled the Bobcat upright with a boat, towed it along the bottom to a launching ramp, and winched it out of the water. Doyle was so embarrassed by the whole thing that he got his buddies together and they worked through the night to tear the Bobcat down and repair it. They had it up and running by morning—an impressive undertaking. The Bahamians have a reputation for being extremely laid-back, but these men displayed intensity of purpose worthy of any culture.

After the Caribbean Marine Research Center was well-established, we were approached by the United States Geological Survey about taking over their 156-foot research vessel, *J. W. Powell*. It was an old, converted commercial utility vessel built to support the oil fields in the Gulf of Mexico. As I understand it, it had been seized by the U.S. Government in a drug bust. The USGS refurbished the ship and added an enormous A-frame on the stern deck. I thought it would be a good addition to our growing program, allowing us to work in the open ocean and throughout the Caribbean. We signed a Memorandum of Understanding with the USGS and took over responsibility for the ship, although the government still owned it. We soon realized that a ship of this size and its cost were going to be a challenge to us. We stationed the *Powell* at the Perry docks in Riviera Beach, Florida, and sailed it to Lee Stocking Island to bring supplies whenever it was on a research cruise in the Bahamas.

The ship was too big to dock at the island, so it had to anchor in protected waters about a quarter-mile away. On one of the early trips, the *Powell* reached the anchorage in the evening. When I got up about 6:30 the next morning and looked out the window, I could see the ship offshore and someone sitting on a pile of luggage on our dock. It was the young son of a friend, who we had agreed to hire as a short-term crewman. But why was he on the dock and not on the ship? My son Bob, who was first mate on the ship, told me that when they anchored the night before the first thing the young man did was jump overboard fully clothed. After the crew fished him out, he went to his cabin, changed into fresh clothes, came back on deck and jumped over again. After pulling him out a second time they asked him why, but he had no explanation.

That same night, when everyone but the watch crew retired, he sneaked to the stern and climbed down into a small, rubber dinghy with an outboard motor that was tied to the ship. He released the rope first, then could not get the motor started and was carried about a mile away by currents. Early the next morning the crew discovered him and the dinghy missing. After a search, they found him sitting

R/V Undersea Hunter *launching research submersible* Deep Rover *in the Exuma Cays, Bahamas.*

in the dinghy being thrown by waves against the rocky shoreline of an adjacent island, Norman's Pond Cay. Once again he was rescued and told the crew he was just "checking out the perimeter." That was it. They packed him and his belongings into a boat and dumped him off at our dock. Bob told me in no uncertain terms that he was banned from the ship and he was now our problem. Over the next few months, the young man displayed more bizarre behavior on the island, to the point other residents complained and we had to send him home.

Over a three-year period, we hustled to lease the *Powell* out to pay for its upkeep and our operations. We leased it to survey and oil companies, and it was occasionally used to support submarine operations. One contract we received was to use the ship as a prop in the James Bond movie *Licence to Kill.* The ship's name was changed from *J.W. Powell* to *Wavekrest*, the bad guy's yacht. I didn't see the movie until it was released and when a scene came up in which the ship crashed into a dock, I gasped. I was witnessing a ship, owned by the USGS and my responsibility, crashing into a dock for the world to see. Fortunately, the movie was not seen by the owners, or they did not recognize their ship, or maybe it just wasn't an issue. It was soon after that we realized it was not serving our research as much as we needed and we returned the *J.W. Powell* to the USGS. It later wound up in the Texas A&M University research fleet.

Our struggles with research vessels continued, when one day a large yacht towing a 28-foot long Blackfin sportfishing boat passed by Lee Stocking Island about a half mile offshore. The larger vessel was cruising at a good pace when the anchor fell off the bow of the smaller boat and grabbed a coral head 70 feet below. When the anchor line stretched tight, the yacht pulled the Blackfin underwater and it sank to the bottom. We dove on the wreck the next day at the owner's request to examine its condition. The boat was sitting on the bottom completely upright with no visible damage and its flag was still flying, so to speak. The view in the clear, tropical waters was surreal; it looked like it belonged resting on the sandy bottom. Several weeks later we bought the boat, as is, from the insurance company for $3,000 and raised it with the crane on the *J. W. Powell*. The boat was refurbished in Florida and was added to our fleet of prized research vessels.

Not long after, a scientist grounded the boat, causing considerable damage, and we were unable to raise the money to again bring it back to operation. So it went.

Future research vessel of the Caribbean Marine Research Center.

39

JOHN PERRY

DURING ALL OF the building phases of the program, John Perry became a regular visitor. He provided startup funds to begin a modest research program and to reconstruct buildings to meet our future needs. John was brilliant and eccentric. His quest for alternative energy systems brought some bizarre activities to the island from his companies in Florida. John had previously owned 35 newspapers and claimed to be the innovator of computerized printing that eliminated the hand-setting of type. He loved to say that he "got the lead out of the newspaper business." I believed it, because we had 25-pound lead bars all over the island, which we used for ballasting everything from subs to a small undersea lab.

John installed three windmills on the island, each about 35 feet high with three large fiberglass blades constructed by his staff. These could actually power the island for a day or two during the early period of the project when the wind was blowing over 12 knots.

The windmills were problematic as the homemade blades would occasionally break and fly off in a heavy wind. They were programmed to turn so they would not get the full force of high winds, but that didn't always work, resulting in a several-hundred-pound missile in the form of a blade flying through the air and crashing into the ground. When that happened, the now-unbalanced windmill, with only two blades left, would rock violently. On several occasions I had to get to the windmill to apply the brakes by shorting the power box attached to the tower. Standing under the rocking steel tower, in what we called the "kill zone," I unhooked one of the large electrical cables and crossed the poles, creating a massive flash and sparking that somehow stopped the turning blades. It was after the first blade failing that we designated an area around the windmill off limits to all but a few of us. Eventually, the island grew far beyond the capabilities of the windmills and they were used solely for Perry's energy research.

John was fond of his wet submersible, *Shark Hunter*, which we kept on the island. The *Shark Hunter* was a two-passenger underwater vehicle that required the operator and passenger to wear scuba gear. It also had a built-in air system that supplied both passengers. An electric motor pushed the sub at speeds just over three knots. Since the sub was open to the sea, the depths of dives were restricted to the limits of a diver and seldom did we go deeper than 100 feet, mostly a lot shallower.

The *Shark Hunter* got its name when John entered a shark tournament in Florida some years before, which he won for the largest shark taken. The *Palm Beach Post* published a photo of him in the first *Shark Hunter* shooting the shark with a spear gun. He told me that he needed some publicity for his new sub, so he hired a fisherman to catch a large tiger shark and tie it to a boat; then he staged the photo of himself. John had no problem pulling a fast one on the public when it came to publicizing his submarines.

One of John's favorite things to do on Lee Stocking Island was to pilot the *Shark Hunter* from the dock around a shallow, half-mile underwater course, which brought him back to his starting point. He delighted in having a passenger in the back seat and would offer a ride to anyone interested. One morning during a visit by some congressional staff, I walked down to the dock to find John ready to be launched off the *Exuma Hunter*. A young lady Senate staffer was in the back seat. I heard John telling her to "just put the regulator in your mouth and breathe." I knew she had no diving training or experience, and I could see she was petrified.

John was dangerous, and part of my job was to make sure he didn't kill a guest, himself, or me.

So, knowing that John paid little attention to the back seat once the ramp started to move, and as we had done before, I told her to get out of the sub just as it was about to be launched. She got out and John went on his way. About 20 minutes later, when the sub was back on the launching ramp, the young lady got back in the seat. As John climbed out he turned to her and said, "How did you enjoy the ride?" She was cool and replied that it was great. John never noticed that she was as dry as a bone after the ride. John was dangerous, and part of my job was to make sure he didn't kill a guest, himself, or me.

In his book, *Never Say Impossible*, John described taking the wife of then-Secretary of Commerce Pete Peterson on a *Shark Hunter* dive with an empty tank during the *Hydro-Lab* project off Freeport, Bahamas. I wouldn't let them go until I checked the air supply. John credited me with saving the life of the secretary's wife. I don't remember much about the incident, but there were so many, it's hard to recall just one.

40

LIVING IN THE PAST—STROMATOLITES

One afternoon in 1986, Bob Dill, a friend and notable marine geologist, and I dove in Adderley Cut, a swift-running channel between Lee Stocking Island and a series of small islands. I had made this dive a number of times before and noticed what I thought were the remnants of dead coral reefs in the middle of the channel. The structures were large, rocky pillars, some jutting out of the sand about eight feet high. The attraction of this dive was the current, which could carry a diver for about a mile with very little effort. The swift current carried us over the structures, and when we came to the surface about 10 minutes later, Bob was sputtering something to me that was completely incoherent. He was yelling and I thought he was having trouble. The boat following us moved closer, and we climbed aboard with Bob still looking and sounding distressed.

"Do you know what those things we passed over may be?" he shouted. "I think they're stromatolites!"

Field of modern stromatolites in a high-energy channel, Exuma Cays, Bahamas.

PHOTO COURTESY ROBERT DILL

PHOTO COURTESY ROBERT DILL

Geologists examining stromatolites in waters off the Exuma Cays, Bahamas.

Say what? was pretty much my reaction. Bob went on to explain it to me and said if they were truly stromatolites, this could be the geological discovery of the year.

Over 3.5 billion years ago, in the Precambrian period, when shallow seas covered the earth, one of the first life forms was a microorganism called cyanobacteria, also known as blue-green algae. The bacteria lived in the ocean and trapped sand particles, or precipitated calcium carbonate, from the seawater. This led to the formation of the first reef structures in the ocean called stromatolites, which dominated the shallow seas for three billion years. The algae associated with stromatolites are believed to be the first contributors of oxygen to our atmosphere and oceans.

About 550 million years ago, many new life forms appeared and the stromatolites began to decline, likely due to predation by newly evolved grazing organisms. In modern times, stromatolites had previously only been found in ancient geological records. Fossils were found all over the world and, until recently, they were considered extinct. Living stromatolites, however, were finally found in the hypersaline Hamelin Pool at Shark Bay, Australia, some 60 years ago. It was thought that these survived by being in a habitat unlivable for algae grazers. Other small sub- and intertidal stromatolites have been found in other places.

Bob took a few samples of the structures back to his lab in California and gave some to his geology colleagues for verification. Sure enough, these were stromatolites—living fossils—the only ones in the world found living in a dynamic system in clear oceanic water, much like those in the Precambrian period. Their size

PHOTO COURTESY ROBERT DILL

Scientists measuring modern stromatolites in the Exuma Cays, Bahamas.

gave them the title of "giant stromatolites," and they became a mecca for geologists from all over the world, who came to see and study them.

From my standpoint, I was smitten by the idea that right in our backyard, in only 20 feet of water and in a relatively active tourist area, we found something incredible. Back in the late sixties or early seventies, I had read a famous oceanographer's remark that most, if not all, of the major ocean discoveries had already been made. He was dead wrong. The world was introduced to these giant stromatolites, which could tell us so much about the history of our planet—evidence of yet another major discovery through diving science.

41

MAYDAY—MAYDAY

When fellow seamen are in trouble, most of us will go to extremes to help. It's an unwritten code of conduct that has prevailed throughout maritime history. However, a couple of rescue experiences in the Bahamas some years ago made me take pause. I learned that rescues are not all simply heroics, and some are actually almost bizarre.

Mid-afternoon one day we heard by radio that a tri-hull sailboat was stuck in the entrance to a channel and was about to be smashed onto a rocky cliff by heavy waves. The sailboat was about 10 miles north of Lee Stocking Island. The radio caller said that his boat was not maneuverable enough to rescue the sailboat, which was anchored very close to the rocks. Adding to the problem, there was a ripping incoming tidal current.

Shawn Bartlett and I jumped into a 20-foot, outboard-powered boat and within 30 minutes arrived at the cut where the sailboat was anchored between two islands. We could see immediately that the boat and the two male crew members were in a perilous position. We estimated that the current in the channel exceeded three knots pulling on the three anchors that they had set. Over six-foot waves were threatening to pound the boat against the rock cliffs only about 30 feet away. To make matters worse, the sailboat had no motor. We couldn't imagine why they attempted to sail out into the sound under these dangerous conditions. We found out later that the two were lovers who had a quarrel, and the owner of the boat decided to bring his now ex-friend to the airport on Great Exuma Island some 35 miles away.

We motored our boat near the stricken vessel, keeping our bow into the current and waves. We instructed the crew to pull up two of the anchors and we would then throw them a towline. Once the line was attached we would steam ahead against the current. The plan was that, when the towline became taut, they would quickly cut the third line and we would pull them across the current away from the cliffs, and then around and back down the channel into calm water. It would have to be a coordinated effort with no hesitation. Being tethered to their boat in the heavy current could put us in a bad position. I didn't think at that time how bad it could be.

Everything went right in the beginning. The two anchors were pulled and we got the towline in place. Once we started to motor hard against the current and the towline was taut, we yelled to them to cut the line to the remaining anchor. Instead, they started trying to pull it up, arguing with each other along the way.

"Cut the damn line!" one of us shouted.

By this time we were struggling to keep the current from swinging us around. The two continued to pull on the anchor with no progress. Seconds later, while we were still tied to the sailboat, the current caught us and swiftly swung us around. We tried to untie the rope, but it all happened too quickly and we found ourselves stopped dead in the water by the towline with our low, flat transom against the current. Within an instant the water flowed over the stern and the current pulled us underwater. I found a knife and at a depth of about five feet I managed to cut the line. We popped to the surface in the flooded boat. No one was hurt as we drifted in the swift current, but I was livid. Those two idiots screwing around with the anchor line put us in jeopardy, not to mention sinking our boat and probably ruining the engine.

Within an instant the water flowed over the stern and the current pulled us underwater.

We later beached the boat, bailed it out, and actually cleaned the water out of the engine enough to get it started and bring us home. Another larger boat came on the scene and was able to finally rescue the two. I didn't want to be anywhere near the sailboat crew when they came in. I would have been way less than cordial, so we left. We came to rescue them and they wound up sinking us. Any lesson in this? Nope.

A couple months later, on a (believe it or not) dark and stormy night, we received a second Mayday call. Gerri and I were having dinner at our house on Lee Stocking Island, when one of our staff banged on our door yelling that someone was in trouble and was calling for help. We turned on the radio and heard, "Mayday, Mayday, I'm sinking."

We immediately responded, "This is '*Bahama Hunter*' answering the Mayday call, please identify yourself. Where are you, what is your condition, describe your boat, are you in immediate personal danger, how many people aboard?" or something like that.

The response was confused, but we learned that the person calling was alone, his 35-foot, wooden sailboat was taking on water, and he could not pump enough to keep ahead of it. He didn't know where he was, but he thought his position was about 10 miles north of our island on the seaward side in Exuma Sound. Besides taking on water, he was being battered by six- to seven-foot seas. No other vessels or individuals responded. The Bahamas Air Sea Rescue Association, BASRA, had not heard the call. It was now up to us to respond.

With staff members Shawn and Digger, I promptly tested a portable pump and loaded it on an open, 20-foot boat with a 90-hp outboard. We prepared for the rescue with tow ropes, throw lines, lights, and such. We weren't eager to navigate 10 miles in pitch-black conditions through the shallow waters behind the Exuma chain of islands, but it would afford us the calmest seas. Under dark and misty conditions the many small islands were almost impossible to see. Their shorelines blended with the surrounding water. In fact, we had to cruise without running lights, which hindered our vision even further.

Gerri set up a communications station to keep in contact with the vessel. Within a short time the three of us were heading north. A stiff wind out of the northeast created a good chop even on the backside of the islands. A couple minutes later we were passing the channel between Lee Stocking Island and Adderly Cay where we could see out to sea. Just by chance we happened to see a light about a mile offshore. Its movement hinted that it was on a mast.

This guy was sinking and he was also stoned. I guess he figured that if he were going down to Davy Jones' locker, he might as well go with a smile on his face.

Although not very hopeful, we called Gerri and asked her to contact the captain of the stricken vessel and instruct him to flash his light on and off several times. Sure enough, the light flashed. Not believing we could be this lucky, we asked him to give us five flashes. The light went on and off five times! Luck was with us—the stricken boat was only about seven to eight minutes away. With a rush of excitement, we headed the boat into the channel and out to sea, directly for the light. Gerri alerted the captain that help was close by. The pounding head seas slowed us down to a few knots, but we still reached the vessel in about 10 minutes.

When we arrived, the boat was low in the water and wallowing in the waves. The mainsail was still up, but luffing in the wind. Shawn maneuvered our boat to the lee side and brought us close enough for Digger and me to jump over and quickly pass the water pump to the sinking vessel.

Although I have long forgotten his name (we later nicknamed him "Shipwreck"), I'll never forget the scene onboard the sailboat. The man, maybe in his mid-50s, was sitting on the top step of the boat's companionway with one hand pumping water and the other raising a lit joint to his mouth, which he pulled on loud enough to hear above the wind whistling through the rigging. The cabin below his feet was flooded within a few feet of the deck. This guy was sinking and he was also stoned. I guess he figured that if he were going down to Davy Jones' locker, he might as well go with a smile on his face.

"Hey, are you okay?" one of us yelled to him.

"Yeah, man, I'm okay," he answered, "getting a little tired of pumping though." A few more tokes on his joint and a grin gave us no confidence that he was going to be any help in his own rescue.

After setting the portable pump on deck, we started it and pushed Shipwreck aside to insert the suction hose into the cabin. We were relieved to see a stream of water coming out of the discharge side of the pump. In less than a minute though, the water stopped flowing even with the motor still running.

Pulling the suction hose out of the cabin revealed that it was clogged solid with plastic food wrapping. There was so much that it would probably take hours to free. We put an underwater light in the cabin and through the murk we could see that there was cellophane wrapping everywhere. I was thinking he must have some kinky relationship with the stuff. Unless we could clear it out of the cabin water, there would be no sense trying to ship another pump from the island. Besides, the boat was going down very soon.

We started to make out breaking waves on a shallow reef about one-half mile offshore. This meant we had already drifted almost a half mile and we were getting perilously close to the reef. There was no time to do anything else but take the sailboat in tow and hope we could make it to shallow water before the boat sank completely. We called to Shawn to bring the rescue boat alongside. I instructed Shipwreck to take down the mainsail, so we would have better towing control. Digger stayed onboard the sailboat and I transferred back to the rescue boat.

We were about to throw a towline when Shipwreck lowered the mainsail and then, to our amazement, he raised the jib. "Pull down all sails, damnit! Why did you raise the jib?" I shouted over the howling wind, but to no avail. The wind immediately caught the jib and sailed the boat right up on the reef.

The sailboat grounded on the reef and careened on its port side. Waves crashed over the decks. Digger started yelling to come and get them, but it was impossible to get any closer without putting us on the reef as well. "Put on your life vests and jump in before the boat breaks up!" we yelled back. It was a hairy situation. Over and over we shouted to them to leave the stricken vessel. Finally, Digger jumped overboard and swam toward us. His swimming was slow, as fear rapidly sapped his energy. When he finally reached our boat, there was nothing left in him. Once we dragged him onboard, he collapsed in the sloshing water in the bottom of the boat.

Our attention turned back to Shipwreck, but no further urging could get him to leave the sailboat. My legs started to shake with the thought that we were about to witness the death of this man. I was about to attempt to swim to the sailboat and throw Shipwreck overboard as a last resort when, miraculously, the wind in the jib, and probably the rocking action caused by the waves, pulled the boat off the reef and into clear water. We pulled alongside and Shawn transferred over. We started the tow around the point of the island and into shallow, protected water.

About a half hour later we reached calm waters and a depth of six feet just offshore, and we let the sailboat rest on the sandy bottom. It careened, but was partially exposed above water. It was high tide and we thought that if we could right the boat with lines from the mast attached to a tractor on shore, at low tide the water would be below the deck line and we could pump the boat dry and refloat it.

It was about three in the morning when we finally finished. Ol' Shipwreck announced that his wallet with all his money was still in the cabin and asked us to get it for him. Although dog-tired, Shawn and I took turns breath-hold diving with a mask and underwater light into the flooded cabin to see what we could find. The cabin was murky with all kinds of floating and partially floating material impeding us. The cellophane wrapping was everywhere. Over and over we dove into the cabin, not finding anything of real value and no wallet. After an hour of this, we decided to make just a few more attempts and then quit. On my last dive, I tried to go deeper into the sleeping quarters of the cabin, but I ran into a mass of floating stuff.

> I turned the light around to illuminate the object and, with a stroke of horror, I was looking at a hideous open mouth with large teeth heading toward me.

As I swam backward out of the cabin, my motions pulled the debris with me, including a large dark object. I turned the light around to illuminate the object and, with a stroke of horror, I was looking at a hideous open mouth with large teeth heading toward me. I yelled out loud underwater and started kicking backward toward the opening of the cabin followed by this thing. Was I hallucinating?

I had never seen anything like it. I came through the cabin door to the surface with the monster almost on top of me, its white teeth gleaming in my light. Catching my breath on the surface, the thing just passively moved by me revealing its identity. "It's a damn bear rug!" I shouted. "Who sails around the islands with a bear rug?"

As we later learned, Shipwreck, once a businessman from San Francisco, had hunted and killed this poor California black bear. Sometime in his career he burned out, dumped out, and became a boat bum, taking his rug with him. This was the end for me. It was almost four in the morning. I was exhausted and emotionally drained; I didn't even have the energy to fantasize about killing Shipwreck.

The next day we urged Shipwreck to prepare his boat and we would help get it refloated. Shipwreck, however, was now in a comfortable house on the island and apparently already settling in, so he decided to rest awhile before attempting any recovery of his boat. We told him that the wind was likely to switch to the northwest and his boat would no longer be in the lee of the island, so we should act soon. He wasn't concerned, and we were not going to do his work for him.

Sure enough, two days later the wind switched, kicking up waves that pounded Shipwreck's boat to pieces. He must have found a new supply of pot, because he didn't show much concern for his boat. He started talking about liking where he was and staying put on the island.

We had other ideas, but it still took over a month to get rid of him and only after threats of physically escorting him off the island. As a parting shot he left us holding the bag for several hundred dollars of his expenses. Even though we saved his life, Shipwreck hated our guts for making him leave—so much for gratitude.

The bastard didn't even give us the bear rug as a souvenir. Gerri and I later found it on the wall of the Fisherman's Inn in Barraterre, six miles by water to our south. That day we raised a glass of beer and declared good riddance to Shipwreck and farewell to my undersea monster that now hung on a barroom wall. Knowing what we know now, would we save Shipwreck again? Yes, but we would probably have dumped him and his rug off at Barraterre the very next day.

42

DROGS FROM THE SEA (AND AIR)

FROM THE VERY day we set foot on Lee Stocking Island to the day we left, it was clear that this part of the world was a major drug-running region. It was common to hear the familiar drone of engines from an old DC-3 and other aircraft with no running lights passing low over the island during the night. The Exuma Islands were used extensively by drug runners to either land planes laden with contraband directly on one of the remote runways found along the chain or drop bags of cocaine and other drugs to waiting boats, sometimes ditching the plane in the process. The U.S. Coast Guard patrolled the islands, but it was a vast area to cover with many islands where boats could hide. Several times during research projects, a fast-moving rubber boat loaded with Coast Guardsmen armed with automatic weapons came ripping out from behind a small cay to board us. We were happy that the Coast Guard was around and did not care about the inconvenience of the occasional boarding operation. We worried that the drug runners would find the large runway on Lee Stocking Island irresistible. We were on our own on the isolated island with a few firearms for protection and nothing else. The lone constable in Barraterre didn't even have a weapon and would be little help to us.

I often wondered what we would do if drug smugglers actually invaded the island. How would we cope? Stories of tourists having been murdered and their boat taken for one run of drugs just a few miles from us were disconcerting. It was well-known that some drug runners were brutal and would do anything to move and protect their cargo. Our mission was to conduct and support marine science, but the drug thing was all around us and we had to, at least, be mindful of the issue.

For the first several years, we placed a couple dozen steel 55-gallon barrels around the 3,000-foot runway in a random pattern, only moving them out of the way when we knew a plane was scheduled to arrive on the island. We were convinced that the barrels would dissuade any pilot from making an unauthorized landing on Lee Stocking Island, especially at night. But one afternoon, with all of the barrels distributed over the length of the runway, a small plane actually landed. Chuck and Lucinda Hepp, who were in charge of the island while we were away, saw the plane about to land and were expecting it to hit some barrels with dire consequences. Unbelievably, the pilot managed to maneuver the plane around the barrels without touching one. Chuck and Lucinda assumed that the plane was up to no good until they met the pilot and his family and found out that he had engine trouble with no choice but to land where he could. He was desperate, and the barrels could have killed them all. After that, the decision was made not to use the barrels anymore. We took our chances with the drug runners.

Late one night, Chuck, who was the island's maintenance supervisor, and I stood on a hill and watched a low-flying plane circle around. It occasionally flashed its lights, which was followed by signal lights coming from the sea. It was obviously a prearranged drug drop from the plane to a boat just off Lee Stocking Island. We watched for a half hour and then we heard the boat rev up and leave. Although we could not actually see what was happening in the dark moonless sky, it was clear that the drop was made. The plane flew north over the shallow side of the island chain. About five miles away we could see its landing lights turn on as the plane headed back toward us, and to our amazement, landed in the sea. From what I can remember, it was a stolen plane that they ditched in 10 feet of water. Its passengers were probably picked up by the same boat that received the drugs. This and other ditched planes were clearly visible in the shallow sea when we flew over the 110-mile Exuma chain toward Nassau.

We found out that drugs like cocaine were commonly placed in two-kilo plastic bags and sealed in waterproof fiberglass cloth and resin, then packed into large burlap bags to be dropped from a plane into the sea. Marijuana was dropped in bales and became known as "square groupers" when they washed up on beaches from time to time.

There were other incidents, and the more we experienced being in the drug corridor from Columbia, South America, to the U.S., the more we felt vulnerable. There were some locals on nearby Great Exuma Island that had the reputation of being involved with the drug trade and we went to great lengths to keep them away. One of our young female employees started dating a man who we suspected of being involved, which gave us fits. I couldn't keep him totally off the island, but he was certainly not welcome to spend the night. It would have been too easy for him to set up a drug pickup or drop in the middle of the night. Of course this caused some dismay for the young lady, but as far as I was concerned there was no negotiation when it came to our safety and the reputation of the island and research center. One drug-related incident involving the island would have been the death knell of our program.

One drug-related incident involving the island would have been the death knell of our program.

Although constantly vigilant, we never imagined being involved in a major incident with "the bad guys." On the evening of March 7, 1985, at around dusk, we

Author removing the shotgun from the R/V Undersea Hunter *used to capture two suspects following the drug bust on Lee Stocking Island.*

had just finished dinner when a typical tropical rainstorm hit the island. There was little wind, but the isolated storm was dumping heavy rain on us. It came down so hard that it was difficult to see more than a few feet in any direction. Gerri and I were sitting on the roofed-over porch, when we thought we heard the muffled sound of an aircraft engine, as if a plane were landing, which seemed to come from the direction of our airstrip. It was difficult to hear anything over the roar of the very heavy rain. I thought it worth checking out and took the island's small van to the airstrip. The rain continued to make visibility difficult, blocking out most of the landing strip. I drove partway up the runway without seeing anything, decided we were probably hearing things, and returned home.

At about 11:15 p.m., after we had gone to bed and the skies had cleared, we again heard the sound of aircraft engines, now different but distinct, as if a plane were taxiing on the runway. We knew something was up at this point. I jumped in the van and drove over a small hill where I could see most of the airstrip. There, in the partial moonlight and to my horror, was a small twin-engine plane sitting in the parking area just below the hill. I couldn't see anyone by the plane, and I decided to return to base for assistance.

We immediately woke Chuck and Lucinda next door and told them about the plane. Chuck got dressed, took the twelve-gauge shotgun, and we returned to the airstrip in the van. Just as we cleared the top of the hill we could make out the forms of two people walking toward us. Chuck stayed in the back seat of the van with the gun out of sight, and I stopped the vehicle and got out to confront the two, now identified as men, in the headlights. I asked them to stop and made it known that there was another person with me. Although I didn't mention that he was armed, I assumed it was implicit to the two. Apparently they had seen me the first time I came to the runway and decided to show themselves. One was a short, middle-aged, rather scruffy-looking man with a fixed, humorless expression who spoke a little English with a Spanish accent, and the other was a young American, maybe in his late 20s.

I asked them why they landed on our runway in the middle of the night and reminded them that it was illegal to fly over these islands after dark. They told me that they were tourists and had lost their way, finally running out of fuel. They saw our runway close by and made an emergency landing. After about 10 minutes of questioning, it was obvious to Chuck and me that they were lying through their teeth. They couldn't even give an accurate account of where they came from and where they were going. We were concerned that there may be others who did not show themselves. Somewhat nervous with the situation, we urged the two to get in the van and come back to our base until we could sort things out. Gerri and Lucinda were waiting back at our house, ready to call the Bahamian authorities if necessary, when we arrived with the men.

We questioned the men for some time and became even more suspicious that they were drug runners. If it had been their plane we heard earlier in the evening during the storm, they would have had ample time to hide any drugs before we realized the plane had landed. The young pilot, Jeff Bissell, asked if he could make a call and we said it would be okay. He picked up the phone and stood there for a time, then hung up the phone and said he didn't know what to say. All this time, Chuck was standing guard on the porch with full view of the room and the fully loaded shotgun cradled in his arms. Our other weapon, a semi-automatic assault rifle, was close by. One of the men, I believe it was Jeff, remarked about "all the guns" on the island. By this time, the other island residents had been alerted, as well as the crew of the *Undersea Hunter*, which was tied up at the dock right outside our house. The crew also had a semi-automatic weapon, so it gave the illusion that we were heavily armed—exactly what we wanted. We inspected the plane and found that the back seats had been removed. By this time it was obvious we needed to go the next step.

We finally told the two men that we were not satisfied with their answers and we were placing them under citizen's arrest and calling the Bahamian authorities in

Nassau. The older man, Alvaro Verplank, who said very little throughout the night and stared at me with a stoic, menacing expression, remained silent as Jeff blurted out, "Can we make a deal?" That was it—I knew these guys were guilty of something and we needed to let the police take over. We called the authorities in Nassau and were informed that there was a strike force in the Exumas and that they would come as soon as possible. We placed the two men in the lounge of the *Undersea Hunter* under armed guard and offered them cookies and drinks. Although I was convinced and downright pissed that they were drug runners, and most likely there were drugs stashed nearby endangering everyone on the island, we decided to treat them cordially until it was all sorted out. With scientists, boat crew, and island staff pressed into service as armed guards and lookouts for more bad guys, we waited nervously for the police to arrive. Everyone gathered by the dock in case we determined it was too dangerous to stay. In that event, we planned to board the *Undersea Hunter* and leave the island.

About four hours later, just before dawn, we heard the faint noise of a boat engine and wondered if it were the police or friends of Verplank and Bissell. Minutes later, a boat operated by one of our Barraterre neighbors arrived with four Bahamian Police Strike Force officers and George Forbes, Police Inspector of the Exuma and Ragged Island District. The strike force officers were big guys in full camouflage uniforms with British Sterling automatic weapons hanging from straps around their necks. They had just come from an operation south of Georgetown. They interviewed us to get a better lay of the land and then turned their attention to the two men on the *Undersea Hunter*.

Some time later they told me to accompany them and the men to the plane. I was to be a witness that they were not going to be abused. After inspecting the plane and finding only a hatchet on the back floor, one of the officers, who obviously had Jeff pegged as the weaker of the two, started to slap the hatchet in his hand saying, "Have you seen the movie *Friday the 13th*, Jeff?" They invited Jeff to come into the bushes and show them where the drugs were hidden. Jeff refused, and was visibly scared. After first light, a search around the runway produced nothing and the policemen loaded the two men, now in handcuffs, and left by boat for a jail cell in Georgetown, 25 miles away.

We were alone once again with the plane still on the runway parking area and convinced that the men had stashed drugs somewhere on the 600-acre island

We were alone once again with the plane still on the runway parking area and convinced that the men had stashed drugs somewhere on the 600-acre island. We felt more vulnerable than ever. To make matters worse, several of the crew on the *Undersea Hunter* defied orders and, convinced that drug runners always carry a suitcase full of payoff cash, sneaked out to the runway to search the surrounding vegetation for hidden treasure. I was livid, but we had bigger problems and I would confront the idiots later. One of the boat's crew turned out in full camouflage uniform, black boots and all, with, believe it or not, handcuffs hanging off his pants. He walked around brandishing an AR-15 from the boat, and I thought this guy was more dangerous than the drug runners—a Walter Mitty militia-wannabe. Another island resident also came dressed in partial camo. I was amazed at how people reacted to this crazy situation, making my position as director of all policy and operations for our program very interesting indeed.

Later in the morning John Perry and his pilot Ralph Knight arrived from West Palm Beach. We gave them a briefing and then started a search along the perimeter of the runway for signs that drugs were on the island. A very short time into the search, someone discovered heavy tracks into dense brush at the far end of the airstrip. I had instructed everyone on the search to not approach any suspicious area, but to report back to me. We called Inspector Forbes in Georgetown, told him what we saw, and asked him to come back to Lee Stocking Island as quickly as possible. Forbes commandeered a private plane and its pilot at the Georgetown airport and arrived an hour or so later.

Accompanied by a few of us, the policeman went to the disturbed site and followed a trampled path straight to a large mound of burlap bags. On top of the bags was a location detector that all planes are required to carry onboard in the

Bahamian police examining captured plane that landed with over 1,500 pounds of cocaine on Lee Stocking Island, Bahamas.

event of a crash or some other emergency. Each burlap bag contained many two-kilo packages of cocaine wrapped in fiberglass. The total weight, we later found out, was 1,523 pounds. It was obvious that the cocaine was prepared to be dropped into the sea from a plane to a waiting boat. When it finally hit us that we were standing next to a fortune in drugs, everyone, including Forbes, became visibly nervous. The location device was placed on the bags to guide someone to the drugs. We were sure, considering the value, it would be soon and the bad guys would go to any lengths to get it all back. In fact, earlier an unidentified plane had circled the island several times and had called us by radio asking for the tail number of the plane that landed.

Forbes instructed us to move the drugs to John Perry's plane and told Ralph Knight that he was to fly it to Georgetown immediately. When Forbes, who only carried a small handgun, took our AR-15 and said that he was going to guard us as we loaded the dope on the plane, we really became nervous. There was talk in the Bahamas about a few officials being involved in the drug trade and we didn't know much about Forbes. We contacted an acquaintance onboard a sailboat in our anchorage and told him of our concern. There we were in the middle of nowhere, in a foreign country with millions of dollars worth of cocaine, and an unknown policeman holding a gun over us. "Suppose he goes batshit," someone said, "and decides to eliminate us to get the drugs."

We were literally defenseless and we didn't think our distrust was unfounded. The boatman, a Vietnam vet, carried a high-powered rifle on his vessel and he agreed to sit hidden and cover us from a hill overlooking the runway. It was a scary thought and a potential non-winning situation. If something did happen and the policeman was shot, how could we explain it? I shuddered at the thought. We were here to study the ocean and coral reefs. How did we get into this mess? During the half hour or so it took to move the drugs to the plane, we kept one eye on our job and one eye on Inspector Forbes. When the plane was loaded, filling the baggage and passenger compartments, Ralph took off with Forbes for Georgetown and the load was placed in a jail cell right across from Bissell and Verplank, who I was told became very agitated. I guess they had hoped that their buddies would have retrieved the drugs from the island by then.

The incident was touted in Nassau newspapers as the largest cocaine bust in Bahamian history and both men were transferred to a Nassau jail without bail pending trial. Over the next week we were concerned about the plane remaining on the island and asked the Georgetown police to send officers to guard us until it was taken away. Some hours later two policemen arrived by boat. One was a seasoned officer carrying a pistol-grip pump shotgun. The other was a very young, skinny kid in a constable's uniform with no weapon. After introductions, I asked the young one why he didn't have a gun and he told me he was not yet qualified to carry one. I couldn't help but ask him if he intended to throw rocks if bad guys came back for the plane or to exact revenge on us. He just laughed and shrugged his shoulders. We didn't have much faith in our police protectors.

To make matters worse, they were friends with some of the Bahamian workers on the island and the two disappeared the next evening for several hours. We later learned that they went fishing with their friends. From then on we kept our weapons close by until the plane was released and flown out. As usual, we felt completely on our own. We were not only responsible for treating injuries and serving as our own Coast Guard and ocean rescue, but we were our own security force as well. Our primary focus of marine research was being pushed into the background. An interesting side note—although we had illegal weapons on the island and we readily displayed them, the police left us alone and never mentioned it.

On April 1st I was summoned to Nassau to testify for the Bahamian police against the two defendants. In the Bahamas, the Commissioner of Police is also the prosecutor. I was fascinated by the Bahamian judicial system, which in this case had no jury. The judge was also the court recorder. He wrote down the testimony of witnesses, who sat close to him, all in longhand. His transcripts only recorded the witness and did not include the questions from either the prosecutor or the defense attorney. Inspector Forbes and I were the only two witnesses.

Before the proceedings, I had only spent about 20 minutes with the police commissioner, which I thought was strange. It was the first time I had any contact with the prosecutor's office and they asked very few questions. When the two defendants were brought into the court, I couldn't help but notice that Verplank's expression was no longer the cocky and menacing look he displayed on Lee Stocking Island. Bissell looked downright scared. After several hours of testimony, during which Inspector Forbes and I were required to describe the incident from beginning to end, the trial was abruptly over. The judge stated that the evidence did not provide a nexus between the accused and the drugs, which had been found in the bushes some hours after the men had been taken from the scene. The two men were acquitted and discharged. I couldn't believe it—these guys were guilty. I wondered why the police hadn't brought drug-sniffing dogs to the plane, which had to have been full of cocaine residue. I guess the drugs just fell from the sky in a neat heap with a locator on top.

I thought that was the end of it all, although I slept with one eye open and a gun next to my bed for a year, wondering if the owners of the cocaine were pissed off enough to come back and seek revenge. I called the local constable in Barraterre to ask for the best way to contact him if there were any other trouble. His answer was priceless and I paraphrase a little here. "Oh no, mon, don't call me," he said. "Those boys play rough and I don't have any ammonishun." I wondered if we should even continue with the project if more incidents like this were possible.

Some of 53 kilos of cocaine that floated onto the beaches of Lee Stocking Island, Bahamas. Spoof photo taken before turning the find over to local police. From left to right: Chuck Hepp, John Clement, Lucinda Hepp, Jane Clement, Gerri Wenz, Rob McGeachin, Bob Wicklund.

A break came for us soon afterward when the U.S. stepped up local drug enforcement. The DEA established a base in Georgetown and brought in several Army Blackhawk helicopters. We heard the low-flying helicopters almost every night. They flew without lights and we saw only brief flashes from the crew's night scopes as they patrolled the long string of Exuma islands for drug smugglers. On several occasions a Blackhawk landed on our runway at night just for practice. As the helicopter sat down, we could only see the eerie spinning light caused by calcium carbonate dust being blown off the runway, hitting and lighting up the huge rotating propellers with millions of tiny sparks.

The number of low-flying, darkened drug planes passing overhead in the middle of the night declined dramatically after the DEA arrived in the Exumas. However, one afternoon a young employee, who grew up in a Midwestern farm area, returned from exploring the beach and told us that there must have been some kind of fishing accident, because there were homemade fishing floats all over the beach in a nearby cove. When we went to see for ourselves, our hearts skipped a beat or two. The so-called floats were fiberglass packages just like the ones in the burlap bags in our drug bust. A drop had been made somewhere close by and a bag broke open, scattering the packages until they floated up onto our beaches.

Luckily it was the weekend and only a few people were on the island. We quietly gathered up the packages and got them to the police before the word got out. In my mind, the most important thing to achieve was to keep Lee Stocking Island out of the drug limelight as much as possible. Once again we called Inspector Forbes, who came immediately by plane, and we presented him with over 53 kilos of cocaine. Forbes left and we never heard a thing about the drugs, where they went, or how they were handled. John and Jane Clement had flown their private plane from Freeport for a visit that day and we all had a good time taking pictures with the pile of drugs before Forbes picked them up.

Several years later, I was contacted by the U.S. Attorney's office in Atlanta, Georgia, and told that the plane involved in the Lee Stocking Island incident had crashed somewhere on the Gulf of Mexico with drugs onboard. I also learned that the Feds had linked Verplank and Bissell to a large Miami drug-smuggling ring, indicted them, and were about to put them on trial with 39 other defendants. Verplank had jumped bail and disappeared, but Bissell would be present at the trial. The U.S. Attorney asked me to testify again and told me it would probably only take about 15 minutes of my time. Perry's pilot, Ralph Knight, was also summoned to testify.

Just before I was called to the witness stand, having passed through two security gates and metal detectors, I was led into a waiting room. There was an older woman sitting across from me and we were the only two in the room. She appeared visibly upset and after a few minutes looked up at me and said, "Thank you for not shooting my son." Startled, I said, "Pardon me?" and she said it again. She was Jeff Bissell's mother. That was all that was said until I left to take the stand. I was very uncomfortable and felt sorry for the woman, but I wondered why she made the statement. I had never, nor had anyone else on my staff, threatened or pointed a weapon at anyone, or even implied any such thing.

"What were you afraid of, that they were going to steal your little fish?" I couldn't help but laugh; so did everyone else in the room.

Once on the stand, I didn't get off for five hours with two attorneys firing questions at me, and accusing me of abusing their clients, acting unlawfully, and so on. I was coached earlier to just tell it like it happened with no elaboration, which I did, and that made it easy. After a few hours the lead defense attorney, who looked like a nice older guy to me, became obviously frustrated and blurted out something like, "Tell me, Mr. Wicklund, why did you act so brashly when my clients landed on the island, with your guns and all. What were you afraid of, that they were going to steal your little fish?" I couldn't help but laugh; so did everyone else in the room.

On another occasion he accused us of pointing a gun into the room and being ready to shoot when we were interrogating the two men. It was true that Chuck

Hepp was outside on the porch with a shotgun, but it was cradled in his arms. The prosecutor followed up, asking me again if we were ready to shoot the men, and I explained that it was a small room containing Gerri, Chuck's wife, Lucinda, me, and the two men. If Chuck fired into the room from where he was standing, the scattergun filled with double-ought buckshot would likely have killed us all, so it was nonsense that Chuck would even come close to shooting. He was there in case there was another unwelcome visitor around we didn't know about.

After the long testimony, I left Atlanta and learned some time later that 40 of the 41 defendants being tried that day, including Jeff Bissell, were convicted, but I never did hear of their sentencing. In a way, I felt sorry for Jeff. He was a 27-year-old bush pilot who got involved with the wrong people for money and now he was going to jail, probably for a long time.

That was the last of the drug problems for us. The DEA and Coast Guard working with the Bahamian authorities pretty much shut down the drug trafficking along the Exuma chain of islands.

During preparation for the first Iraq war, the military called back the Blackhawk helicopters. When one was passing Lee Stocking Island on its way back to the States, it lost one of its two jet engines and was forced to make an emergency landing on our runway. For the next two days, we put the crew up and assisted them in changing engines when a new one was flown in. We were sorry to see them go.

Later on, we met a new foreign officer assigned to the U.S. Embassy in Nassau under Ambassador Chic Hecht. He learned of our involvement in the drug bust and recommended to the ambassador that we receive a citation from the U.S. Government. Apparently, Mr. Hecht, who was previously a one-term senator from Nevada, had no interest. We never heard from him. Knowing his reputation as ambassador to the Bahamas, this was not surprising.

43

SUPPORTING SCIENCE WITH A BANG

I THOUGHT I KNEW what it took to support a scientific operation and science in general until we hooked up with deepwater geologists on the island. Bob Ginsburg, a well-known marine geologist from the Rosenstiel School of Marine and Atmospheric Sciences, applied for a project to look at the geological history of the deep drop-off in Exuma Sound. It would require a small submersible to place C-4 explosives into shallow caves down to depths of 1,000 feet.

Bob got all the necessary permits to purchase and transport the explosives to Lee Stocking Island from the U.S. and Bahamian governments. We hired the two-man *Delta* submersible and placed it aboard our research vessel, *Undersea Hunter,* which then sailed from Florida to Exuma Sound to start the project.

Under Bob's direction, the *Delta* crew placed C-4 explosives at different locations on the almost vertical wall along the sound. A long primer cord attached to the explosives was connected to the sub's surface-support ship. Once in place and the sub recovered aboard the ship, the C-4 package was set off, creating a large explosion that shattered the rocks inside the cave. The sub was then re-launched to recover small rocks from the site with its hydraulic manipulator system.

Bob got his samples. Of course, we biologists were concerned about the damage the explosives did to the deep ecosystem, but we didn't have enough funding for extra sub dives to observe the explosion sites.

After the project, Bob realized that he had over-bought the C-4 and was concerned about bringing the leftovers back to the States. He had a whole box of explosives, caps, and primer cord and asked if we could store it on the island for future use. In my naiveté, I said sure and stored the box under my desk with the caps in a drawer. C-4, I assumed, was benign until it was set off with the caps and primer cord.

So for almost a year the explosives served as my footrest, until one day I was reading about how lightning or even static electricity could set off the caps. Even if they were not in direct contact, the explosives could be detonated. I looked under my desk and at the drawer where the caps were—only about five feet away—and jumped up and away from the desk. Oh man, I thought, here were enough explosives to wipe out this whole end of the island. I grabbed the box of C-4 and moved it to another part of the island, away from all of us and the caps. I wished that directions had come along with the package.

A year or so later we built a house that needed a septic system. This required the use of explosives to blast through hard limestone. I figured with all the C-4 on the island and to save money, who needed an explosives expert? So I called Gene Shinn, a marine geologist with the U.S.G.S., and received a 15-minute lesson over the phone on how to place the explosive and rig it up to blast the rock at the septic system site.

Our island maintenance manager, Carlton, and I placed pieces of the C-4 in holes previously drilled by geologists taking core samples around the island to identify sediment layers. We plugged the primer cord into the explosives as instructed, rolled it out a few feet, attached the caps, and ran 50 feet of electrical wire from the caps to us. We used a dump truck for protection and its battery for setting off the charge.

After checking my notes quite a few times to make sure all was right, it was time. I took the two bare ends of the wire and touched them to the poles of the battery. Both of us instinctively jumped under the truck, but nothing happened. Carlton and I were now a bit nervous. What did we do wrong? We were, of course, out of our realm and sat down to discuss our next move.

I still had the two ends of the wire in my hands and, while we were talking, I inadvertently reversed the wires and touched the battery poles. BLAM! The sky was filled with a few tons of shattered rock and dust. Carlton and I once again jumped under the truck, but way too late to be of any help. Our hearts were beating wildly. We were successful—no one was hurt—and we now considered ourselves to be explosive experts. We were pumped—we wanted to blow up something else.

Thankfully, the last of the explosives on the island was used to dispose of one of our older research vessels, a rather bizarre ending to something so important to my early diving and marine science career. The *Challenger*, which had been the primary research vessel for the Sandy Hook Marine Lab and captained by my father, Irv, was decommissioned and sold as a fishing boat sometime in the 70s. By some strange coincidence, my brother Don later bought it and contracted with the State of New Jersey to take kids from inner cities on marine science cruises. When we downsized our fleet of large vessels, we bought the now very inexpensive *Challenger*. Don stayed on as captain for a while, since he knew all the old boat's idiosyncrasies.

The *Challenger*, once again, did its job as a research and cargo vessel for the Caribbean Marine Research Center. Two years later, during a trip from Florida with a full load of cargo and in heavy seas, the old wooden hull finally gave out, twisting the vessel's keel. After a thorough inspection, we decided the *Challenger* was finished.

When some of our Bahamian neighbors found out that we were going to get rid of the boat, we had a number of offers to buy it, but considering the condition of the keel, it was too unsafe to sell.

Gerri and I were now based stateside. The new island manager, Bill Head, and his staff wanted to take the *Challenger* to deep water, burn it, and sink it, but thinking the fire might attract too much attention, they decided to use the remainder of the C-4 explosives to blow it to bits. A lot of people heard the explosion and called around to see what had happened. Fortunately, it ended there and the poor old *Challenger*, almost a member of the family, slipped into the sea and into history.

44
HAITI

One of our major projects on Lee Stocking Island was marine aquaculture or, more precisely, mariculture. We believed that the depletion of wild stocks would make fish farming an important source of seafood in the future. Following an assessment of different species such as grouper, snapper, and conch, we decided that a tilapia species was worth exploring. Tilapia is a group of over a hundred freshwater species originating in many regions of Africa. At the time, tilapia was considered a trash fish which had been imported into the U.S. to control aquatic weeds in waterways, ponds, and such. Escaped tilapia established unwanted populations in many warm regions of the country. The tilapia was, on the other hand, a fast-growing, resilient species with a good-tasting flesh and, most importantly, it ate just about anything, including algae.

Although we originally rejected the possibility of ever making this fish a viable marine farming candidate, we capitulated when our research discovered a hybrid that could tolerate living in brackish water. Over the next few years, the project, headed by Wade Watanabe, became a success. We adapted the fish to live and thrive in full seawater after spawning them in freshwater, and then grew thousands of tilapia in seawater ponds and cages. One of our concerns was the possibility that escapees could establish a population in Bahamian waters, so the fish were sex-reversed to make them all males. We also conducted research to see if they could spawn in full seawater at salinity levels of 36 parts per thousand. Fortunately, the Exuma Islands were surrounded by full-salinity, sometimes higher, oceanic seawater. Even so, there were no guarantees that the species would not be introduced into local waters.

Following the success of the tilapia mariculture project, we wanted to extend our knowledge to Bahamians interested in starting fish farms, as well as to other Caribbean islands. But, it was Haiti that caught our attention. We thought that bringing our mariculture technology there would make the most impact.

Haiti is only about 500 miles from Lee Stocking Island and it's the poorest nation in the western hemisphere. It is a nation of over six million people with just about all but a few living in serious poverty. A longtime victim of greed and its own politics, Haiti at one time was rich in resources and contributed in no small way to France's wealth. For over 100 years, Haiti supplied France with sugar, rum, coffee, and cotton, based on a slave economy. A slave rebellion led to a 13-year war of liberation against Haitian colonists and Napoleon's army, resulting in Haiti becoming the hemisphere's second independent republic in 1804.

Troubles racked the country, including a long civil war. The U.S. occupied Haiti for 13 years in the early twentieth century to maintain some order. After many troubled years, Dr. François "Papa Doc" Duvalier declared himself President-for-Life in 1964 and formed the vicious and corrupt Tonton Macoute, a paramilitary group that carried out his policies, striking fear in all Haitians. Duvalier's dictatorship marked one of the worst periods in Haitian history. Many Haitians were killed or exiled under his rule, and some simply disappeared. He later turned the country over to his son "Baby Doc" and things only got worse. When his son finally fled the country, it was left in financial ruin. The problems in Haiti persist and, while it was our intention to help the Haitians, we were about to be given a lesson in reality.

Our first attempt to talk to Haitian officials led nowhere. The government was in its usual turmoil and getting a project established in the country would require another tactic. Just by chance, some American visitors to Lee Stocking were

Raising saltwater-tolerant tilapia off the coast of Haiti.

PHOTO COURTESY ROBERT WICKLUND

volunteers with a Baptist missionary project in Haiti. When we told them of our interest in extending our fish farming techniques to Haiti, they were very excited and invited us to tour the country with them and explore the possibilities of teaching Haitians how to raise their own fish. Gerri, Bori Olla, his wife, Jill, who was also a marine biologist, and I made our first trip to Haiti.

Our mission was to scope out the need and possibilities in extending our aquaculture program to teach Haitians how to grow their own fish for subsistence and possibly for commercialization. We were, at first, taken aback by the obvious and abject poverty everywhere. Children, as well as adults, followed us everywhere, constantly begging for money, our watches, and even our shoes. When we toured a salt marsh as a possible site to grow fish, at least 30 locals appeared out of nowhere to accompany us. In some of the remotest places, followers were there out of curiosity, not necessarily to ask for something. Many people had rarely seen foreigners.

During our first visit to the island nation, we saw malnourishment everywhere. Many young people had orange hair and extended stomachs, sure signs of severe malnutrition. It was heartbreaking and strengthened our resolve to try to help them. If we could get just a few people to grow the salt-tolerant tilapia on their own, we thought it might develop into something bigger, perhaps a cottage industry that would bring cash as well as food to these poor people.

Our plan was simple. We would provide a one-meter-cubed floating cage with enough tilapia fry and food to grow the fish to about one pound in six months to each person who wanted to participate. We would also train them in general husbandry of the fish. The Haitians would care for and feed the fish twice a day until harvest, at which time they could either eat them or sell all or some for cash. Two of our staff scientists prepared to move to Haiti to oversee the project and conduct research.

We spent a lot of time on the Haitian coasts, talking to fishermen and breath-hold diving along the shallow shorelines. We never saw any fish larger than several inches long, whether in the water or on the beaches where the fishermen were drying their catches in the sun. The waters were virtually fished out, but interestingly the local fishermen told us there were plenty of fish available. This perception by fishermen of abundance is not unlike many other parts of the world. Even in the face of obviously declining fish stocks, fishermen will argue that things are alright. Maybe it's just protecting their turf from regulation or maybe they just don't know. In the case of the Haitian fishermen, it's most likely that they have lived so long with so little left in the sea that it's all relative to them.

During our tour of villages we met a so-called "Mayor," who was obviously a tough guy and controlled the village with an iron hand. He welcomed us and assured us that the locals would cooperate with our project. We later heard that he was suspected by some to be a former member of Papa Doc's notorious Tonton

Macoute. Many Haitians believed, although it supposedly disappeared with Papa Doc, that the organization was still alive but much more segmented and secretive.

After several trips and meeting Haitian families through the Baptist church in Fort Liberté on the northern coast, we found people who were eager to participate. We selected the growing sites along the adjoining bay and set out to build cages and spawn tilapia fry on Lee Stocking Island for the project. The connection to the church gave us a base from which to work. Churches were really the only sources of infrastructure in the countryside. Although the population of the country is about 90 percent Catholic (and 100 percent voodoo), the Baptist church had an agricultural compound on the north coast that best suited our needs. We worked out a deal with them to lease an apartment on the compound and some equipment, including a boat and vehicle, for one of our scientists during the project. The connection also gave us access to the missionary flights that flew in and out of Haiti several times a week. Missionary flights were also the only way to travel by air within the country. There were commercial flights from Miami and other locations into Port-au-Prince, but none beyond that.

The connection to the church gave us a base from which to work. Churches were really the only sources of infrastructure in the countryside.

We were in this strange foreign country and, except for our dealings with Immigration and Customs as we traveled into and out of Haiti, we had no contact with any government official. As far as anyone was concerned, we were missionaries. Most of our travel to and from Haiti was either on the Perry plane or on an old missionary DC-3 to Cap-Haitien, not far from Fort Liberté and also on the north coast.

On one of the early trips, we brought about a thousand pounds of frozen tilapia from our ponds on Lee Stocking Island to distribute in Haitian villages. Half of the fish never got past the custom officials. They took the boxes from us and carried them away. It was the price we had to pay to get the remaining fish and ourselves into the county with as little hassle as possible. The distribution of the fish was also problematic. With a few missionaries from West Virginia and the pastor of the local church, we went to a small village just outside Fort Liberté to hand out the remaining 500 pounds or so of tilapia.

The word got out within minutes of our arrival, and we were surrounded by people pushing and yelling for their share. It quickly became chaotic and potentially dangerous. We tried our best to give fish to as many people as possible, but they started to push further and grab at the boxes. We could do nothing more than step back and let it all play out. When the last fish disappeared, we left the village somewhat shaken by the experience and wiser to the absolute desperation of these poor people. The next time we brought fish to Haiti, we added enough for the customs people and then gave them to the church to quietly distribute to their parishioners.

Finally, the project was underway. We flew into Cap-Haitien with the first batch of cages and fish, traveled to Fort Liberté, and set the cages up in the bay, each with enough fry to grow at least a hundred pounds of tilapia in about six months. We hit our first snafu when we met with the families selected by the church to begin the process.

It turned out that, to a person, the Haitians selected were deathly afraid of the water and were not willing to get in a boat, much less wade off the beach to service the cages. We couldn't believe it. No one thought to mention this to us when we met the groups earlier. We had even shown them pictures of fish cages floating in the water. I almost lost it. Our project was going down the tubes without even beginning and we were left holding the proverbial bag. Fear of the ocean was not uncommon among people of the West Indies—we should have known. Michael Rust, one of our scientists who moved to Haiti to oversee the project, quickly approached a group of local fishermen to see if they were interested in being involved. Spending much of their time on the water, it should have been easy for them. They said they would be interested, but only if paid a salary. They told us once again that they could catch all the fish they wanted and growing fish in cages for their own use was not worth their time. Strange logic, but we were backed into a corner and agreed to a pay several fishermen a monthly salary to oversee and care for 10 cages for the duration of the project.

It turned out that, to a person, the Haitians selected were deathly afraid of the water and were not willing to get in a boat, much less wade off the beach to service the cages.

Over the next few months the project seemed to be moving along. Jane Brass, a sociologist working for the center, joined Michael to conduct a socio-economic study on the feasibility of saltwater cage culture of tilapia in Haiti.

Over time, things started to get ugly politically. For various reasons there were protests all over the country and roadblocks by machete-wielding men set up close to our working area. Attempting to cross them could be fatal to anyone. We started to worry about Michael and Jane living and working in Fort Liberté. If they were caught on the wrong side of a roadblock, they could be prevented from reaching the compound, food, and water for several weeks.

A second, non-lethal but worrisome problem was that within just a couple of months the tilapia were much larger than most fish caught in the ocean, and the locals wanted to harvest them long before they were big enough to be of any commercial value. It was a hard sell to people who were hungry to wait another few months to eat or sell the fish.

The increasing threat of violence was making it difficult to continue the project. I saw it personally early one morning, waiting to fly from Port-au-Prince to Cap-Haitien. Following a commercial flight from Miami, I arranged to fly to Cap-Haitien with a missionary pilot in a single-engine plane the next morning. I arrived at the general aviation section of the airport about 6:00 a.m. and waited in a room alone with a sleepy soldier sitting at a desk holding an automatic weapon. Several minutes later, a Haitian came into the room and started arguing with the soldier. They shouted at each other in Creo-French, which, of course, I didn't understand. I tried to ignore it all, but the argument became more violent until the soldier picked up his gun and pointed it at the man. My heart jumped as I imagined being the only witness to a shooting and the soldier turning his gun on me as well.

My heart jumped as I imagined being the only witness to a shooting and the soldier turning his gun on me as well.

I looked around for the nearest exit. If shots were fired, I would beat feet to the nearest door and run like hell. I was sitting frozen in my seat waiting for something to happen, when the man suddenly turned around and left. The soldier put the weapon down, smiled at me, and went back to sleep, leaving me sitting in my own sweat. I believe it could have been a disaster, but on the other hand, maybe I just didn't understand the Haitian mind. In any event, it was unnerving.

The missionary pilot arrived with two other passengers. We went out to the plane and were asked to hold hands under the wing and pray. Standing there with heads bowed, I hoped there was going to be more to the pre-flight check than just a "wing and a prayer." There were safety checks after all, and the small plane successfully cleared the 9,000-foot-high mountains all the way to Cap-Haitien.

Along the way we saw the devastation caused by the Haitian charcoal industry. Charcoal is used almost exclusively by the Haitians for cooking, which has led to the almost complete destruction of the forests. We could see smoke coming from the tops of even the highest peaks, where people were making charcoal from the few trees left. The charcoal would eventually be carried down the mountains to local villages on their backs.

The desperation of the people and destruction of this country were difficult to witness. No trees, no fish, no infrastructure, and malnutrition everywhere. The poorest country in the western hemisphere was less than 600 miles from the richest in the world, which made it all that more tragic.

The combination of events and our concerns for the safety of our two scientists living and working in Haiti prompted us to terminate the project after a long year and bring our people back to Lee Stocking Island.

In our paper published in the *Journal of the World Aquaculture Society*, we concluded that, at least preliminarily, in the comparison of production costs to potential market prices, saltwater cage culture of tilapia was not economically feasible on an artisanal scale and it was a high financial risk on a commercial scale. Even so, we believed that further study could reveal ways to cut back on costs using local feeds, and if a transportation system were to be incorporated into a business, prospects for success would increase.

Although Haiti has not changed much since our project, I still hope to go back some day.

45

MARINE ANIMALS SHOW THEIR STUFF

THE VASTNESS OF the three dimensional sea makes observations and descriptions of even the largest of creatures difficult at best. Consider the giant squid, one of the largest animals on earth and most likely quite common, living within reach of much of our technology. Even though submersibles have spent a significant number of hours in the giant squid's habitat, around 3,000 feet deep and in different regions of the oceans, none of the animals has ever been seen from one. The squid has never been seen alive or photographed in its natural habitat, except for a few brief, distant photographs taken by Japanese scientists in 2005. The giant squid and the even bigger colossal squid remain great mysteries of the sea.

Only two specimens of colossal squid have been collected, one caught in a fishing net in the waters of Antarctica. These differ from the giant squid in that they have hooks, which rotate 360 degrees, on the end of some tentacles—an awesome, scary killing machine. Both squids grow to enormous sizes, exceeding 60 feet long and possibly weighing over a ton.

While giant squid are occasionally caught in nets or washed ashore, much of what we know about them comes from records of whaling ships. These squid are a mainstay of the sperm whale's diet and remnants have been found in captured whale's stomachs.

Dan Aspenleiter, captain of the research vessel *Cape Fear* owned by the University of North Carolina Wilmington, described some interesting catches when he fished commercially from this same boat years before. He fished specifically for wreckfish in water about 3,000 feet deep off the east coast. The caught fish would occasionally spit up pieces of giant squid and one time an entire squid beak, the size of a baseball, appeared on the vessel's deck. The wreckfish, averaging about 60–100 pounds, were obviously not capable of attacking and devouring a giant squid. However, Captain Dan said they occasionally caught a sixgill shark in the same area, and we speculate that these are large enough to kill a giant squid, with the opportunistic wreckfish picking up leftover pieces. At the same time, the wreckfish are probably the main diet of the squid, which is the reason they are in the same location.

Why have these marine giants only been seen alive once in their natural surroundings? I don't find it so puzzling considering I have lived for years where black bears are fairly common, but I have only spotted a few, and then only for very brief moments. This is in a place where I can see for miles and where I am fairly mobile. The vastness of the three-dimensional and totally dark, deep sea makes observations very difficult at best. Submersibles or ROVs moving around in the giant squid's turf use lights and are noisy. The squids, with their dinner-plate-sized eyes, are most likely repelled by light and, as prey of sperm whales, they would be wary of noise and movements of large objects.

Much of my time underwater was spent observing marine life firsthand in relatively shallow water, and even there the sea gives up its mysteries reluctantly. When swimming equipment down to the *Hydro-Lab* in preparation for a scientific mission, I could not help being distracted by some fish or crab going about its business and revealing it secrets. The only times I would not let myself be distracted were when I was responsible for someone's safety, perhaps a novice diver, or as a buddy diver in deep water, or during the occasional emergency. But my thousands of hours underwater over the years gave me many opportunities to learn how marine animals made their living. Some of these observations have never been formally documented and are published here for the first time.

Flounder Deception

Strangely, the flatfishes called flounders share their name with the word that means to move clumsily. The fish, in fact, does just the opposite. During quiet dives on the tropical reefs, I would occasionally see a lone peacock flounder partially buried in the sand. The flounder would swim away when approached and if I pursued the fish aggressively and got too close, it would suddenly dive into the bottom with a puff of sand and disappear. I often tried to flush the fish out right where I saw it dive into the bottom. I never found the fish and I could not figure out how the flounder became so cryptic, so quickly.

Over the years, I encountered several dozen peacock flounder under these circumstances and in each case the fish would dive into the sand and disappear. If the flounder were on hard bottom without sand, it did not attempt to dive; it would simply seek shelter around a rock or coral head.

Over time I sought and observed many of the juvenile flounders and I was finally able to piece together the fascinating strategy that flounders use to escape predators.

On one occasion, I was lying on a sandy bottom watching fish around a small coral head when I spotted a juvenile peacock flounder just a few feet away. The fish was only about three inches long and was lying quietly on the bottom and partially covered with sand. When I approached the flounder, it moved away and dove into the sand just like its adult counterparts. Almost immediately after disappearing into the sand, a partially covered tiny pair of eyes appeared about two feet closer to me. It was the same fish. It did the same thing when again disturbed.

Over time I sought and observed many of the juvenile flounders and I was finally able to piece together the fascinating strategy that flounders use to escape predators. When pursued and closed in on by a predator, the flounder comes up slightly off the bottom and at the same time twists around to face back at 180 degrees, all the while using its fins to stir up the sand. The flounder, now concealed by the disturbed sediment, moves smoothly back and under its pursuer and stops, covered with sand.

The predator, fixed on the spot where the fish disappeared, does not see its quarry slip underneath and behind it and ends up attacking an empty spot. Once the flounder stops, it has averaged about seven body lengths back in the opposite direction. This is why I could not see the adults after they made their move. They were actually behind me.

When a predator gets too close, a flounder about one foot long swims back seven feet, tricking its pursuer. The juvenile flounder, on the other hand, only moves back two feet or less, making it possible for me to see it. The predator avoidance strategies evolved by the peacock flounder and, I later learned, other flatfish species that use the same techniques are as clever as I have ever had the fortunate opportunity to observe. They are, in all respects, the "Houdinis of the sea."

School of Survival

Prey have developed many different strategies for survival from a predator attack. Sometimes it is simply by hiding or by changing colors and blending into the surrounding landscape. Others have developed markings or behaviors that make them look like a larger or dangerous creature. Small fish that are prey for just about everything in the sea have evolved the strategy of large numbers and staying together in schools. Being one of a large number gives an individual less chance of being eaten. By schooling, the species is offered a number of advantages.

I watched a school of small silversides in the Bahamas form a tight school of many thousands of individual fish. Shaped like a ball, the school moved as if it were a single organism. Snapper, jacks, and other predators circled around the school, which, for the most part, moved up, down, and horizontally with no apparent lead fish. Signals passed through the school so fast that the entire group appeared to move in instant unison. When one or more of the predators attacked the school, the prey scattered in all directions away from the oncoming fish. This action served to confuse the predators, making it almost impossible for them to snatch a mouthful. They often came up with nothing. Following the attack, the school quickly regrouped and continued its schooling behavior.

A fish by itself in the ocean does not have the advantage of being only one of many choices for a predator, nor the ability to work as a group to avoid enemies. A lone individual encountered by a predator will almost certainly be eaten. Although being part of a school presents safety in numbers, it can still be hazardous for an individual that is injured or sick and unable to keep up with its partners.

On a number of dives I observed a large, tight school of silversides being harassed by several snapper. The snapper would approach the school quickly, but not attack. During the predator's approach, the entire school would turn away in unison and only move several feet ahead of the approaching fish with a rushing sound. There would often be a handful of stragglers desperately trying to catch up, some visibly injured or deformed, others looking okay, but slow. The moment the school of silversides moved ahead leaving behind some of their brethren, the snapper moved in and swallowed up the unfortunate prey.

After watching this behavior for some time, two thoughts came to mind. First, the school actually benefitted by losing its weakest members. It assured that the strongest survived. Second, the snapper appeared to make these false attacks on purpose to expose the stragglers and, therefore, capture an easy meal. Could this be true? Or was it the strategy of the school to purposefully sacrifice its weakest for the sake of the whole? We may never know for sure, but it was clear that both predator and prey, with the exception of the victims, benefitted from the arrangement.

The Nassau Grouper—Einstein of the Coral Reef

The intelligence of animals at all levels is becoming more and more of interest to science—dolphins and whales, dogs that can recognize hundreds of words, apes of many species that can conduct complex tasks. But little is known about the so-called lower forms of life. After years of observing marine life, my perception is that we humans shortchange the intelligence levels of fish and other species of the sea. That is not to say it is the same as human intelligence, but intelligence nonetheless. The author Henry Beston captured the essence of this in his book *Outermost House* back in 1928 through the following quote:

> We need another and a wiser and perhaps a more mystical concept of animals. Remote from universal nature, and living by complicated artifice, man in civilization surveys the creature through the glass of his knowledge and sees thereby a feather magnified and the whole image in distortion. We patronize them for their incompleteness, for their tragic fate of having taken form so far below ourselves. And therein we err, and greatly err. For the animal shall not be measured by man. In a world older and more complete than ours they move finished and complete, gifted with extensions of the senses we have lost or never obtained, living by voices we shall never hear. They are not brethren, they are not underlings; they are other nations, caught with ourselves

Typical adult Nassau grouper.

in the net of life and time, fellow prisoners of the splendour and travail of the earth.

Of all the creatures I encountered in the sea, few can measure up to the groupers, and particularly the Nassau grouper, in terms of displayed intelligence and a most agreeable personality. (It is tough not to anthropomorphize when describing these animals.) Marine taxonomists named the Nassau grouper *Epinephelus striatus* of the family Serranidae. In common terms, these are groupers belonging to the large family of seabasses with members ranging in size from a few inches, such as the little fairy basslet and tobaccofish found in the Caribbean, to the Pacific seabass, which grows over 12 feet long and weighs over 1,000 pounds. The Atlantic goliath is somewhat smaller than its Pacific brethren, reaching about 700 pounds.

My first encounter with a grouper was in 1968 during the record saturation dive from the *Deep Diver* lockout submersible. It was a 20- to 25-pound black grouper that lived on the mid-depth reef in 120 feet of water off Little Whale Cay, Berry Islands, Bahamas. It was obvious that the fish had little or no contact with humans. It displayed no fear of me and actually became a pest, pushing against me and glaring into the glass window of my diving helmet. Groupers that have not been hunted or otherwise harassed by divers seem to display this behavior commonly. Either they are studying the diver's eyes or they see a reflection of themselves. Since I have not seen one attack a faceplate, it's fun to imagine that they are actually admiring their own image instead of seeing it as an adversary. When it comes to grouper behavior, anything is possible.

The black grouper stayed with me for hours that day, often getting in my way as I tried to inventory some of the fish species on the reef. Around noon I returned to the *Deep Diver* for a lunch break and rest. I had a leftover peanut butter and jelly sandwich, which I decided to feed to the fish on the next dive. The grouper was waiting for me and bumped against my knee as I emerged from the lockout chamber.

Standing on the bottom, I took half of the sandwich from the plastic bag and held it out for the grouper. Without hesitation, the fish literally inhaled the food from my hand and immediately wanted more. It became fixated on my bare knee and nipped at it several times when I kept it from getting the other half-sandwich. After several games of keep-away, the crafty fish must have figured out my strategy of behind-the-back and hand-to-hand. With a quick movement, the grouper had the sandwich, still in the bag, in its mouth.

Part of a Nassau grouper spawning aggregation, swimming upward and releasing eggs and milt. Note the partial black coloration that indicates courtship behavior.

PHOTO COURTESY PAT COLIN

Alarmed that this might harm the fish, I tried pulling at the little bit of bag not yet swallowed, to no avail. I was distressed. My new and loyal friend had stayed with me on my lonely dives, and now I may be responsible for its harm. The grouper stayed away from me but within sight for the duration of the dive. On my third dive, my friend was still around and miraculously the bag was sitting on the bottom near the sub—more miraculously, the sandwich was gone. Groupers surely crawled into my heart that day.

Perhaps I'm short-shrifting other species of the family, such as this black grouper, but my diving throughout the years has been mostly in the realm of the Nassau grouper from their shallow nursery grounds to the outer reef systems, so it is this species which is most familiar to me.

Grouper Group Sex

Adults of the Nassau grouper in the Caribbean gather in spawning aggregations for one week during the full moon in February and March of each year. Tagged specimens demonstrated that they travel for at least 90 miles, and probably much more, to meet and reproduce. Dr. Pat Colin discovered in 1989 that at Long Island, Bahamas, the groupers become very active around late dusk in almost complete darkness. Twenty to fifty, males and females together, would rush upward spewing eggs and milt into the open water. The then-fertilized eggs—those not eaten by giant whale sharks swimming through the egg masses with open mouths and other smaller species—soon float to the surface and are carried by the currents for a couple of days. They are carried by currents for another 35 days or so as larvae, until they seek shallow water and safety in some grassbed-bottom habitat. By spawning at dusk, the groupers give the mass of eggs a chance to disburse throughout the night unseen by most predators.

The spawning behavior of these fish obviously evolved over many thousands or millions of years and is very efficient, but in recent years local fishermen learned about the aggregations and converged on the fish, catching them by the thousands. In some regions of the Caribbean, the spawning aggregations became extinct after only a few years of heavy fishing pressure—another stupid, short-sighted action fueled by human greed. There is no more effective way to wipe out a fish species than to catch them on their spawning grounds. Tight regulations have since been placed on the spawning aggregations in some regions of the Caribbean, but as usual, enforcement continues to be a problem.

Few Nassau grouper larvae are lucky enough to reach their nursery grounds. Once in the open ocean, their fate over the next 35 days or so is determined to a large extent by oceanographic conditions. Advective, density, and wind-driven currents will determine the fate of the eggs and larvae. Some marine eggs, believe it or not, are not just passive particles in the water column, but are capable of changing their buoyancy to stay at a certain depth and possible current regime for a better chance of survival. It is not known if Nassau grouper eggs can do this.

It is believed the strategy of a spawning aggregation is to be located where the eggs and larvae have the best chance to reach a nursery. The site of the spawning aggregations in the Long Island region is washed by currents moving north to and along the Exuma chain, where tidal currents carry larvae into the back shallows and nurseries of the Great Bahama Bank. Any part of this process can be disrupted by a storm or strong winds that generate offshore currents, carrying the larvae away from their destination and into deep waters where they cannot survive.

Once on the nursery grounds, the larval grouper seek the bottom and go through metamorphosis. At this point, the tiny juveniles become cryptic and bury in the sandy bottom, usually under an object such as a shell. About a month later the grouper, now about one-two inches long, seek a home on the shallow-water *Thalassia* grass beds, often in abandoned conch shells. It was in this setting that I observed a remarkable behavior of the young Nassau grouper, described here for the first time, which furthers my belief that this particular species of fish is very intelligent.

A Clean Home is a Safe Home

On a sunny afternoon in June, I was swimming in about 10 feet of water with a clipboard, still camera, and video camera to conduct my monthly survey of the grouper population on the western side of the Exuma islands in the Bahamas. My eye caught an old, abandoned conch shell with a juvenile Nassau grouper, about two inches long, in its opening. This was the fifth juvenile I observed that day that had adopted an empty conch shell as its home. All stayed close to the opening of the shell and were extremely aggressive toward other fish swimming close by. Some of the fish attacked by the small Nassau grouper were many times bigger.

Lying fairly still on the bottom, I watched the grouper for about 15 minutes when a large stingray swam behind me. When I turned to take a photo of the ray, my swim fins inadvertently kicked sand and bottom debris into the conch shell. When I turned back toward the shell, I could see that the young grouper had become visibly agitated, swimming back and forth in quick bursts of speed, even making what appeared to be threatening moves toward me. Instead of leaving the now useless shelter, the fish displayed some remarkable behavior over the next 10 minutes or so.

While I watched from a short distance, the juvenile grouper took mouthfuls of sand from inside the shell and with puffed cheeks swam off a few feet and spit the sand out. In between the sand removal, it picked up long sticks of dead gorgonian and blades of dead *Thalassia* grass. The grouper grabbed the sticks like a dog carrying a bone and methodically placed them a short distance from the shell.

PHOTO COURTESY ROBERT WICKLUND

Juvenile Nassau grouper sweeping sand from its conch shell home with its tail fin.

This went on for several minutes. When all of the debris and most of the sand were removed, it entered the shell opening, lay on its side, and, with rapid movements of its tail fin, swept the remaining sand from the shell. Now with its home in order, the fish resumed its position and again started defending its territory from all comers. The little fish looked at me as if to say, "Don't try that again, buster."

It may appear rather cruel that, after all the hard work by the grouper, my scientific curiosity kicked in and I purposefully pushed more debris and sand into the shell. I was curious to see if the fish would react in the same way; it did. I later observed other individual juvenile Nassau groupers in other conch shells displaying the very same behavior. Although interesting from a human's standpoint, and pronounced "cute" by some people, this behavior is dead serious and critical to the young grouper's survival.

During subsequent population surveys I conducted in the region, the juvenile Nassau grouper were sparsely distributed about one every two to three acres, most likely due to the lack of suitable habitat for this stage of the grouper's life history. Empty conch shells were rare as were other suitable habitats.

These nursery grounds are typically shallow grass beds vulnerable to high winds and large wave action, which could move sand and debris into conch shells or other shelters that the young fish occupy. These fish have learned several techniques to keep their homes usable. If sand or other sediment is the problem, they have learned to "shovel" with their mouths or "sweep" with their tail fins. If it is other debris, they have learned to pick it up and carry it off. Without this behavior, and the safety of shelter, the fish would likely perish.

When the Nassau grouper grow to four to five inches long, which eliminates their vulnerability to many potential predators and the need for shelter, they move into shallow coral reefs for two years and then often onto deeper reef areas. We have never seen adult grouper display the behavior described here.

Tricky Fish

During the *Hydro-Lab* project in 1974, I observed another amazing display of intelligence by the Nassau grouper. Denny Breese and I used the *Hydro-Lab* to watch how reef fish react to traps of various shapes, sizes, and types of bait. Some of the traps were fashioned from wire mesh into a cube shape, others were triangular, and some were built of conventional wooden slats common to the Caribbean region. We also experimented with biodegradable panels that would fall apart after a short time, allowing catch to escape if the trap were lost.

Juvenile Nassau grouper cleaning out its conch shell home. It has picked up a grass blade in its mouth and is swimming it away from the shell.

PHOTO COURTESY ROBERT WICKLUND

One of the experimental traps was a Cuban design built of chicken wire with one rather small opening only capable of capturing fish around two to three pounds. This trap was baited with the remains of a small filleted fish.

The Cuban trap was placed in 50 feet of water right in front of the main window of the *Hydro-Lab*. This allowed us to sit inside the habitat without being detected by the fish we were watching. Soon, an adult Nassau grouper, about 5–6 pounds, swam up to the trap and stopped for a moment. We could see its eyes moving rapidly as it appeared to be surveying the trap and its contents.

The fish slowly circled the trap and attempted to go through the small opening. After several attempts, the grouper again circled looking for another opening. It stopped by the end of the trap where the bait was laid and hit the cage several times trying to get at the food. When this failed the grouper remained motionless for some time, seemingly analyzing the situation.

After several minutes, the grouper moved to the bottom next to the bait, turned onto its side with its tail fin facing the trap, and began rapidly moving its tail up and down, washing the bait to the opposite side of the trap. During this process it would raise itself up on a pectoral fin and, while still on its side, bend its upper body so with one eye it could see what was happening in the trap behind it. When the bait was washed across the trap, the grouper immediately swam to the other side and repeated the washing motion. Back and forth, the grouper made about 10 attempts to wash the bait from the trap, then finally gave up and left.

This fish probably had a whole repertoire of techniques to obtain food and we saw just a sampling that day. Groupers, like most other predators, are also scavengers and probably use the washing technique to move food out of the many holes and nooks that make up a coral reef. It displayed intelligence in its ability to solve a problem, not only by using its tail fin to move an object, but also by rising up on its pectoral fin to observe and mentally track its progress.

Schooling Grouper

Other than gathering in spawning aggregations once or twice a year, groupers are primarily solitary animals from the time they go through metamorphosis through the rest of their lives. I have seen several living around a coral head, but always in separate holes or crevices.

During experiments to artificially spawn and raise Nassau grouper in captivity, Dr. Wade Watanabe, a renowned marine aquaculture scientist, placed several thousand juveniles in round tanks, ten feet in diameter and four feet deep. The tanks were smooth-walled all around with no hiding places for the fish. To our amazement the young grouper quickly gathered into a tight group and swam around the tank like any other schooling fish. Although this is something that we have never seen, nor do we expect to see, in the wild, substituting schooling as protection in the absence of their normal bottom habitat was obviously triggered by their survival instincts.

This behavior of the Nassau grouper is still a mystery and it poses the question: Do all fish have a schooling instinct that serves as a substitute for protection when other means are not available? The grouper is a bottom dweller and, for the most part, lives a solitary life. There seems to be little chance that conditions in the wild would allow the fish to learn how to form schools, so observations alone will not give us the needed clues to this strange behavior. Experiments under controlled conditions may answer this question.

The Queen Conch

During our years on Lee Stocking Island we became intrigued with the queen conch, a beautiful marine snail that has been an important part of the dietary requirements of Caribbean inhabitants. In my opinion, the queen conch, designated *Strombus gigas* by scientists, is one of the best-tasting food species in the sea. With a firm, white meat that needs to be tenderized and a large shell that is used to make cameo and other jewelry, the queen conch was, until just a few years ago, one of the most valuable marine resources in the West Indies. But, like many other popular species, it is now severely depleted throughout the tropics.

Bahamians told us that not too long ago a person could wade out into waist-deep water anytime and pick up as many conch as they could hold in their arms. Commercial fisherman would breath-hold dive into shallow water from a small boat and pick up hundreds in a day just about anywhere in the West Indies. The Florida Keys were, at one time, noted for their conch and Key West is still known as the "Conch Republic." But there are few conch to be had in the Keys today. Over 15 years ago the conch came under protection in the Keys with the hope the population would come back, but that has not happened. It appears that the population was so depleted that it cannot recover.

Throughout the Exuma islands and around Lee Stocking Island, our scientists found nursery grounds of the queen conch. In fact, close to the nursery grounds there were hundreds of conch middens on the beaches, consisting of many thousands of shells each. When we carbon-dated shells from the bottom of the piles, some were over 500 years old, indicating that indigenous peoples fished for queen conch in the same places with probably the same techniques long before Europeans set foot in the New World.

When we first started to study conch in 1985, they were reasonably abundant throughout the Exumas. Over a 10-year period, however, the adult conch became scarcer and scarcer as fishing boats from Nassau and other Bahamian ports started to extend their range in search of the valuable animal. On the other hand, the young conch, up to three years old and protected by law, were still plentiful. As time went

Author observing mating pair of queen conch in 80-foot depth off Lee Stocking Island, Bahamas.

on we were finding less of the adults and more freshly cleaned, illegal-sized shells. This was a clear indication that even in these out islands the locals were forced to turn to poaching the plentiful young conch as the adults became scarce.

Our research on the queen conch focused on their early life history. Headed by Al Stoner, a CMRC scientist, with Bori Olla as scientific advisor, the conch program became one of our largest and longest-running projects. We found that following spawning the conch larvae, called veligers, are carried on surface currents for about 35 days and when they reach a suitable nursery in shallow water, they go through metamorphosis and bury in the sandy bottom. Later, at about an inch or so, the young conch move mostly to grass beds where they feed on tiny epiphytes accumulated on the blades of grass. The conch stay in this habitat until they reach maturity in four years, at which time most move off. We found a lot of older conch offshore as deep as 80 feet. The depth protects them from most fishermen, who are only allowed to breath-hold dive. It is illegal to spear or capture fish or other animals with scuba gear in the Bahamas.

During our dives on the conch nursery grounds, we discovered an incredible behavior of the young conch, which had not been previously documented in scientific literature. While snorkeling around a shallow nursery area early one morning, we noticed a wide swath of young conch, most about four inches long, gathered

PHOTO COURTESY GERRI WENZ

Mass migration of juvenile one- to two-year-old queen conch in the Exuma chain, Bahamas.

together by the thousands. The swath was about 20 feet wide and extended in a snake-like form into the distance and out of sight. We designated this phenomenon a "conch wave" based on its wave-like appearance. We followed the wave for several hundred feet and estimated there were well over a hundred thousand conch, all moving slowly in the same direction, perpendicular to the length of the swath, like a legion of soldiers marching to battle. At the back of the 20-foot swath, conch could be seen left behind in a rather sparse array.

We observed this behavior only a few times and concluded that when the nursery area gets too crowded and food becomes scarce, the young conch form up in the swath configuration and actually redistribute themselves over a larger area. Rather than random movement by individuals looking for food, the conch evolved a strategy that distributes their population over the feeding grounds in an orderly and efficient fashion.

By 2007 conch had become very scarce throughout the Caribbean and had not repopulated in the Florida Keys. The future looks grim for the species unless there is a West Indies-wide moratorium on catching and selling them, followed by strict international laws and enforcement of quotas after, and if, the populations recover.

46

THE DECLINE OF THE CORAL REEFS

FROM MY FIRST view of them over 40 years ago, tropical coral reefs, with their beauty and species richness, have for me epitomized the oceans. They are the most diverse of all biosystems, yet they cover only a fraction of the global surface. Their value, in terms of dollars from fishing, diving, and general tourism, to many nations is enormous, and their contribution to protecting shorelines from storms is incalculable. Incredibly, and in spite of their enormous popularity, only about half of all species associated with coral reefs are known to science.

Millions of years of reef building have created one of the earth's ecological marvels. Hard corals, soft corals such as sea fans and gorgonians, and many species of sponges create a dazzling, multi-colored display. But, more importantly, coral reefs are home to a diversity of life not even rivaled by a tropical rain forest. Hundreds of fish species and other marine organisms, some more colorful than the corals, thrive in, over, and among the reef system. The shallow reefs in crystal clear waters are lit up by the tropical sun, with the shallowest parts of the reef displaying the entire spectrum of colors. The deeper a coral is found, the less color is visible. Moving downward through the water column, colors are absorbed, first the reds, then yellows, and at about 100 feet deep only blue remains. Much deeper everything becomes black and white or gray, and then into the abyss, the world of eternal darkness.

Most modern coral reefs in shallow tropical waters in the Atlantic, Caribbean, Pacific, and Indian Oceans are thousands of years old. The hard, calcareous skeleton that forms around millions of coral polyps slowly builds the reefs over the centuries. Shallow-water corals thrive in warm seas within a very narrow range of temperature, around 15–30°C in most places. Corals are unable to tolerate much above or below their threshold temperature regimes without becoming stressed.

They are also stressed by other things, including poor water quality, low oxygen levels, high levels of suspended sediment and other particulates, heavy seas associated with storms, boat anchors, and heavy intrusions of divers. When corals are stressed they often expel attached beneficial unicellular plants called zooxanthellae.

These pigmented plants give corals most of their color. When they are expelled, the coral skeleton displays all white, a phenomenon commonly called "bleaching." Zooxanthellae aid in the production of calcium carbonate by the corals, and it is believed that, as with terrestrial plants which need sunlight to photosynthesize, the low light levels in the deeper ocean limit most tropical corals to the coastal shallows. There are some species of coral in the deep, cold ocean that do not live symbiotically with algae.

During our early years on Lee Stocking Island, we were impressed by the healthy coral heads and reefs all around the Exuma chain of islands. There were coral species ranging from just a few feet of water, with some of these being exposed to air during low tides, down to around 200 feet. Even at this depth light still penetrated the clear water, but at a much reduced intensity. In fact, during many excursions down to 1,000 feet in a submarine, we could still see a distance of 30 feet or so with just ambient light.

There were, however, early warning signs that corals were being affected, not only by natural forces such as hurricanes, diseases, and a Caribbean-wide die-off of the beneficial sea urchin *Diadema,* but also by increasing human activities. Pollution from runoff and ocean sewer outfalls caused decline in coral reefs close to urban areas, and overfishing was upsetting the balance of the coral reef ecosystems. When

Almost fully bleached club coral among partially bleached staghorn coral in Exuma Sound, Bahamas, 1987.

PHOTO COURTESY ROBERT DILL

the urchins that prevented the overgrowth of algae on the reefs began dying off in 1982–83, it was the job of grazing fish to keep the reefs clean. But as fishing pressure continued, the grazer population declined, allowing the algae to compete for space with the coral polyps. The remoteness of Lee Stocking Island and the Exuma islands in general kept the surrounding coral reefs from being affected by many of these problems.

In late summer 1987 everything changed. A slow, almost undetectable increase in ocean temperatures crept into the Caribbean like a plague. We were monitoring temperatures on a number of shallow and deeper reefs and noticed that the numbers were high, but we had no idea of the consequences. In late August, when the temperatures usually peaked in the Exumas, we were measuring over one-and-a-half degrees Celsius higher than in previous years. The surface temperatures were exceeding 86°F, virtually "bathtub water." No more than curious about the warm water, we went about our business studying the reef systems until we started to realize that an inordinately high number of corals were losing their color and turning white.

We knew that new growth on some corals, such as the elkhorn and staghorn, was not immediately populated by the zooxanthellae algae and they normally displayed some of their white skeleton, but we were curious enough to set up a casual monitoring program. We asked the many scientists who dove on the reefs on a regular basis to report any signs of whitening of the corals. In the meantime, we researched reports of a bleaching event on South Pacific reefs around 1983 and wondered if we were witnessing the same phenomenon.

We were soon getting regular observations of bleaching from our scientists, and we saw it firsthand. The coral reefs were turning white in many places with entire heads sometimes being affected. It wasn't long before we heard from scientists throughout the Caribbean that corals were bleaching in large numbers.

Was this a Caribbean-wide outbreak of a disease? It didn't make sense. Diseases like the one that wiped out the sea urchins usually started in one area and spread. In this case the corals were affected in different places throughout the Caribbean and West Indies all at once. Our attention turned to the high temperatures, and with a rudimentary knowledge that coral could be affected by overly heated water, we monitored recording thermometers on the surface, shallow, and deep reefs. In all cases the recorders indicated that the temperatures were extraordinarily high. This was also true in most reported regions of the Caribbean.

Once we learned that corals will expel their symbiotic algae, zooxanthellae, and subsequently lose their color, we knew we were witnessing a historic "mass bleaching" of Bahamian reefs and a widespread phenomenon, at least in the Caribbean region. Based on our records of high seawater temperatures measured during the bleaching, we surmised that the corals were being stressed by the warm water. For the next few weeks most of our attention turned to diving surveys of the reefs in the local area to see the extent the bleaching.

We recorded bleaching of coral from the shallows of only a few feet deep to almost 200 feet. Other species of soft corals, gorgonians, anemones, and many sponges also showed clear signs of bleaching. A large percentage of the reefs were affected and continued to be affected throughout the remaining few weeks of the summer and into the early fall. By winter, when the temperatures declined, many corals and sponges regained their population of algae and appeared to have survived the bleaching event. However, there was a large number of all affected species that did not survive, and we estimated the mortality rate at roughly 10 percent.

This was devastating to us. In the blink of an eye, we witnessed previously healthy reefs suddenly become stressed and die in relatively large numbers.

This was devastating to us. In the blink of an eye, we witnessed previously healthy reefs suddenly become stressed and die in relatively large numbers. We suspected that this was not a one-time event. We also knew that even though the scientific community was aware of the problem, it would be prudent to get the federal government involved right away. I contacted my old boss, Lowell Weicker, who was then chairman of the Senate Appropriations Subcommittee with funding jurisdiction over ocean programs. Lowell acted immediately and set the first congressional hearings in motion on the issue of coral bleaching. There wasn't much scientific data on the bleaching phenomena available at that time, but enough firsthand observations from credible scientists existed to at least begin to understand the severity of the problem.

The next major bleaching event in the Exumas took place in 1990 and again it was reported from other regions of the Caribbean and the Florida Keys. This time we had more information about the ecology of corals and associated species. We now knew that corals cannot tolerate temperatures just a few degrees above their threshold levels and that this is true as well on the deeper reefs where the temperatures are cooler. It is all relative.

During our diving surveys we discovered undersea waterfalls of relatively hot water cascading down the steep slopes of the shelf where the deepwater corals and other species were most affected. This occurred in the vicinity of channels during outgoing tides where shallow bank water, which was hypersaline from evaporation, flowed out to sea. Warm water is normally lighter than cold, but in this case the high salinity of the water made it denser than even the cooler water offshore. When this water rushed out of the channel, it sank and flowed down the slope carrying the warm temperature with it to a depth of about 140 feet. At that point the density of the flowing water was the same as the ambient water and it stopped sinking.

This was not the first time I experienced this phenomenon. During an excursion in the *Deep Diver* submersible off Andros Island some years before, a similar current actually carried the sub down in an uncontrolled descent almost 80

Bleached boulder coral in 1987 off the coast of the Exuma Cays, Bahamas.

feet. It was scary at first until the pilot maneuvered the sub away from the slope and out of the undersea falls. In that case it was winter and the falls were colder, thus denser, than the surrounding water.

When the sea temperatures decreased following the 1990 incident, many of the stony and soft corals, sponges, and anemones again recovered, but many also died. The bleaching incidents over the years have taken a collectively high toll on the reefs. In some places around the Caribbean, less than half of the corals are alive and the future looks bleak.

The hot seas are considered the result of global warming, which is now a long-term problem. Carbon dioxide and other chemical compounds emitted into the atmosphere from human activities have been identified by the majority of climate and other scientists as the main cause of global warming. Increased ocean acidification has also resulted, and this has had a detrimental effect as well on the stony corals.

I have been asked over and over how a minute change in temperature could cause corals to stress. We have documented that just a 1–2°C seawater temperature rise over the corals' threshold level will set off a bleaching event. Residents of the ocean in general, and corals in particular, maintain in a fragile window of temperature. The oceans, unlike the atmosphere, absorb and dissipate temperature very slowly and shallow-water corals live in parts of the oceans subjected to relatively small changes in temperature. Many mobile species, such as finfish, migrate away from large swings in temperature to stay within their tolerance levels, but corals, sponges, and other immobile species can only survive where the temperatures are relatively stable throughout the seasons.

This then is the dilemma—corals and many of their associated species are, for better or worse, prisoners of the habitat to which evolution assigned them. So, as the oceans continue to warm because of our unchecked behavior of choosing comfort over survival, the coral reefs as we knew them just a few years ago are already gone, and what remains may be completely wiped out within our children's lifetimes.

Is there hope that the trend can be reversed before it's too late, and can the coral reefs start the slow road back to health? Perhaps, but I wouldn't wager my life on it. In any case, it is bound to get worse before it gets better.

EPILOGUE

Why does Neptune weep?

I was preparing for a dive off the coast of St. Croix in the Virgin Islands on a winter day in 2007. On the surface, everything looked the same. The waters were as clear as aquarium glass. Muted shades of green reflected from the shallow, sandy bottom and graduated to the turquoise and then dark blues of the deeper waters off the island shelf. Yet it was all deceptive. I knew that once I was underwater everything would change.

I was hoping for a miracle. Maybe this time the reefs would be okay or at least the damage wouldn't be as bad. Maybe they would have begun, in their steady, incremental way, to repair themselves. Maybe there would be groupers this time, or a barracuda or some parrotfish. Maybe the macroalgae would be less invasive. Maybe life would have begun to bring color back to the bleached bones of the coral.

Maybe.

I adjusted my tank straps, mask, and regulator and eased into the warm sea. I swam down to the St. Croix reef—no miracle had occurred. The fish population was nearly gone; there was only a smattering of live coral between the spreading macroalgae and the rocky outcroppings of coral skeletons. Things looked no better, probably worse, since my last dive in St. Croix the year before. At least half, maybe more, of the live corals were gone. How different it was from the magnificence of the reefs 40 years ago, during that first dive in the Bahamas.

The reality of rapidly declining reefs is pretty much the same throughout the West Indies and, in fact, all tropical seas of the world. A recent global survey of coral reefs revealed only one left in the world considered pristine—off the coast of Madagascar in the Indian Ocean. Overly warm ocean water, however, had begun to stress even those remote reefs, and they were displaying widespread bleaching.

Some estimates indicate that in many places 40–70 percent of live coral coverage on reefs has disappeared. This includes all shallow tropical coral reefs worldwide. The Great Barrier Reef off the coast of Australia is affected; the second largest barrier reef off the coast of Belize, Central America, is affected; reefs in Palau and Micronesia and Guam are affected; and reefs around the 700 islands of the Bahamas are affected. Within my lifetime of diving, coral reefs have gone from healthy to gravely threatened. They may well be one of the first complete marine ecosystems to become extinct.

Corals are only a part of the story. The oceans are under siege. Increasing demand for seafood, new fishing technologies, ineffectual management, habitat destruction, and diminished water quality create a deadly combination that is leading to the predicted and predictable collapse of many of the world's major commercial fisheries. Most commercially important species are already affected. The mighty codfish, at one time so abundant that a person could imagine walking across their backs in the waters off the northeastern U.S. and Canada, now has gone the way of the American buffalo.

The magnificent giant bluefin and some other tunas, many of the sharks, groupers, conch, haddock, blue claw crabs, and oysters are all grossly overfished. Populations of so-called fodder species used for chicken and aquaculture feed, including anchovies, some herrings, and krill are being fished and reduced relentlessly.

Recent predictions are that all global commercial fish stocks will severely diminish or fail completely by the mid-21st century, not much more than 40 years from the time of this writing. The greed and shortsightedness of mankind is at the core, whether it is overharvesting the wild populations of fish and other species, coastal pollution from farm and urban runoff, chemical discharges and oil spills, or heating of the seas through global warming.

The future of the human species, and most likely all species in the world, is tied to the health of our oceans, which are at our mercy. Although we talk endlessly about the problems, the crisis goes on. The arrogance of our collective self-indulgence keeps the oceans in a downward spiral.

The oceans gave birth to and supported life for billions of years. Stromatolites, found in fossilized remains from some 3.5 billion years ago, dominated the ancient, shallow seas and not long ago were believed to be extinct, but a few still live in scattered waters of the world. Those we recently found in the waters of the Bahamas underscore the importance of research and discovery.

There are still many thousands of marine species waiting to be discovered—the biodiversity of the sea is seemingly endless. But, dark times loom ominously. I have seen little to be optimistic about. The decline in marine populations on a global scale has been well known for decades, and now our coral reef ecosystems worldwide are in steep decline. It appears that the degradation of our oceans has been accelerating over the past 50 years or so.

As human population continues to explode, the demand for natural resources from both the sea and land is increasing. The encroachment on the globe by this relentless march of humanity pollutes and renders rivers, streams, farmland, and coastal waters unfit for the most fragile of creatures at first, and now toxic algae and chemicals threaten the health of us all. An increasingly hungry world hunts the seas for species that just a few years ago would have been considered trash food in much of the world. When these animals, called "bycatch," were caught incidentally along with targeted commercially marketable species, they were discarded overboard. Over the years, many millions of tons of fish and other marine species, including mammals, died on the deck of fishing vessels and were simply shoveled back into the sea.

At a congressional hearing I attended some years ago, a U.S. Government official made the outrageous comment that dolphins caught accidentally in nets by tuna fishermen were "returned to the ecosystem"—dead, of course, like this official's brain. Sharks are captured and, after having their fins cut off, are released alive to die a slow death. These are, in my opinion, immoral acts of the first order and black marks on the human spirit. Laws passed by Congress in the 1970s have helped somewhat, but the situation remains grim. Some species, fished to almost commercial extinction, may never recover.

Laws passed by the U.S. will not help marine populations that are under siege in the waters of other countries. In fact, even with the new laws, American fishing practices are still way out of sync with establishing a sustainable industry, much less a healthy population for most species. It's unbelievable to me that in spite of all we know about the condition of the world fisheries, restaurants still commonly promote "all you can eat" seafood menus. For a relatively small amount of money, one can consume copious amounts of fish, shrimp, crab, lobster, scallops, etc. This defies logic. Discussion of the declining oceans would take the writing of many books, and solutions to saving the seas are as complex as anything we have tackled in human history. Reducing runoff from cities and farms, cutting emissions from cars and power plants, truly stopping illegal and overfishing, reducing oil, chemical, and trash spills are all logical and necessary steps that can stem the tide of destruction of the oceans, but at high costs and likely taking many decades to accomplish. A rush by nations to discover and drill new oil fields is underway, which will likely increase worldwide oil consumption, at least in the near future, probably offsetting any reductions in carbon emissions that new alternative energy systems may provide. This, with the lack of real global effort to stabilize the environment, assures the long-term decline of the oceans.

In April 2010, a British Petroleum (BP)-operated oil rig, *Deepwater Horizon,* blew up in the Gulf of Mexico, killing 11 people and spilling millions of gallons of crude oil into Gulf waters for months. This was just after President Obama announced that large areas of the U.S. East Coast would be opened for drilling, after a several-decade moratorium.

The cause of the explosion is not yet clear, but there is speculation that a faulty cementing operation caused the release of gas hydrates from the 5,000-foot-deep ocean sediments. All of the so-called fail-safe systems were not able to shut down the oil flowing from the wellhead.

The Gulf of Mexico will suffer environmentally and economically for a long time, and it's not the first time. While employed in the Senate in 1979, I was assigned a fact-finding mission to the IXTOC 1 oil drilling explosion in the Bay of Campeche, Gulf of Mexico. The Mexican-owned operation was reporting that the spill was under control. During a flight over the site in a Coast Guard plane, I could see a huge upwelling of oil, which was also on fire. The spill was nowhere near under control and, in fact, lasted for almost 10 months—the second largest oil spill in history. As a side note, the IXTOC 1 drilling operation was in fairly shallow water. Divers were used to help stem the spill and, as I understand it, one was caught in the massive flow of oil to the surface and died from the uncontrolled ascent.

The IXTOC 1 blowout was caused by the loss of drilling mud circulation, allowing a buildup of hydrocarbons in the pipe. This appears to be a completely different reason from the BP incident, pointing out the fragile nature of the systems—the industry cannot guarantee their integrity. Oil production in the oceans is a losing game; there will always be devastating spills adding more nails to the ocean's coffin.

There are a number of Marine Protected Areas in the waters of the United States and around the world. They come in many forms and are a rather recent idea. The establishment of many more protected areas on a global scale may very well be the easiest, most positive action we can take right now. Their creation needs to be ramped up dramatically to add many critical areas to the system. Research to determine where they should be established, such as recruitment-rich nursery grounds and spawning regions, is essential.

Radicalization of no-take zones within the protected areas will also be necessary to allow marine species and populations to recover, no matter what negative effects it may have on jobs and local economies. This is a relatively small step in the overall scheme, but one that can bring quick returns. Like the highly successful U.S. National Park System, Marine Protected Areas can be a catalyst for sustainable systems, but on a far larger global scale. Sylvia Earle, who has long recognized the importance of Marine Protected Areas, is now focusing on these issues and has made significant progress promoting them in Hawaii and elsewhere.

Many people probably see the oceans as fierce, cold, mysterious places that produce storms and sink ships—places full of large, dangerous creatures like sharks and giant squid. But, when swimming around a coral reef in the tropics or a rocky ledge in the North Atlantic, or peering out a port of a submarine in cold, deep water, it becomes clear that the sea is a beautiful, fragile place and its future—and ours—is in our hands. Fate handed us a planet rich in water and life. By simple rules of survival, the human species must live in concert with the many other species in our world. So far, we have conducted ourselves poorly, as if only humans really matter. We already know this has been a huge mistake. It's time we stopped treating the oceans as an alien world to be exploited or ignored. Our oceans need our help—all of us—and it must be now. It must be considered a priority higher than just about anything else we do in the coming years. Ultimately, we are inseparable from the sea. Whatever we do to it, we do to ourselves. It is not too late to change, but the clock is ticking—and Neptune continues to weep.

INDEX

H

I

J

K

L

M

Y

Z

ABOUT THE AUTHOR

ROBERT "BOB" WICKLUND is a true undersea pioneer. His amazing career (over 50 years) included many "firsts." As director and co-founder of the *Hydro-Lab* Undersea Research Program (1971–75), Bob's team saturated 343 scientists and policymakers, enabling them to live and work on the bottom of the ocean. His seven years with the U.S. Senate working on legislation for diving science and ocean protection included the building of the *Aquarius* undersea laboratory.

Bob was co-founder and executive director of the Caribbean Marine Research Center in the Bahamas (1984–95), which conducted thousands of scientific dives every year. He also held the directorship of the National Undersea Research Program in the Caribbean, and later the Southeast and Gulf of Mexico Region. His dives included nine saturation missions, two of which are records—the first saturation dive from a submarine and the first saturation dive under the Arctic ice.

Wicklund began his career at the Sandy Hook Marine Laboratory in 1961 as a researcher and the Northeast diving examiner for the Bureau of Sport Fisheries and Wildlife, Department of the Interior.

In 1990, Bob Wicklund was presented with the NOGI Award for Diving Science. The NOGI is the oldest and most prestigious award in the diving industry, dating back to 1960. The roster of NOGI recipients has become a virtual "Who's Who in the Ocean World."

Bob has met and enjoyed the company of many interesting and influential people over the years, but it is his time spent in the sea that he treasures the most. Sharing time and space with fish and other sea creatures gives him a deep appreciation for the importance of the ocean to our own well-being.

Bob is presently the director of Federal Programs for the University of North Carolina Wilmington and resides with his wife, Gerri Wenz, on their farm in Virginia.